POLICING THE
SECOND AMENDMENT

POLICING THE SECOND AMENDMENT

GUNS, LAW ENFORCEMENT, AND THE POLITICS OF RACE

JENNIFER CARLSON

PRINCETON UNIVERSITY PRESS

Princeton and Oxford

Published by Princeton University Press
41 William Street, Princeton, New Jersey 08540
6 Oxford Street, Woodstock, Oxfordshire OX20 1TR

press.princeton.edu

All Rights Reserved
ISBN 9780691183855
ISBN (e-book) 9780691205861

Library of Congress Cataloging-in-Publication Data
Names: Carlson, Jennifer, author.
Title: Policing the second amendment : guns, law enforcement, and
the politics of race / Jennifer Carlson.
Description: Princeton : Princeton University Press, [2020] |
Includes bibliographical references and index.
Identifiers: LCCN 2020011510 (print) | LCCN 2020011511 (ebook) |
ISBN 9780691183855 (hardcover ; alk. paper) | ISBN 9780691205861
(ebook) Subjects: LCSH: Firearms ownership—United States. | Gun control—
United States. | Police—United States. | African Americans—Violence
against. | Discrimination in law enforcement—United States. |
United States—Race relations.
Classification: LCC HV8059 .C373 2020 (print) | LCC HV8059 (ebook) |
DDC 363.330973—dc23
LC record available at https://lccn.loc.gov/2020011510
LC ebook record available at https://lccn.loc.gov/2020011511

British Library Cataloging-in-Publication Data is available

Editorial: Meagan Levinson, Jacqueline Delaney
Production Editorial: Terri O'Prey
Text Design: Carmina Alvarez
Jacket/Cover Design: Karl Spurzem
Production: Erin Suydam
Publicity: Kathryn Stevens, Maria Whelan
Copyeditor: Madeleine Adams

Jacket/Cover Credit: Shutterstock

This book has been composed in Charis

Printed on acid-free paper. ∞

Printed in the United States of America

10 9 8 7 6 5 4 3 2 1

To those who must struggle over terms they did not choose

Contents

A Note to Readers

This book is an attempt to unravel the relationship among legitimate violence, public law enforcement, and race through the lens of gun politics and gun policy. It is animated by data in three forms: newspaper and archive analysis, interviews with police chiefs, and observations of gun licensing processes. Data involving people and their lived experience are unruly and often contradictory. Sociological analysis demands that we—its authors—subordinate the messiness of lived experience, and the uneven schema used to navigate and make sense of it, to develop our parsimonious theoretical claims. But people, and their experiences, are not merely sociological categories, and unruly data are not just objects of analysis or grounds for narrative elaboration. Data and analysis always also stand as ethical claims, moral proclamations, and political stances. For different readers with their own distinctive experiences with guns, policing, and the politics of race, different portions of this book may be difficult to read and absorb. As author, I do not take for granted, and deeply appreciate, your willingness to tread these waters. Thank you.

Acknowledgments

I wrote this book in the two and a half years that my father lived with, and then died from, ALS. ALS is a relentless disease; it always ends in death, but that's not the worst part. On a monthly, then weekly, then seemingly daily basis, my dad lost function. Each step in this graduated decline—not being able to feed himself; not being able to walk; not being able to swallow; not being able to speak; not being able to hold up his own head; finally, not being able to even blink yes or no—signaled a physical loss but also a deeply social one. We have an easy way of measuring biological death; social death, not so much—and we're wary to face such slow and severe deterioration head-on.

As my father's illness undid him, there were too many moments of sadness, loss, and despair—but also remarkable moments of gratitude, happiness, and connection. The awareness granted by the impending death of a loved one can affect people in many ways; I found myself recognizing life anew—and increasingly refusing to entertain the fear, anxiety, hastiness, or any other emotion that can rob us of the joy of what we do and what we achieve. Although I could not have known it at the time that I was collecting interviews and observations for what would become this manuscript, this book became my refuge. It provided a space for me to recognize the pleasure of losing oneself in reading and writing; to acknowledge the exuberance of being able to objectify my thoughts and ideas into the written word; and to greet the privilege of contributing to a conversation beyond myself. I am deeply grateful to be able to do this work. My ability to do so is a testament to my father's perseverance and example in ways I am only now starting to grapple with.

This book would not have been possible without the generosity and goodwill of dozens of police chiefs who agreed to share their perspectives and experiences on gun politics, gun policy, gun violence, and gun law enforcement. Although my pledge to keep participants anonymous precludes me from acknowledging them by name, I am grateful that they took the time to speak with me, and that they shared their insights honestly and frankly. I hope that they (and readers more broadly) find in this book a serious, and sincere, sociological attempt to understand the crucial ways in which police make sense of, and engage with, guns in America.

Many people contributed their own intellectual labor to this book. I want to especially thank Kristin Goss, Nikki Jones, Cal Morrill, and Maria Smith for reading and rethinking this manuscript with me at a book workshop at the University of California, Berkeley. I am also grateful to Jennifer Alexander, Stefano Bloch, Liz Chiarello, Jessica Cobb, Randol Contreras, Phil Goodman, Kimberly Hoang, Neda Maghbouleh, Dan Martinez, Jordanna Matlon, Josh Page, Poulami Roychowdhury, Forrest Stuart, and Laurel Westbrook, who provided pivotal feedback on early versions of chapter drafts. Chessa Rae Johnson rescued many ideas in the manuscript with her attention to lyricism and empiricism (as well as definite articles and helping verbs). In addition, portions of this book were presented at Boston College; Duke University; University of Arizona; University of California, Berkeley; University of California, Irvine; University of California, Riverside; University of Chicago; University of Georgia; University of Massachusetts, Amherst; University of New Mexico; University of Ottawa; University of Rochester; and University of Toronto. The engaged feedback I received at these venues helped me to increase the clarity of the book's core arguments. Versions of some of the arguments in this book have appeared in the *American Journal of Sociology, Social Problems, Gender and Society,* and *Law and Society Review*; I want to thank the editorial staff and reviewers at each of these journals for shepherding my articles through the peer-review process. I also want to thank Madison Armstrong for diligently reading and copyediting an early draft of the manuscript.

The support from Princeton University Press has been incredible and indispensable. From the start of manuscript development, Meagan Levinson provided hands-on guidance, coaching me on narrative voice, theoretical accessibility, and analytical cogency. Her patient attention allowed me to grow as a writer and a thinker, especially as I tried out new approaches to writing. Overall, Meagan, along with the Princeton team she assembled and the anonymous reviewers she arranged, provided vital insights into organizing the book's core structure, tightening the book's arguments, and smoothing out the prose. And in particular, Madeleine Adams provided crucial wordsmithing on the final version of the manuscript. I could not ask for a more responsive, more thoughtful, and more compassionate team than Princeton's.

I am also grateful for the funding that made this book possible. This includes a Connaught Small Faculty Grant from the University of Toronto; a Visiting Assistant Professorship at the University of California, Irvine; and a Social and Behavioral Sciences Research Institute Faculty Small Grant from the University of Arizona. Likewise, I gratefully acknowledge the tireless support of the staff at the University of Arizona's School of Sociology, without whom this book would have not been possible: thank you Jesse Castillo, Elena Cruz, Vienna DeLuca, Raquel Fareio, Lauren Jacobson, Miguel Larios, and Juliana Reddick.

My unstoppable friends, colleagues, and mentors—many have been all three—have provided me with support, love, and patience during the journey of this book, which necessarily entailed so much more than "just" a book. Thank you for being there at a moment's notice; for listening and listening and listening—and always without judgment; for melding heart and mind and pushing me to embrace both without reservation; for teaching me how to be a better thinker, a better friend, and a better person; for taking my ideas seriously enough to pull them apart and help put them back together; for reminding me that life is full—tragic and beautiful. Whether I could do this without all of you is beside the point; it simply wouldn't be worth doing any other way.

Jessica Cobb, Bradley Coffman, Jenn Earl, Kristin Goss, Kimberly Hoang, Chessa Rae Johnson, Sarah Macdonald, Raka Ray, Jaime Tollefson—and especially Nick Danford: thank you for your friendship.

Mom, dad, sister, brother: thank you for teaching me, even after so many years, the value of family.

And Jeremy Cripps: thank you for the power of partnership.

Finally, the University of Arizona, where I work and wrote this book, is sited on the homelands of the Tohono O'odham Nation and the Pascua Yaqui tribe. I acknowledge the historical and present-day social, political, and economic relations that have made possible the circumstances of today's United States. This includes the genocide of Native peoples and the appropriation of their land; the enslavement of African peoples and the exploitation of their labor; as well as the ongoing relations of racial and economic domination undergirded by white supremacy.

POLICING THE
SECOND AMENDMENT

INTRODUCTION
AN ARMED SOCIETY IS A POLICED SOCIETY

In the summer of 2016, Philando Castile—a school cafeteria supervisor, a father, a fiancé, an African American—is driving his family in a suburb of Minneapolis. He is pulled over by police. This is one of millions of interactions that civilians in the United States would have with police in 2016, and it is one of dozens Castile himself has had over the course of his life. As police's audio-recording just before the stop reveals, Castile is pulled over because the officer believes he fits the description of a robbery suspect.[1]

Castile has experienced this kind of stop before. Aware of the rules of engagement when a black man is pulled over by police, he is careful to explain that he is lawfully armed: Castile is a concealed pistol license holder.

Castile understands that his license to carry a firearm is granted on terms shaped by his racial identity. He recognizes that, as an armed African American man, he foremost has to "comply" with police. His mother later recalled that, in a conversation on the very day he was killed, Castile insisted on compliance: "That's the key thing in order to survive being stopped by the police." His sister was apprehensive about being armed and black: as she told the press in the aftermath of her brother's death, "I really don't even want to carry my gun because I'm afraid they'll shoot me first and then ask questions later."[2]

And Castile strives to comply as he navigates the stop later that evening. Dissecting his movements for the officer, he explains that he is lawfully armed but not reaching for his gun; rather, he clarifies, he is removing his driver's license and car registration for the officer. But attempting to submit to the law as a legally armed black man, Castile is put in the impossible position—what the former prosecutor Paul

Butler calls the "chokehold"[3]—in which complying with the law (e.g., reaching for his car registration, as demanded by police) means further submitting to its coercive power (i.e., being framed as an armed— and therefore dangerous—black man). For Castile, there is no space for compliance, no real opportunity to submit without being misrecognized as a violent threat; the officer is already holding Castile at gunpoint. By the time Castile exclaims, "I wasn't reaching for it [the gun]," Officer Jeronimo Yanez of the Falcon Heights Police Department has already mortally shot him.

Castile's killer had undergone twenty hours of "Bulletproof Warrior"[4] training that taught him that police who hesitate on the job could end up losing their lives, and during that stop, he quickly decides to pull the trigger. That decision aligns with an ideology of gun militarism that stipulates black men as not just suspect criminals but dangerous gun wielders—rather than legally armed as Castile was. In the process, Castile's right to keep and bear arms is done away with—the very right that many Americans, especially American conservatives, hold dear.

Nonetheless, the National Rifle Association (NRA)—despite fashioning itself as the bulwark of gun rights—only timidly speaks out about the case after being pressed by some of its members. Perhaps concerned about appearing antipolice, the organization euphemistically refers to "troubling . . . reports in Minnesota."[5] Nevertheless, as the case unfolds, some NRA members demand answers about an apparent racial double standard in defending the gun rights of Americans.

The proliferation of guns disproportionately harms African Americans who are feloniously killed, injured, and traumatized by them at rates that exceed manyfold those of other racial groups in the United States. Is it just a cruel irony of American gun law that, as African Americans turn to the very thing—the gun—that many in American society celebrate as the ultimate protection against violence and the ultimate indicator of full citizenship, they are more likely to be punitively harassed by the state—police stops, arrests, jail time, prison time, probation, and even death—on account of it?

A year later, Castile's killer is acquitted of all major charges.

On the political right, some, such as the *National Review,* bemoaned the verdict as a "miscarriage of justice."[6] Some police chiefs told me that they were deeply troubled by the facts of the case and its outcome. Ultimately, though, it was the political left that defended Castile most loudly. By the time of his death, the Black Lives Matter movement had already become a major political force to spur public debate regarding the undue and unjust killings of people of color.[7] Though the movement began in the aftermath of the acquittal of the private civilian George Zimmerman in the killing of Trayvon Martin, it soon became focused on the issue of police killings of people of color. Juxtaposed with local law enforcement's initial decision to release George Zimmerman without arrest, Castile's death intimated a lethal double standard in law enforcement's treatment of armed civilians. Castile's death electrified street protests and public outcry. *The Atlantic* declared Philando Castile, Alton Sterling, and other armed African Americans as "The Second Amendment's Second-Class Citizens."[8] A *New York Times* op-ed, titled "Philando Castile and the Terror of an Ordinary Day,"[9] implicitly conceded that gun carry was "ordinary" for Americans, even as "black people still struggle to hold on to the ordinary." Memes proliferated that maintained that arming black people was a surefire way to enact gun control.

The racial politics of guns suddenly, but only momentarily, shifted the liberal left and the conservative right to otherwise uncomfortable sides of the gun debate in the context of Castile's death. Because of the way race and gun rights intersected in this tragedy, the Castile case had the potential to create strange bedfellows and a different public discourse concerning race, guns, and policing. But ultimately, this did not and could not happen. Why not is the subject of this book.

• • •

Philando Castile was not the only one who tragically died that summer week in 2016. A day before Castile was killed, two officers approached Alton Sterling and pinned him to the floor of a convenience store in Baton Rouge, Louisiana; one of the officers yelled that Sterling had a gun, and Sterling was shot to death. Then, the day after Philando

Castile died, protesters held a Black Lives Matter rally in Dallas, Texas. There, a lone gunman targeted police in a revenge ambush, allegedly in response to the spate of police homicides leading up to that day: five Dallas Police Department officers, including Lorne Ahrens, Michael Krol, Michael Smith, Brent Thompson, and Patricio Zamarripa, were executed while on duty at the protest, protecting the right of the people gathered there to peacefully protest—in this case, peacefully protest the police.

A few days later, I interviewed Chief Raymond (a pseudonym) in a wealthy white hamlet in Northern California. Chief Raymond was exasperated: "I am not sure what can be done. I think we need some kind of divine intervention, like a Mother Teresa." I responded with my own exasperation at the run-up to the 2016 U.S. presidential election: "So, not Donald Trump or Hillary Clinton?" "No," he responded, "we need divine intervention. A spiritual fix."

Chief Raymond was hard to pin down during my hour and a half with him. He was skeptical about top-down government fixes, sardonically mocking his own chosen profession: "We're the government, and we're here to help!" In his view, people were "entitled" to own guns. He couldn't help but believe that when guns are outlawed, only outlaws will have guns: "If you tell people they can't buy guns, only law-abiding people are not going to buy a gun. I totally sympathize with that. Then the question is, what's practical?" Guns were practical, it seemed, because guns had always been a part of his life, and so it was difficult for him to imagine life without them—not just for him, but for others, too: "I am totally comfortable with a gun. I have one at home. I lock it up at all times, but I have it at home. And people should be able to have it at home, and they should lock it up." If people wanted to feel secure, he reasoned, they should be able to have guns, safely stored.

But when I brought up concealed carrying of guns into public, he seemed perplexed: "Carrying, that is a little more problematic. Philosophically . . ." There was an awkwardly long pause, which seemed to be interrupted by the weight of current events. He explained: "I put myself in the position from the perspective of law enforcement: where someone says, 'I have a gun,' and the officer says, 'let me see your hands,' and the guy reaches for a gun. Like what happened this last week in Minnesota." He notably didn't say the name Philando Castile, but we both knew what he was talking about. Then he shifted his frame of reference; he was now the concealed carrier: "I know that if I am stopped, my hands are on the wheel, and my hands are even out of the car if that's what the officer wants, and I'm doing everything that officer wants me to do. He can even 'felony' stop[10] me. Whatever he needs to feel safe."

His commitment to law and order was steadfast, as was his condemnation of lackluster enforcement. Gun bans for people deemed prohibited possessors, like people with violent felony convictions? "If we stuck to it, it'd be effective! Somehow, people manage to get their guns back— it's broken, like the courts." Gun bans for people under domestic violence protection orders? "My sense is that the courts aren't issuing them enough. They tend to minimize the severity and seriousness of domestic violence." Outright bans on entire classes of guns, such as so-called assault rifles or magazines that can hold more than ten rounds of ammunition? "It is not effective at all. Once again, we have laws on the books already, but they are not being enforced. And no, those guns [assault rifles] don't bother me." Mandatory minimums for gun-involved crimes? "If someone goes away for twenty-five years because of a gun, that's a deterrent. Sorry if we have to build bigger prisons. Ship them somewhere cheap, like Kansas or Wyoming. Warehouse them. I don't care." And he was bewildered by "all of the violence"—even, he admitted, cops "shooting people in the back." But for Philando Castile and the question of gun carrying, he couldn't give "a definitive answer except to say, it is extremely difficult to expect police officers to not use deadly force on someone they know to have a gun."

GUN POLITICS AS THE POLITICS OF THE POLICE

Police are aware that guns are lethal tools that threaten emotional, physical, legal, and financial wreckage. They understand that guns irreversibly kill. They know that their working *and* personal lives are indelibly marked by having so many guns in so many hands. And they recognize that problems, even high-stakes confrontations, can be—and often should be—solved without recourse to guns.[11] These sentiments are sometimes captured by newsmakers as evidence of police's natural alliance with gun control, as suggested by recent headlines in the *New York Times* ("As states expand gun rights, the police object"), the *Washington Post* ("Houston police chief on gun control: If not now, when?"), *USA Today* ("Gabby Giffords' gun-control group gets new law enforcement allies"), and elsewhere. From greater gun regulation, police stand to gain safer working conditions, enhanced enforcement tools, and clearer jurisdiction over their mandate as armed enforcers of the law.

The problem, though, with the assertion that police across the United States would be better off without the widespread proliferation of civilian guns is that *police themselves do not buy it*. An expansive Pew survey on police attitudes shows that police support gun rights, and in percentages that outpace the U.S. public.[12] The general public has been split 50–50 on prioritizing gun rights versus gun control, but police favor gun rights over gun control by a ratio of 3:1. Meanwhile, though police widely support gun tracking mechanisms—including expanded background checks—they also oppose outright bans. In stark contrast to the two-thirds support for an assault weapons ban among the general public, less than a third of police support the outlawing of these weapons.

It is easy to imagine how far fewer police and far fewer of *those policed* would be hurt and killed in the course of law enforcement work without guns in the holsters of civilians (or, for that matter, in the holsters of police),[13] but police nevertheless appear willing to live with the consequences of a widely armed society. How and why do many police embrace expanded gun rights? For whom do they embrace gun rights? And what are the social consequences of this embrace?

We will never know how Chief Raymond would have actually reacted upon stopping a legally armed civilian. What we do know, though, is that he, other police, and the public in general have inherited particular, racialized ideas and expectations about perpetrators and victims, about blameworthiness and innocence, about chaos and social order. None of us created these ideas out of whole cloth, but most of us have been raised and socialized to believe that they form an indispensable part of the society we live in. And, whether we like it or not, we are charged with navigating these ideas accordingly. To be clear, this is not an indictment of police except to the extent that it is an indictment of all of us; it is a recognition of the ways in which ideas about race constitutively shape our collective understandings of a wide variety of social phenomena, including the boundaries of legitimate violence.

Legitimate violence describes a kind of physical coercion that appears justifiable within the broader society where it takes place. As used in the context of this book, *legitimate violence* is not a normative term that justifies a particular act of violence; rather, it is a term that opens up the questions of *how, to what extent,* and *in what contexts do certain acts of violence become justified and thus legitimate.* The sociological approach in this book assumes that things are not simply as they appear to be; they are produced, and reproduced, through specific mechanisms and practices undertaken by real people, often coordinated by the social institutions they inhabit.

There are a number of ways violence can be justified—through law, justice, and authority.[14] Classical sociology—starting with Max Weber[15]— has long held up the state as the institution uniquely charged with the prerogative to distinguish between legitimate and illegitimate violence, including violence occurring in the private sphere and enacted by private individuals. In the contemporary context, legitimate violence has included acts perpetrated by police in the name of law and order and by private civilians in the name of defense and protection. The legal and societal norms surrounding legitimate violence, of course, do not always line up: a violent act may be deemed lawful by the state but inspire massive public outcry—as in the case of Philando Castile's death.

The controversy over designating certain acts of private violence as legitimate is at the heart of contemporary American debates about guns in society, including the proliferation of lawful guns into everyday life (e.g., gun carry), the vetting of individuals wishing to access guns (e.g., background checks), and the appropriate punishments for gun-involved infractions (e.g., enhanced sentencing for gun-involved crime). Roughly

330 million guns are owned by around one-third of American households; at least eighteen million Americans are licensed by their state of residency to carry a gun concealed, and millions more can carry under "permitless regimes"; 72 percent of Americans have shot a gun at least once.[16] White American men are disproportionately likely to own and carry guns and find in them a source of empowerment;[17] African American men also own and carry guns lawfully for protection and empowerment,[18] but they are disproportionately likely to be involved in gun-involved crimes, whether as victims or suspects.[19]

Oriented around questions of legitimate violence, this book traces contemporary American gun politics, gun policy, and gun practice across state and society (and back again). It argues that race shapes not only how gun politics unfold but also how public policies regarding guns are mobilized to distinguish between legitimate violence and criminal violence. This distinction has profound consequences for how we live and die by, and how we debate and deliberate about, guns— whether guns on the hips of private civilians or guns in the hands of police.

By attending to racial frames of legitimate violence, this book claims that within the United States, coercive social control is organized by racialized understandings of gun violence. And it shows that, although the contemporary terrain reflects a historical legacy of racial domination in the United States, the racial delineations between *legitimate* versus *illegitimate* violence and between *public* versus *private* legitimate violence are actively reproduced and, at times, resisted.

Accordingly, this book centers on three key brokers that play crucial roles in staking out the boundaries of legitimate violence for private *and* public gun wielders. The first is the NRA. Although the organization is known for its transformation of the cultural and legal landscape of gun rights among private civilians, it has also advocated on behalf of police as professional gun wielders since the early twentieth century. The second is police chiefs. Although they may not be on the front lines of gun law enforcement in the sense of conducting regular stops and searches, they are uniquely and acutely attuned to the complex politics surrounding gun policy by virtue of their accountability to their respective agencies, to the politicians who appoint them, and to the broader public on whose behalf they serve. The third is gun board administrators who issue, reject, revoke, and suspend gun carry licenses. Although gun boards exist in only a few states,[20] they provide a rare window into understanding how representatives of the state— here again, public law enforcement—broker the boundaries of legitimate violence for private civilians looking to wield legitimate violence in the form of a concealed firearm.

Each of these brokers provides a vital vantage point to unravel "gun talk." Gun talk refers to the discourses through which we make sense of guns, including criminal guns and lawful guns as well as private civilian guns and police guns. Accordingly, gun talk provides a means of tracing sensibilities regarding the social dynamics of legitimate violence. Who has the capacity for it, and based on what statuses or qualifications? In what contexts? And according to what norms, justifications, or authority?

By studying the NRA, police chiefs, and gun boards, this book examines two brands of "gun talk" that link the politics of guns with the politics of the police: gun militarism and gun populism. I hope to convince the reader that these terms are more useful than the usual terms of the gun debate (i.e., "gun control" and "gun rights") for understanding the surprising affinities and aversions among those invested in the politics of guns. Under gun militarism, the division between state and society is deepened with regard to legitimate violence, and this chasm is galvanized by racialized imagery of a "bad guy with a gun" to justify aggressive gun law enforcement. In contrast, under gun populism, the boundary between state and society is blurred with regard to legitimate violence, and the putatively color-blind imagery of the "good guy with a gun" is mobilized to justify expanded gun access. Always coexisting, oftentimes complementary, and sometimes dueling,[21] these two racial frames serve as guideposts in mapping out contemporary gun talk. As such, they clarify the stakes in today's gun debate. Much more than a disagreement over private gun regulation, the U.S. gun debate is fundamentally a debate about the license for and the limit of legitimate violence—of private civilians as well as of the state.

GUN MILITARISM

Since the 1960s, the war on crime has left urban America pockmarked with busted doors, shattered windows, and broken lives. A variety of government initiatives have deepened ties between the police and the military: local police departments have vied for military equipment; they have sought out training by military experts; they have recruited military veterans to fill their ranks. This transformation has been labeled "police militarization." As the criminologist Peter Kraska describes, this is "the process whereby civilian *police* increasingly draw from, and pattern themselves around, the tenets of militarism and the military model."[22] What has resulted is a distinctive frame for understanding police-civilian relations in militarized terms, a frame that emphasizes a strong police monopoly on legitimate violence as the preferred mechanism to wage a war on crime. This book calls this frame "gun militarism."

The "Warrior mindset" is a powerful starting point for understanding gun militarism. As the former law enforcement officer and legal scholar Seth Stoughton writes, this mindset "refers to a deep-bone commitment to survive a bad situation no matter the odds or difficulty, to not give up even when it is mentally and physically easier to do so."[23] This mindset is what Philando Castile's killer learned when he attended auxiliary "Bulletproof Warrior" training. According to a *New York Times* summary, the training treats police work as combat, portrays "a world of constant and increased threat to officers," and encourages officers to fully embrace their prerogative to use force. (As the *New York Times* notes, the course labels as "myth" the notion that "the officer must use the minimal amount of force necessary to affect their lawful law enforcement objectives.")[24] From the perspective of the Warrior, gun regulation becomes a mechanism to disarm the enemy, thereby stacking the odds in the Warrior's favor.

With the Warrior brand of policing unleashed on urban streets across the United States, black Americans have learned from an early age— from the police who stopped, frisked, questioned, and arrested them as well as from parents and community members who struggled to protect their lives and their childhood innocence[25]—that their skin color made them suspicious; their clothing, body language, and words were under protracted surveillance for evidence of presumed criminality; and therefore there was no such thing as an unnecessary precaution in performing black deference to police authority. And although black and brown girls and women are frequently the target of police abuse, sexual assault, and violence and are denied status as deserving victims as compared to their white counterparts,[26] the specter of hyperaggressive, hypersexual masculinity became central to suturing criminality to blackness. Black boys and men are disproportionately likely to be stopped, frisked, arrested, incarcerated, and killed by state agents.[27]

These were all lessons that Philando Castile knew well. As a legally armed black man, Philando Castile should have upset the stereotypes that stipulated black men as criminals (a felony conviction, after all, would have barred him from gun possession, let alone gun carry). Gun militarism nevertheless rendered his life unlivable because it left no room for firearms in the hands of private civilians already racialized as potential criminals. As a racial frame[28] used by public actors to define and demarcate the boundaries of public versus private legitimate violence, gun militarism reveals that the U.S. state is invested in a state monopoly on legitimate violence—at least with respect to the specter of racialized criminality.

But this is not the only frame of legitimate violence at stake in the United States.

GUN POPULISM

Millions of Americans carry guns every day. Many of them are stopped by police without incident. That reality raises the question of whether Philando Castile could have been understood differently—not as a threat to the prerogatives of law enforcement but as a collaborator in social order. From the perspective of gun carriers, this was often the purpose of a lawfully carried firearm: to provide a stopgap between those precious moments between a violent crime's commission and the police's arrival.[29] From this perspective, Castile was not a threat to police or public safety; he was an asset. As an armed citizen-protector,[30] he was someone willing to use lethal force to save innocent life and, therefore, someone aligned with police in pursuit of public order or, at the very least, public safety. Accordingly, a license to carry *should* have provided a credential of respectability for its carrier.[31]

The notion of police looking to private legitimate violence as an asset rather than a threat may surprise some. It certainly goes against the commonplace presumption that the police are defined by "the gun and the badge," so to speak. But it is entirely in line with much of the gun talk that the NRA crafts, that police chiefs embrace, and that gun boards enact. And it is also in line with American history.[32] The historian Pieter Spierenburg reminds us that "in the United States as a whole and throughout most of its history, the social pressures favoring a monopolization of force have been weak in comparison with those in European national societies."[33] In a book provocatively titled *The Six-Shooter State*, the political scientist Jonathan Obert argues that private and public forms of legitimate violence have co-constituted and reinforced one another in response to major social upheavals, from industrializing Chicago to the Reconstruction South to Western settlement.[34] Even the earliest forms of U.S. state-making—namely, Anglo settler militias who violently pushed the lines of U.S. sovereignty deeper and deeper into Native lands through dispossession and genocide[35]—often took the form of private initiative in pursuit of public interest. And in the contemporary period, scholars studying phenomena as diverse as a "no rules" weapons fighting groups, borderland militias, and armed citizen patrols find that legitimate violence percolates across state and society, often buttressing state prerogatives in the process.[36]

We risk sketching out a very incomplete picture of the contours of legitimate violence in the United States if we focus exclusively on gun militarism. The opposite of gun militarism is not merely a *lack* of aggressive policing. Rather, it is a different way of demarcating legitimate violence and of understanding the significance of guns in private possession, which I unravel in this book as "gun populism."[37] Gun populism helps explain why much of law enforcement supports expanded gun rights; why many police see armed civilians as collaborators in fending off threats; and why the celebration of "good guys with guns" enhances the legitimacy of police and private wielders of violence alike. Under *this* brand of gun talk, armed civilians are not threats but assets to the state, and police, for their part, understand themselves not so much as Warriors who hunt criminals but as Guardians who save victims.

Gun populism is embedded in an alternative, and underappreciated, policy impulse of the war on crime. Since the 1980s, firearms laws involving gun carry (such as "shall-issue" laws) and the defensive use of guns (such as Stand Your Ground) have largely expanded gun access and use. As with "tough on crime" politics that embolden the state to punish criminal offenders, this set of policies champions the rights of law-abiding civilians over those of would-be criminals. However, these policies presume the state's incapacity to solve the problem of crime for ordinary Americans.[38] Unlike gun militarism, which deepens the divide between police and private civilians with respect to legitimate violence, gun populism blurs this line by recognizing certain forms of private violence as legitimate, often in an effort to protect "the people" from threats from below (e.g., political, economic, and cultural threats posed by marginalized groups) and above (e.g., political, economic, and cultural threats posed by elites).

Gun populism often appears alongside color-blind ideals of lawfulness and innocence that nevertheless reflect values, dispositions, and sensibilities associated with whiteness.[39] Indeed, the very expectation that one's gun will be recognized as legitimate is one example of why the legal scholar Cheryl Harris[40] sees whiteness as a form of property that can compel certain kinds of recognition from legal authorities. While most policing scholarship reduces race to black and brown bodies, gun populism urges us to unpack the relationship among whiteness, legitimate violence, and policing. Despite its naturalized invisibility,[41] whiteness is a contingent social achievement[42] that does not merely disadvantage some but also "craft[s] advantages"[43]—for example, the advantage of having one's acts of violence recognized as legitimate. Throughout American history, institutional arrangements have benefited whites by redistributing resources from people of color.[44] Such arrangements have also established the structural and discursive shill for justifying this redistribution—such as the construction of black and brown boys and men as criminal "thugs."[45] Finally, as this book unravels, such arrangements have effectively deputized whites (and those who adhere to the color-blind politics of racial respectability) as legitimate carriers of law and order and validated the racial distribution of legitimate violence that sustains it.

Centered on public law enforcement but not restricted to it, this book analyzes the social life of gun populism and gun militarism. These bifurcated racial frames of legitimate violence (namely, a militarized bent and a populist bent) help unlock the contemporary politics of the police and the present terrain of gun politics—and the urgency of considering them as deeply intertwined, rather than distinctly separate, concerns.[46]

POLICING THE SECOND AMENDMENT

Chief Raymond and police across the United States chose the profession of law enforcement, but they did not choose its history. Today's law enforcement entered the profession during and after its ascendance as a central institution for the color-blind pursuit of law and order. Although race overtly undergirded the origins and manifestations of policing projects in the South, the North, and the West in their early incarnations, policing became increasingly color-blind as the twentieth century marched forward. With the assistance of late nineteenth- and early twentieth-century sociologists and criminologists who pioneered statistical analyses of crime as a scientific venture that nevertheless attempted to justify racial inferiority,[47] crime (rather than race per se) became a central concern of what would develop by the latter half of the twentieth century into a vast and complex carceral state.

This emphasis on crime would be the basis whereby police transformed from a corrupt and inept state institution dependent on outside support (whether charities in the North,[48] white supremacists in the South,[49] or private security firms in the West[50]) into an institution singularly defined by its professional commitment to eradicate crime. Police work has historically been highly localized and uneven, but during the twentieth century, it became more standardized, while the discourses used to *talk* about police—as heroic crime fighters sworn to protect and serve—became increasingly monolithic among the police and public alike. Crime thus became a dog whistle both to justify the aggressive pursuit of "law and order" in black and brown communities as well as to flag a particular kind of state authority captured in the figure of the uniformed police officer.

Following Ibram X. Kendi's caution that we should not approach the history of race in America as a history of racial progress,[51] this book does not conceptualize the contemporary contours of either the politics of policing or gun politics as a monolithic march toward, or away from, greater justice, equality, and order. Instead, it considers these politics as contingent and mutually reinforcing. As such, this book aims to trace different impulses—gun militarism and gun populism—with regard to the organization of legitimate violence, public law enforcement, and gun access in the United States. To "police" the Second Amendment is not merely to regulate guns; it is to forward particular visions of social order that reflect particular understandings of both what *constitutes* legitimate violence and *how it should be distributed* across society, visions that are embedded—often implicitly but sometimes explicitly as well—in racial ideas surrounding law and order. To "police" the Second Amendment means negotiating gun militarism and gun populism amid long-standing and revamped ideas about criminality and innocence, as Chief Raymond did as he negotiated his own use of force in relation to his delicate support for civilian access to firearms.

Evidence

This book develops gun militarism and gun populism as racial frames of legitimate violence that link together the politics of guns and the politics of the police. To unravel this linkage, I rely on newspaper accounts from local and national newspapers; interviews with police chiefs across Arizona, Michigan, and California; and observations made at gun licensing boards in Michigan. This evidence allows me to explore the relationship among gun violence, gun politics, gun policy, and gun law enforcement.

I focus on three kinds of actors that broker the relationship between the politics of guns and the politics of the police. The first involves gun lobby organizations. Since the early twentieth century, the NRA in particular has acted as what the sociologists Roberto Fernandez and Roger Gould call an "itinerant broker."[52] This kind of broker links actors involved in the same social arena, but the broker itself is not actually part of that social arena. This book shows that the NRA plays a role in coordinating the attitudes and, to a much more limited degree, the actions of law enforcement officers across jurisdictions, even though the NRA itself is not a state entity. Second, this book considers the administrators (themselves law enforcement) who populate gun boards as "gatekeeper brokers"[53] insofar as they decide the terms on which a particular resource—in this case, legitimate violence in the form of the capacity to lawfully carry a firearm—is distributed to private, nonstate actors. Third, this book looks at police chiefs as "representative brokers"[54] because they must navigate the competing demands coming from both *outside* and *within* their respective agencies.

The population of police chiefs, it is important to note, is not interchangeable with law enforcement at large. Chiefs should not be generalized to the whole of public law enforcement. Nevertheless, their vantage point is key to understanding the social construction of gun violence within public law enforcement and its impact on police practice, as police chiefs play critical roles in training, managing, and disciplining officers within their jurisdictions. Hailing from an earlier generation of police, chiefs are older, and they tend to have less racial and gender diversity. My interviewees were overwhelmingly white, middle-aged men split across urban, suburban, and rural jurisdictions. In addition, most police spend their careers involved in patrol activities, whereas in many agencies, chiefs neither regularly engage in patrol nor have done so for years. (That said, many of the chiefs I interviewed in smaller and medium-sized locales attested to regularly engaging in patrol activities.) Police chiefs and line officers are widely known to differ in their political profiles, with line officers generally more conservative than top brass. Accordingly, as candid as police chiefs were during my interviews, the findings in this book likely *underestimate rather than oversell* the pull of gun populism and gun militarism in shaping police's stance on guns. (For those who are interested, I describe my methodological approach as well as present detailed aggregated data on sample characteristics in appendix A.)

This book traces gun militarism and gun populism across three states with similar politics of crime and punishment but dissimilar politics of guns. Arizona, California, and Michigan are racially diverse and socioeconomically unequal states characterized by punitive politics of policing and punishment. The politics of crime and punishment in each state reflects the punitive turn in criminal justice since the 1960s as well as an increasing proliferation of criminal justice practices and sensibilities beyond criminal justice proper.[55] Over the past five decades, these states have rallied "tough on crime" policies to address issues of immigration, racial inequality, socioeconomic restructuring, and public disinvestment.[56] Nonetheless, their respective politics of guns—and gun cultures—are strikingly divergent.

Arizona

Arizona is "gun-lax": there are few restrictions on gun use and gun ownership in Arizona, and the state has even passed a law aimed at superseding federal regulation of guns produced and sold within state lines. Outpacing states popularly associated with gun rights (such as Texas or Florida), Arizona represents a small but growing number of states that have abolished restrictions in favor of expanded gun access and resisted laws that would enhance regulations. Arizona receives an F from the Giffords Law Center to Prevent Gun Violence, a gun-safety organization;[57] it has frequently been ranked #1 by the magazine *Guns & Ammo* as the best state for gun owners. As the magazine notes, "It's hard to improve upon Arizona's gun laws but they seem to make an effort every year."[58] Legally, the state boasts an unprecedented apparatus—or lack thereof—for gun law enforcement, and pro-gun groups like the Arizona Citizens Defense League press to ensure that the state's laws remain favorable to gun rights proponents. There is no required licensing procedure to vet civilians who carry firearms within the state (a licensing apparatus exists for individuals wishing to carry out-of-state), nor is there a firearm registry or permitting system for gun ownership. Background checks are not required for private sales. Legally, an eighteen-year-old can possess (provided it is obtained via private sale) and openly carry a pistol without a license; anyone twenty-one or older can carry any gun they legally possess either openly or concealed. Arizona not only has Stand Your Ground, but also a law designating what constitutes the lawful display of firearms for defensive purposes (effectively legalizing "brandishing" for the purpose of protection). There are no Red Flag laws that facilitate the seizure of guns from those posing a danger to themselves or others, and—by virtue of eased due process standards—those under personal protection orders for domestic violence are not automatically required to relinquish their firearms, despite federal regulatory efforts in this regard.

Despite being ranked in the top third of U.S. states for gun violence,[59] high-profile acts of gun violence (such as the 2002 University of Arizona Nursing School shooting and the 2011 Gabrielle Giffords shooting), and pockets of gun-safety advocacy (including a surge in activism in the aftermath of the Giffords shooting), pro–gun rights sentiments saturate the social life of Arizona from a variety of angles. Economically, the state is deeply intertwined with the gun industry. With a Ruger factory in Prescott and countless niche gun and gun accessory manufacturers, gunsmiths, and self-defense schools, the state has been described as a "Mecca" for gun makers.[60] Culturally, Arizona is shaped by its deep frontier history of gunslingers and vigilantes; this history is visible in arenas as distinct as the state's constitution[61] and its contemporary tourist campaigns—Tombstone, Arizona, for example, recently proclaimed itself America's "Second Amendment City." Politically, the state's pro–gun rights sentiments not only shape debates directly about guns but also inflect other issues, including responses to the politics of migration; the relationship between the United

States and sovereign Native peoples; and the relationship between local and state politics and federal politics, particularly with respect to the U.S. military.

Michigan

In contrast to Arizona, Michigan represents a state apparatus best characterized as "gun-permissive." Michigan is representative of the majority of states in that it is both regulatory (i.e., licensing systems are in place) *and* permissive. Residents can legally own handguns and long guns as well as fully automatic guns, although they must register handguns with local police (unless they have an exemption) and register fully automatic firearms with the federal Bureau of Alcohol, Tobacco, Firearms and Explosives (ATF) and the Michigan State Police. Like the majority of other states, Michigan has a shall-issue concealed carry licensing system, which means that the state grants civilians a license to carry a gun on a nondiscretionary basis; these laws vastly expand the number of lawful gun carriers within states that pass them. Michigan passed Stand Your Ground legislation in 2006, and unlicensed open carry remains legal in the state. And although the state bars anyone under a domestic-violence–related personal protection from possessing a firearm, any protocols and resources for actually seizing the firearms fall largely onto local police jurisdictions. Meanwhile, efforts by gun control advocates to pass Red Flag laws that would facilitate gun seizures have been considered but stalled in the state legislature.

Michigan has a multifaceted gun culture. Hunting is huge: in 2017, the state counted more than seven hundred thousand licensed hunters, trailing only Texas and Pennsylvania.[62] Furthermore, hunting accounts for billions of dollars of the state economy and 170,000 jobs.[63] Meanwhile, Michigan has a vibrant defensive gun culture; the state receives more than six million dollars a year in concealed pistol license (CPL) fees, and with more than six hundred thousand active CPL holders, roughly 8 percent of the adult population are licensed to legally carry firearms in public.[64] Whether in the rural Upper Peninsula or urban Detroit, it is difficult to drive far without seeing billboards, bumper stickers, or storefronts embracing firearms as everyday objects of recreation and protection. Shooting ranges, gun shops, and mom-and-pop firearms training schools do not just allow Michiganders to enjoy gun culture; they also allow entrepreneurial residents to transform gun culture into personal businesses. Meanwhile, the state has a bustling gun rights political community, including the Michigan Coalition for Responsible Gun Owners and Michigan Open Carry.

Alongside this vibrant gun culture is an uneven terrain of gun violence. Though the state experienced overall declining rates of gun violence—it now ranks at the median of states in terms of the firearms death rate[65]—gun violence remains starkly concentrated in a few areas of the state. Detroit, Flint, and Saginaw frequently top lists of the most dangerous cities in the United States. Furthermore, despite the state's pro-gun politics, it is a historically blue state—the home of labor struggles that gave rise to the United States' most vibrant union organizing. This blend of politics helps explain the state's interesting mix of gun policy—better described as permissive than lax. The state received a C from the Giffords Law Center to Prevent Gun Violence,[66] and *Guns & Ammo* ranked the state twenty-seventh in its 2017 list of the "Best States for Gun Owners."[67]

California

Finally, California is "gun-restrictive." California administers its own background check system alongside the federal system, and the state heavily restricts gun ownership, has its own state-level assault weapon ban, and has made efforts to regulate both magazine capacity and ammunition. Not only does California actively maintain and enforce a "prohibited persons" list to remove guns from unlawful possessors, but it has also passed Red Flag laws such as the Gun Violence Restraining Order Act (AB1014), which expands the conditions under which law enforcement may seize guns from gun owners.[68] Needless to say, the state has not followed the majority of states in passing Stand Your Ground laws or implementing a statewide shall-issue concealed carry licensing system; instead, the state has banned both loaded and unloaded open carry. California represents approximately a dozen states in which guns are highly regulated *and* highly restricted. In light of the state's efforts at gun restrictions, some firearms manufacturers have pulled their operations out of California;[69] others have ceased selling in the state altogether for reasons of politics as well as profits.[70]

As the state devolves responsibility for issuing concealed pistol licenses onto local police chiefs and county sheriffs under the state's may-issue system,[71] California gun culture has some meaningful variation within the state. Politically represented by the CalGuns Foundation, there is an active community of gun owners in California, especially in rural areas where police chiefs and county sheriffs are more likely to issue licenses to qualifying residents. Especially in urban coastal areas, however, the state is politically and culturally aligned with gun control as compared to the rest of the United States. Ranked forty-third in terms of gun deaths per 100,000 residents,[72] California receives an A from the Giffords Law Center to Prevent Gun Violence.[73] Not surprisingly, *Guns & Ammo* ranks the state at forty-sixth for "Best States for Gun Owners," commenting that "what was a very restrictive state for gun owners to live in has become outright hostile."[74]

OUTLINE OF BOOK

This book starts by reconstructing twentieth-century gun politics from the vantage point of the police. Chapter 1 focuses on the relationship between the National Rifle Association and U.S. public law enforcement. Although police may be popularly defined by "the gun and the badge," it was the NRA that helped to establish the handgun as a tool of police expertise in the early twentieth century. As the NRA courted, then antagonized, and then courted again public law enforcement in the twentieth century and into the twenty-first century, it harnessed a racial politics of crime, touting a "tough on crime" agenda for urban gun offenders while decrying efforts to regulate American gun owners seen as otherwise upstanding. This chapter establishes that the NRA, rather than acting merely as an advocate of the firearms industry or a shaper of American gun culture, serves a critical role in linking together gun politics, public law enforcement, and the racial politics of crime. Chapter 2 shifts focus to police chiefs in Arizona, California, and Michigan to examine their broad support for gun militarism in the form of aggressive "tough on crime" policies amid the specter of urban gun crime. This chapter shows that gun policy has been indelibly marked by the war on crime, rendering it intimately intertwined with the politics of race.

Whereas chapters 1 and 2 document how racialized tropes have animated understandings of urban gun violence and justified particular intersections between gun politics and the politics of the police, chapter 3 focuses on a new threat of gun violence that erupted in public and police consciousness alike in the late 1990s: active shootings. As compared to urban gun violence, active shootings are popularly associated with white perpetrators, white victims, and suburban and rural contexts. The racial politics of this new threat opened the door for police to reconceptualize themselves and their own guns. Instead of Warriors,[75] the police chiefs I interviewed situated themselves vis-à-vis active shootings as Guardians, and rather than objects of urban warfare, they saw their guns as tools of hardened care work necessary for protecting innocent victims from this newfound threat. They borrowed from the language of gun rights to make sense of their own obligations as police; they embraced the importance of their role as first responders in these crisis events, blurring the line between themselves and ordinary civilians; and they even at times embraced armed law-abiding citizens as allies and potential contributors to public safety. After explaining in chapter 3 how active shootings have affected how police chiefs understood their own prerogatives as police, chapter 4 explores how police chiefs articulate gun populism to make sense of their relationship with armed private civilians, often reflecting the sociolegal contexts in which police chiefs were embedded. In gun-restrictive California, police chiefs articulated an anti-elitist stance against lawmakers and legislators looking to unduly disturb or disarm "the people." In gun-permissive Michigan, police chiefs understood ordinary civilians as potential crime fighters and saw the gun license as a color-blind indicator of respectability.[76] And finally, Arizona chiefs found—at times begrudgingly—that Arizona's lax gun laws could enhance police response and public safety, appreciating the armed private civilian as potentially productive of social order.

The first four chapters of the book lay the foundation for understanding gun militarism and gun populism as racial frames that circulate in national, state, and local debates about guns (chapter 1) and in the attitudes of police chiefs (chapters 2, 3, and 4). Chapter 5 addresses the question of how these racial frames shape what law enforcers actually do. Unraveling how these racial frames operate in practice and with what consequences, this chapter examines two county-level gun licensing boards that operated in Michigan until the end of 2015. Largely staffed by public law enforcement, these gun boards reflected gun populism insofar as they appeared motivated to issue concealed pistol licenses to would-be licensees, but they also reflected gun militarism to the extent that they nevertheless disproportionately disadvantaged—and degraded—claimants of color seeking concealed pistol licenses as compared to white claimants.

The book concludes by turning to the promises and pitfalls of reform—both with regard to guns and with regard to the police. Attending to gun militarism and gun populism as coexisting racial frames of legitimate violence, this book shows that an armed society need not necessarily be a "polite" society, as gun rights advocates claim, but it is most certainly a "policed society." For far too long, Americans have argued about gun politics and the politics of the police as if they are separate debates. They are not—and we insist on their separation at our own peril.

CHAPTER 1

GUN POLITICS IN BLUE

Police officers will go through a wall for politicians
who have their back.
—James Pasco, Executive Director of the Fraternal Order of Police,
commenting on the Trump presidential campaign on National Public Radio's
Diane Rehm Show (2016)

The police will forgive me.
The National Rifle Association never forgets.
—Anonymous U.S. Congressman, commenting on the proposed
ban of "cop-killer" bullets, *Sun Sentinel* (1985)

In 1994, then-President Bill Clinton signed into law the Violent Crime Control and Law Enforcement Act with a flank of police officers standing behind him. It was a sweeping "law-and-order" bill: the Act would toughen criminal penalties, expand the federal death penalty, increase the number of police on the streets, establish financial support for investigating and preventing violence against women, and, finally, prohibit the manufacture of legally classified "assault weapons" and cap the capacity of newly manufactured magazines at ten rounds. This last portion of the bill was officially labeled the Public Safety and Recreational Firearms Use Protection Act, but publicly, the moniker *assault weapons ban* stuck.

Wedging gun control into the broader agenda of law and order, the Act signaled not just Democrats' embrace of "tough on crime" politics but also the emergence of new, credible allies for them: the police. By 1994, police boldly came out in support of Clinton's gun control measures, with the Fraternal Order of Police, the International Association of Chiefs of Police, and other law enforcement groups pledging a unified front.

Just a couple of decades later, the presumption that the law enforcement community largely supports gun control would be unsustainable. Today's surveys of police suggest that law enforcement largely opposes an assault weapons ban, embraces licensed concealed carry, and supports gun rights over gun control.[1] In those intervening decades, the Fraternal Order of Police (FOP) has weakened its embrace of gun control, while other law enforcement groups—e.g., the Law Enforcement Alliance of America and the Constitutional Sheriffs and Peace Officers Association—have emerged to represent the interests of pro–gun rights law enforcement. Although survey data indicate support among police for some gun control measures popular among the general public, such as universal background checks, public law enforcement as a whole can no longer be characterized as allies of the gun control lobby.

The NRA, for its part, has welcomed the law enforcement community with open arms, even though this affinity is rarely noticed in public debates about guns. Writing for *The American Rifleman* on the fiftieth anniversary of the NRA's founding of the Law Enforcement Division, Angus McClellan notes, "The NRA is well-known for its efforts in protecting the individual Right to Keep and Bear Arms, but its achievements in helping to train and prepare those to whom we've granted the power to enforce the law are relatively unknown to the public at large."[2] Starting in 1916 with Frank Kahr's call for police firearms training in the NRA's magazine *Arms and the Man*, the NRA has embraced working with public law enforcement as part of its mandate. Over the years, this has at different times meant providing police with training, funds for police equipment, and expert advice on patrol weapons; brokering gun sales between the federal government and local police agencies; publicly endorsing stiff criminal penalties for illegal gun use; proactively defending police from public criticism; and providing individual police with line-of-duty death insurance and college scholarships for the dependents of fallen officers.

Those who think of the gun rights lobby and police interests as diametrically opposed may be surprised to learn that the NRA has shaped public law enforcement in a variety of ways. Indeed, the organization helped popularize the notion that police *needed* guns (as opposed to billy clubs or anything else) to competently perform their duties. It pressed the idea that police should "qualify" on their guns as a mark of their professional proficiency. And the NRA espoused the view that police should embrace guns not just on duty as professional tools but also off duty, whether as competitive sporting gear or as means of defense and protection. From its early calls for police to be properly trained with guns[3] to its direct support to police departments[4] to its ongoing training and competitive shooting programs specifically geared at police,[5] the NRA has had an overt interest in police and their guns for more than a century.

The appeal of guns and gun rights to police, as to the public, reflects the broader contours of the politics of crime. Although police may have straddled both sides of the gun debate over the course of the twentieth century and into the twenty-first century, their embrace of gun rights and gun control alike have centered on particular notions of crime, policing, and criminal justice often informed by popularized tropes of disorderly, unruly, and criminally inclined black and brown delinquents. A historical look at the gun debate from the perspective of police reveals the heightened impact of the racial politics of crime in shaping police attitudes on guns, and it also shows how the NRA has harnessed these racial politics to reshape the meanings attached not just to guns in the hands of civilians but also to guns in the holsters of police. Over time, it has courted public law enforcement by blending together two frames for talking about the proper place of legitimate violence in society: gun militarism, which emphasizes aggressive gun law enforcement against armed criminals, and gun populism, which embraces law-abiding civilians (including police) as enhancing, rather than detracting from, the fight against crime. Placing public law enforcement at the center of debates about gun politics—that is, viewing "gun politics in blue"—clarifies how "law and order" politics has deeply shaped the politics of guns, and it also helps make sense of how officers sustain a politics of guns that entails *both* an embrace of aggressive enforcement *and* an openness to civilian gun access.

In addition to a lobbying group aimed at influencing interest groups adjacent to its gun rights platform (such as police), the NRA can also be understood as a *broker*, given its focus on *building the political foundations of the alliance* between gun rights proponents and police interests.[6] This chapter examines the relationship among the NRA, public law enforcement, and gun politics, tracing how the racial politics of crime shapes the intersection of gun politics and the politics of the police—and the role that gun control and, especially, gun rights lobbies have played in that process. Understanding that the racial contours of legitimate violence are rooted in historically situated social practices and institutions, this chapter starts with a brief history that delineates the early, inchoate forms that U.S. policing took in the eighteenth and nineteenth centuries. It then turns to the early twentieth century as the starting point for unraveling the relationship between gun politics and the politics of the police, highlighting the unique role the NRA has played as a broker in shaping legitimate violence across the state *and* society. Over the course of the twentieth century, the NRA learned a crucial lesson: that police officers are the kind of political ally that the NRA can ill afford to lose. And in acting on that lesson into the twenty-first century, the NRA has helped to shape—to the organization's own advantage—the personal and professional interests of public law enforcement in gun policy and gun politics.

FROM POLICING TO PUBLIC LAW ENFORCEMENT

Criminologists—especially those with a historical long view—point out that the apparent "police monopoly on policing" of the second half of the twentieth century may, in fact, be a blip:[7] historically, police have not monopolized policing, and today, this waning monopoly is visible in the proliferation of private policing, neighborhood watch groups, home security systems, and private gun ownership.[8]

The earliest forms of public law enforcement in the United States looked less like institutionalized public law enforcement and more like private action undertaken in pursuit of expulsion, extermination, and containment. Compared to the taken-for-granted nature of today's institutionalized and permanent police forces, early policing prerogatives could be short-lived, amorphous, and, at the same time, expansive. With no such thing as a "police officer," early white Anglo-Saxon American men (and some women) responded to the "hue and cry," served on night watch, formed militias for an array of acute and generalized issues of public order, and took it upon themselves to exercise police power where they saw fit. As early as the seventeenth century, when both Anglo-Saxons and Africans were subject to conditions of indenture and slavery, any colonist could stop strangers to demand that they identify themselves; once slavery depended entirely on black labor, slave codes emerged that allowed white colonists to police blacks—free or enslaved—by demanding identification and physically assaulting and even killing them if they did not adequately "comply."[9] As the police historian Martin Alan Greenberg notes, "during much of the seventeenth century, slave patrols did not exist. The control and discipline of slaves were considered the responsibility of any free and responsible citizen."[10] By the eighteenth and into the nineteenth centuries, however, slaveowners' agitation over runaway slaves and slave rebellions led to a form of policing that extended the coercive power of the plantation: the slave patrol. Eventually, these brutal slave patrols worked alongside, and to some degree became institutionalized as, some of the earliest public law enforcement entities in the United States, including the New Orleans Police Department in 1853. In the second half of the nineteenth century, public law enforcement in the South developed alongside virulent white supremacist militias that emerged in the aftermath of the Civil War.[11] The Ku Klux Klan (KKK) largely resembled the slave patrols of the antebellum period; though the Klan did not enjoy the formal legal immunity that earlier slave patrols did, white and black Southerners alike treated them as interchangeable, given "the straightforward adoption of [slave patrol] methods by the Ku Klux Klan and other vigilante groups of the postwar period."[12] This was convenient for Southern institutions—such as public law enforcement—

looking to reinforce racial order while also complying with Northern demands. As the historian Sally E. Hadden notes,

> The more random and ruthless aspects of slave patrolling passed into the hands of vigilante groups like the Klan. The KKK provided an outlet for the racial aggression that white Southerners could no longer legally inflict through patrolling or slave ownership. Both the methods and the targeted victims of Klan violence—denounced by federal officials—were secretly approved of by many white Southerners who came to see the Klan as the South's true "law enforcers." Meanwhile, policemen in Southern towns continued to carry out those aspects of urban slave patrolling that seemed race-neutral but that in reality were applied selectively.[13]

Thus, the KKK and other white vigilante groups provided beneficial (to adherents of white supremacy) opportunities for collusion amid pressures on police to "appear . . . racially unbiased."[14] This arrangement illustrates not just a lack of state monopoly on policing in the period leading up to and during the Jim Crow era; it also illuminates how the coordination across different private and public arenas provided a means for legitimate violence to reinforce racial domination and white supremacy, despite legal formalities putatively requiring otherwise.[15]

The relationship between racial control and early policing forms took different form in the North. There, policing was characterized by early "watch and ward committees" composed of unpaid volunteers[16] before taking shape as what scholars have understood as "class-control policing."[17] Private and later public efforts focused on patrolling the vices of immigrants that offended the sensibilities of more established Americans: "Wealthy Protestant nativists feared and resented the new immigrants, who were often Catholic, uneducated, disorderly, politically militant, and prone to voting Democrat."[18] Policing working class people to adhere to bourgeois norms would presumably make for a more efficient workforce,[19] but this was not just a class project. As early as the first half of the nineteenth century, Northerners opted for expulsion and coercive containment of black Americans, adhering to segregationist tactics, strategies, and policies before the South discovered them in the context of Jim Crow.[20] Accordingly, African American ghettos became criminal havens by design by the late nineteenth and early twentieth centuries, as Khalil Gibran Muhammad shows in *The Condemnation of Blackness*. In an effort to cleanse ethnic white communities and assuage the anxieties of white elites, institutions of vice became concentrated in black communities, and lawlessness—among both white patrons and white police, and sometimes in concert—reigned. With black ghettos subject to routine physical abuse by whites (whether private civilians or police) with little recourse to the law's protective function, it was African American reformers who, in the 1930s, first called for a brand of "community policing"—whereby African Americans would police themselves.[21]

If Northern policing emerged as an exclusionary impulse for the moral uplift of Eastern and Southern European immigrants and Southern policing centered on the coercive impulse to enforce the racial foundations of slavery (even after its formal abolition), then policing in the West introduced a different kind of racial project: that of colonial settlement and primitive accumulation at the edges of law and order. Policing efforts in the West enforced a variety of racial and class divisions, but the contexts—and stakes—were different from those in the North and the South. Western lands were not empty; settlement depended on the forced, often brutal, removal of Native Americans and Mexican Americans, and it was political violence in the form of genocide, rather than the stylized interpersonal violence of "Dodge City" and other fables of Western lawlessness, that largely shaped the West. This genocidal violence entailed the widespread physical, cultural, political, and legal butchery of Native peoples, on the one hand, and cultural and legal impunity for white settlers who committed heinous and excessive acts of violence, on the other hand. These settlers knew not only that they would never be held to account for their acts in a court of law but also that their actions would largely be condoned if not celebrated by whites who saw Native peoples as inferior and deserving of degradation. These conditions spurred a particular organization of legitimate violence. The expanse of land, the low population density, the degradation of Native peoples and the impunity for violence exacted against them, and the lack of formal and informal oversight mechanisms all facilitated "rapid, informal and harsh"[22] justice from settlers, vigilante groups, and, eventually, private policing firms that operated on behalf of railroad and mining companies. In addition to the statutory recognition of anti–horse theft societies[23] as well as high levels of legal tolerance for violence allegedly undertaken for self-defense or defense of property,[24] Western jurisdictions introduced and expanded *posse comitatus*. This doctrine is rooted in ninth-century England and recognizes the common-law authority of a sheriff and other local officials to conscript able-bodied men (who joined a "posse") to assist in law enforcement activities.[25] Accordingly, the early law enforcement agencies in Los Angeles and San Francisco of the mid-1800s can be traced to volunteer vigilante groups.[26] Early law enforcement efforts in the West also borrowed from other regions in the United States: lynch mobs and white vigilante groups ensured that the terror of Jim Crow would extend into the Western frontier (for example, the widely covered execution of the black teenage farmhand Jesse Washington by a white lynch mob occurred in Waco, Texas, in 1916), and the volunteer militia Texas Rangers played a key role in enforcing the caste system of segregation between Tejanos and Anglo-Americans known as "Juan Crow," which continued well into the mid-twentieth century.[27]

In the North, South, and West, these early policing forms slowly transformed into more institutionalized mechanisms to quell fears and realities of social disorder amid the growth of new social arrangements—industrialization in the North, chattel slavery in the South, genocidal settlement in the West.[28] A clear takeaway emerges: historically, policing—whether in the North, the South, or the West—has been a project not just *for* the community but also *of* the community, with community defined narrowly in nativist, white settler, and bourgeois terms.[29] Instead of a state monopoly on legitimate violence, then, American history reveals a dynamic distribution of legitimate violence, sometimes dispersed in the hands of ordinary whites (think: whites serving in slave-catching efforts before more formalized slave patrols); sometimes concentrated in emerging, though still informal, institutions of law, order, and racial domination (e.g., deputized slave patrols or the early Texas Rangers);[30] sometimes handed off to nonstate actors in contexts where state actors could not overtly engage in legitimate violence as such (e.g., lynch mobs); and sometimes concentrated in the hands of formal, institutionalized, and explicitly state-sanctioned state agents.

Only by the late 1800s and early 1990s did law enforcement begin to establish itself, professionalize, and—with the standardization of handguns as part of the police uniform—arm itself as the seat of legitimate violence poised to manage not just problems of social order but of racial order as well.

THE WAR ON ALCOHOL

By the turn of the twentieth century, American police were situated on the forefront of a color line increasingly understood and enforced through criminality. In the South, lynchings of black men and women were justified through appeals to law and order, and white accusations— especially regarding rape of white women—were taken at face value to indicate the guilt of the alleged perpetrator. In the North, whites also experienced impunity in practicing "street justice" against African Americans in urban ghettos, while African Americans attempting to defend themselves from white aggression were informed—through the fist and the billy club of private citizens and police alike—that *they* were, in fact, the criminals.[31] The increasing concentration of gambling halls, saloons, and other "vice" institutions in African American neighborhoods exacerbated black vulnerability.[32] *Though* these institutions often catered to whites, their location conflated blackness and criminality, and *because* these institutions often catered to whites, they effectively increased the likelihood of white-on-black violence. While early criminologists and sociologists produced statistical accounts to demonstrate (and, less often, contest) the conflation of blackness with criminality, non-elite whites were already forging this line as part of the texture of everyday life.

This backdrop is critical for appreciating the impact of Prohibition on the racial politics of policing that would emerge in the 1920s. Popu-

lar understandings of Prohibition-era law and order often focus on ro-
manticized tales of Italian and Jewish gangsters, with their iconic
tommy guns, trafficking alcohol from Canada to illicit speakeasies and
blind pigs (slang for illegal liquor establishments) in Chicago, Detroit,
Harlem, and elsewhere. Gun crime dramatically increased in tandem
with Prohibition, which was repealed in 1933.[33] The gun violence associated with these criminal gangs resulted in acute debate regarding
national gun policies and, most directly, the enactment of the National
Firearms Act of 1934, which taxed sawed-off shotguns and fully automatic firearms. A few years later, the Federal Firearms Act of 1938
established a licensing system for firearms dealers and prohibited the
transfer of firearms to "prohibited persons" such as those convicted of
a felony.

If Prohibition created the conditions for a moral panic regarding gun
violence among gangsters, its deeper appeal played on broader white
anxieties about the so-called disorderly classes. Outlawing alcohol was
seen as a way to stamp out the moral laxity associated with European
Catholics, African Americans, Asian Americans, Mexican Americans, and
other racialized groups.[34] Liquor law violation arrestees were disproportionately black; intoxication provided a convenient pretext for police
to stop and arrest "suspicious" individuals.[35] As the historian Jeffrey
Adler writes, "Race control became embedded in the crime-control
crusade, shifting the enforcement of a racialized definition of law and
order from popular justice and white mobs to legal institutions and the
police."[36] Police employed dragnets to apprehend and search "all suspicious negroes" for concealed weapons;[37] used so-called clean-up squads
focused on African Americans and the working class;[38] and "applied
the law unequally, obtained dubious search warrants, and used deadly
force with impunity."[39] As the historian Lisa McGirr writes, "Abuse of
law in policing minority and poor communities was so widespread
as to be invisible."[40] The incompleteness of the popular imagery of
Prohibition-era policing, which emphasizes gangsters while omitting
how ordinary people got swept up in its net, is itself a historical legacy
of what McGirr calls "selective" and "uneven" enforcement: "Uneven
enforcement was the hidden reason the white, urbane upper-middle

class could laugh at the antics of Izzy Einstein and Moe Smith, while Mexicans, poor European immigrants, African Americans, poor whites in the South, and the unlucky experienced the full brunt of Prohibition enforcement's deadly reality."[41]

Prohibition-era policing did more than simply solidify law enforcement as the primary institution for the installation of racial control through crime and justice. It also provided law enforcement with the very tools that now define the profession: in this era, police increasingly turned to guns, rather than billy clubs, as the tool and symbol of law and order. The decade of the 1920s is critical for understanding the sociolegal life of guns, not only because the era led to what is largely treated as the first federal gun control in the United States but also because it represents the era in which guns became embedded in the work of American public law enforcement—thanks to the NRA.

The NRA was formed and consolidated with the expressed purpose of enhancing marksmanship; the organization's 1871 charter from New York State allowed the organization to host firearms competitions, organize rifle clubs, and assist in training and education for civilian enthusiasts and military members alike. Fully in line with this orientation, the NRA helped create the notion that police not just *should* but *must* be armed to fully achieve their potential as crime fighters. As early as 1916, the NRA's Frank J. Kahr explained the necessity of police guns in the organization's then-flagship magazine, *Arms and the Man*:

> When the time comes and every policeman is capable of drawing his revolver or pistol with the least possible delay and shooting it accurately, the lawbreakers, who now hold little fear of the policeman's aim, will think twice before drawing their fire. Then, and not until then, will the criminal element have respect for the policeman's revolver.[42]

Kahr's call to police arms came at a particularly opportune moment. On the one hand, World War I dramatically increased the availability of guns in the United States due to leftover service guns that returned with soldiers.[43] On the other hand, police themselves had little standardized training or even protocols with regard to firearms. Around the beginning of the twentieth century, the then-president of the New York Police Department Board of Police Commissioners Theodore Roosevelt moved to standardize that agency's firearms with a purchase of 4,500 Colt New Police revolvers,[44] but this was an exception in that time. More often, police agencies lacked formal training with firearms, and police officers themselves often used their own private sidearms while on police duty "as often as not as a matter of personal choice."[45] As Kahr himself explained,[46]

> The average policeman has some rather vague notions about shooting. In his responsible position of protector of homes and human life he is called upon frequently to use his head, his club or the revolver or pistol furnished him when he takes his place on the force. . . . We are far from that state of Arcadia where we may place complete confidence in our police force and its ability to protect life and property under all conditions. . . . [The policeman] is still far short of being a hundred per cent perfect unless he is qualified in the art of shooting.

At the beginning of the 1920s, an NRA-administered survey of all police departments serving jurisdictions with more than twenty-five thousand residents found that only three police agencies had what constituted, according to the NRA, coherent firearms training programs.[47] Over the course of the next ten years, the NRA proactively focused on changing that. The organization encouraged police to become NRA members, undergo NRA training, and return to their local agencies to start up rifle clubs and teach firearms proficiency. As the criminologist Gregory Morrison notes,[48]

> The significance of this development cannot be overemphasized, for it propelled the NRA into the role of national sanctioning body for police firearms training. By as early as the mid-1920s, officers who managed to fire minimum scores on an NRA course became "qualified." This was a significant development in the evolving nexus of police firearms, training and competency.

The NRA's focus on the police during this decade reflected the marksmanship orientation of the organization at the time, but it also represented a protracted attempt by the organization to situate itself as a "law and order" organization allied with the police. As the NRA executive vice-president noted in 1926, "The National Rifle Association feels that there is no angle of the shooting game and no angle of the crime suppression movement which is of greater importance than the angle dealing with the subject of police pistol marksmanship, and we intend to bend every effort toward promoting such marksmanship and toward co-operating with all department heads in this direction."[49] By 1925, the NRA had established a police school "emphasizing handgun proficiency and stressing instructor preparation [as well as] to varying degrees . . . other firearms, hand to hand fighting, and riot control."[50]

Throughout the 1920s, the organization held in-person and postal competitions aimed at the public law enforcement community. From the perspective of the police, the NRA's training provided a number of benefits: NRA-organized matches and competitions provided an opportunity for police to develop and broadcast their newfound handgun proficiency and define their professional identities by a crime-fighting mentality centered on firearms. The extent to which American police work became professionalized around the gun owes a great deal to the NRA's work during this period.

Politically, this alliance had an obvious payoff for the NRA. Many police in this period publicly took a prohibitionist view on guns. In 1922, the International Association of Chiefs of Police recommended the adoption of uniform state laws on gun restrictions.[51] Meanwhile, a 1927 *New York Times* article titled "Plan to Bar Arms to All Criminals" revealed that the sixteen police chiefs gathered for a subcommittee of the National Crime Commission agreed that guns "were a 'disadvantage' for any citizens who owned them."[52] The deputy superintendent of Chicago police noted that "Chicago authorities think weapons are unnecessary except for policemen . . . owning or carrying a gun by a citizen ought to be a felony. Gun toters should go to prison."[53] Meanwhile, the chief of Detroit rhetorically asked, "Do you know of any laymen who have really helped themselves by using pistols for self-protection? No. The idea that they do help themselves is a popular fallacy."[54] Against the backdrop of these sentiments, the NRA's police-oriented outreach, according to Morrison, "paid a variety of benefits, including making it more difficult to paint NRA, by virtue of its widespread firearms activities, into the crime picture itself."[55]

Crucial in shaping ideas about how and the extent to which police should and would be trained in handgun proficiency, the NRA was soon a victim of its own success. By 1935, the FBI had outfitted its agents with handguns and took over firearms training. Guns were now so centrally embedded in what it meant to be a government agent that the NRA no longer needed to broker the symbolic relationship between guns and the state.[56] It would not be until 1960 that the NRA would again so deliberately forge a relationship with the police—a relationship that would be soon strained under the caustic politics of crime and disorder that would overwhelm U.S. statecraft in the second half of the twentieth century.[57]

THE WAR ON CRIME

At the dawn of the 1960s, the NRA was not yet Washington's most powerful lobby; the police were not yet a militarized force; and the racialized tropes of "crack addicts," "gangbangers," and "superpredators"[58] threatening the streets of urban America had not yet arrested the American imagination regarding crime and its control (that would come in the 1980s and 1990s). Although the leftist slogan that "times are a'changin'" reflected changing sentiments about the Vietnam War, civil rights, and other progressive issues, the mantra could have just as well applied to the NRA—and the changes it was about to undergo.

In the early 1960s, the NRA was still broadly understood as an all-American organization focused on training and discipline; many police tested their firepower not on the streets but in competitions held by the NRA; and Americans felt generally safe. As a 1962 editorial in the *St. Louis Dispatch* noted,[59]

> I am a member of the National Rifle Association and mighty proud of it; I'm also proud of the fact that my son was taught how to shoot. . . . I wonder if [legislators proposing regulations on firearms]

know about the countless dads and police officers who coach young men in the use of firearms—and without pay?

This sentiment—from the perspective of the NRA, the police, and the public—helps to explain why the NRA founded its Law Enforcement Division with little public fanfare. As an article appearing in *Police Magazine* on the fiftieth anniversary of the Division explains,

> In 1960, the NRA changed its law enforcement firearms training strategy. The NRA's leadership decided that the best way to reach individual officers was to provide better training for police firearms instructors and let them take what they learned back to their students. . . . For the last 50 years, the NRA has been fine-tuning its law enforcement programs. Since 1960, the NRA's Law Enforcement Firearm Instructor Training program has graduated 50,000 firearms instructors. The program is now also open to military instructors, which brings the organization full circle from its roots.[60]

As the NRA championed police training, they also were slowly beginning to come into their own as a hard-line gun rights organization. In 1963, the organization developed a national drive to oppose a putative ban on guns, insisting that "we surround the criminal with every safeguard, yet we propose to lay penalties on people who would arm themselves for defense . . . of their loved ones or for sport."[61] By the mid-1960s, the NRA's actions were already credited with preventing the passage of meaningful federal gun control proposals.[62]

While the NRA was finding its voice as a hard-line gun rights defender, it was also testing out its position on enforcement and criminalization, advocating for more enforcement, more support for law enforcement, and stronger consequences for illegal gun use. As a 1967 op-ed in the *Detroit Free Press* insisted, "The NRA fights against the criminal and for the law-abiding citizen and police officer."[63] Coverage of the 1965 NRA convention likewise suggests a concerted effort to position the organization as an ally of law enforcement:

> The NRA also will support properly drawn legislation to impose heavy penalties on crimes involving the misuse of firearms and urge

better enforcement of laws at all levels of government. . . . Harlon B. Carter, newly elected president of the association, said the board of directors and the executive committee formulated plans to further the war on crime and accidents on many fronts. He said that the association now has 600 police departments among its 12,000 member clubs and organizations and made plans to expand its police training program in the year ahead.[64]

Then-president Harlon Carter's statements on law enforcement are worth situating within his own personal biography. The son of a Texan border patrol agent, Carter joined the NRA at the age of sixteen in 1930. In that period, hundreds of Tejano (Mexican American) residents were killed by Texas Rangers, border patrols, and citizens. Like lynchings of African Americans, these killings were often justified by accusations of crime, but the underlying motivation was control over the contested borderlands between the United States and Mexico. A year after joining the NRA as a teenager, Carter killed a Tejano boy he claimed posed a threat, and he was convicted of murder. On appeal, the murder conviction was overturned as self-defense, and Carter went on to join the U.S. Border Patrol, become a police chief, and, by 1965, the president of the NRA. Carter, famously, would go on to head the NRA's Institute for Legislative Action (ILA) in 1975 before transforming the NRA as its executive vice president from 1977 on. Against this biographical backdrop, it is not surprising that Carter would presume an alliance between the NRA's obligation to protect gun rights and the police's prerogative to ensure social order.

While the NRA was finding its singular voice on the issue of gun policy, police were equivocal and ambivalent. For example, one 1965 op-ed reads: "As a former deputy commissioner and deputy superintendent of the Chicago police department with many years of service, I know regulations such as proposed will have little effect on the criminal. On the other hand such a firearm regulation may result in the harassment and alienation of the law abiding citizen."[65] Some dipped their toes in the water in support of federal gun control law, including the police chief of Washington, DC, who called for gun registration to "help District police in their fight against crime."[66] Still others began pivoting the gun debate around the police, especially after the 1964 FBI Uniform Crime Report, released in 1965, revealed that "in the period 1960–64 there were 225 officers killed by criminal action. Firearms were used in 96 percent of killings of police, with hand guns predominating."[67] Almost a decade later, one 1975 story from the *Detroit Free Press* reports,

> The campaign for [gun] legislation [has grown] stronger as murder and armed robbery rates have risen, as more and more police officers have been gunned down . . . and as city dwellers, black and white, have become more alarmed at the carnage around them. . . . [S]ince 1970, more than 400 police officers have been killed with pistols.[68]

As federal efforts to further regulate guns stalled and gun violence in the streets surged, statistics on gun violence against the police became an increasing feature of debates about guns.

With rising cynicism among police regarding the efficacy of regulatory efforts, the NRA appealed to more immediate responses than congressional action—such as enhancing police's own arsenal. Six-shot revolvers were the standard issue for police, but the NRA put forward suggestions about more powerful arms, taking credit in one outlet for the police's turn toward the more powerful .41 magnum revolver.[69] In some cases, the NRA even helped broker gun deals for police: the organization's membership had long enjoyed special deals on military surplus weaponry, but the federal government ended police programs for the same. When riots broke out in Detroit in 1967, for example, police first turned to local gun stores to borrow rifles on an emergency basis; after that, officers in Detroit joined the NRA en masse in order to personally purchase discounted military carbines that their agency could neither afford nor access.[70]

Harking back to the early forms of policing in the United States, this bottom-up push for more (and bigger) guns was a trend that extended beyond public law enforcement; throughout the United States, people—whether private civilians, militants, police, or activists—began stocking guns. As one story noted,

> More and more, America seems to be dividing into armed camps. Big city police forces are stocking up on a variety of terrifying weapons. . . . Negro militants are equipping themselves with firearms in an apparent determination to sell their lives as dearly as possible. Gun clubs and sporting clubs are . . . training [members] as vigilantes. . . . The National Rifle Association benevolently blesses all this lethal activity as an ideal form of "community stabilization."[71]

This echoes the NRA's now-familiar claim[72] that guns fill the essential gap between crime and police response. As one contemporaneous summary of an NRA editorial noted,

> The National Rifle Association has not only been fighting against any decent federal gun legislation, but in the latest issue of its magazine, the NRA recommends that citizens arm themselves and join posses and unorganized militia to protect American communities against riots. The NRA editorial goes on to say that the police cannot do the job and it's essential that everyone buy a gun.[73]

Reading these excerpts closely reveals a subtle shift: guns were not simply to be seen as "equalizers" but as "stabilizers," and thus not just *protective* of individuals but also *productive* of social order. Some high-profile police agreed, including the Los Angeles police chief Edward Davis, who received a standing ovation at the NRA's 1975 National Convention in San Diego.[74] He encouraged civilians to get armed, and even saw guns as a bulwark against foreign invaders along the California coastline.[75] This narrative resonated with popularized stories of police training housewives in self-defense, which became a cliché by the late 1960s. But among police, this sensibility appeared to be deeper than a cliché and more pervasive than the eccentric stances of a few celebrity police: the sociologists Gary Marx and Dane Archer report that in a survey of local police regarding the self-defense groups that had emerged in the 1960s, police saw as many as 61 percent of these groups as "pro-police," and 43 percent of police "reported they were glad the groups existed."[76] Law enforcement also saw a prosocial role for these groups: "Police felt that 36% of the groups had improved police-community relations; 29% were seen as actually cutting down on crime; and 18% had helped to prevent or deflate riots."[77] Only 25 percent of surveyed police "wished that the groups did not exist."[78]

In the early 1960s, the NRA reportedly had "more than 600,000 members";[79] the organization entered the 1970s one million members strong.[80] As the organization grew, it adopted an increasingly hard-line stance—one that some police were willing to openly embrace at the time. Many police agreed that strong penalties and reliable enforcement were just as important as gun regulations, if not more so. But by the dawn of the 1980s, police began to doubt that the NRA had the police's best interests at heart. At the same time, lobbyists and politicians began pushing for gun regulations whose main beneficiaries wouldn't be civilians, but police. And when the NRA blocked that regulation, the gun control lobby found itself an unlikely ally in the police.

COPS FOR GUN CONTROL

By the 1980s and 1990s, the war on crime had escalated.[81] Police leaders and policymakers agreed[82] that battering rams, armored military vehicles, patrol rifles, riot gear, and other kinds of militarized equipment were necessary to battle what police and the public understood as a "war" waged by "thugs," "superpredators," and "gangbangers" who putatively roamed urban space.[83] The public, for its part, acquiesced. Different tactics and distinctive motivations notwithstanding, white communities and communities of color alike organized around the issue of crime and embraced "tough on crime" policies.[84] Popular imagery and commentary from the 1980s and into the 1990s featured African Americans, particularly African American boys and men, as the key aggressors in violent turf wars endemic to the crack epidemic unfolding across U.S. urban centers. Popular accounts spotlighted the ruthless feuds of gangs like the Los Angeles–area Bloods and Crips as evidence of just how out of control U.S. urban centers had become. And they sparked moral panic about the sexual and violent threat posed by boys and men of color to justify aggressive punishment, as evidenced in Donald Trump's full-page advertisement in the New York press calling to "Bring back the death penalty! Bring back the police!" in the wake of the brutal Central Park jogger sexual assault of 1989.[85] Cop dramas, reality TV shows, and newsreels featuring aggressive policing became wildly popular—and, particularly for white boys and men,[86] consumption of cop dramas increased positive attitudes toward police. One 1997 study concluded that "much of public opinion in this domain [crime] is influenced by racial concerns."[87]

At the same time, scholars and politicians began elaborating a "culture of poverty" argument that explained—in the words of John DiIulio in 1995—a generation of "superpredators" as the inevitable result of "fatherless, godless, and jobless"[88] teens teeming in urban America. But the preteens and teenagers DiIulio singled out were not fatherless or jobless because of a pathological culture but because of pernicious policies; these reputed "superpredators" represented a generation of marginalized kids who grew up in the era of public disinvestment and a war on crime that relocated their parents from their homes into prison. As Patricia Hill Collins notes, tropes such as the superpredator, the thug, the gangbanger, and the drug dealer all have served as "controlling images":[89] they stereotype marginalized people into caricatures and, in the process, justify their marginalization. DiIulio's predictions were ultimately wrong—crime would drop dramatically in the years to come—but his rhetoric animated political discourse toward "tough on crime" solutions and emboldened police. It also provided a political foundation for gun control advocates to persuasively promote restrictive gun policies to public law enforcement as in their professional interest.

California law enforcement was at the center of the intersection of expanding police militarization[90] and rising support for gun control. In the aftermath of the 1965 Watts riot, Daryl Gates, along with a group of fellow Los Angeles law enforcement officers, came up with the idea of the specialized weapons and tactics (SWAT) team. The Los Angeles Police Department (LAPD) prioritized the development of elite tactical units,[91] and after Gates became its chief in 1978, the LAPD would soon earn a reputation as "one of the more paramilitary departments in the nation," according to the legal scholar Jody David Armour.[92] By the 1980s, the LAPD's efforts were reinforced with national policy; the Ronald Reagan administration would deepen the war on crime, embrace saturation policing, introduce mandatory minimums for gun and drug possession, and incentivize aggressive policing of drugs through asset forfeiture. Under the George H. W. Bush administration, a special program—subsequently known as the 1033 Program—would be set up to transfer the military equipment rendered surplus by the end of the Cold War to local police departments.

The depth of support among police for gun control measures during this era had at least as much to do with growing police militarization as it did with a level-headed analysis of gun policy. This was understandable from the perspective of rank-and-file officers: police were outgunned—and they were dying. In San Jose in 1984, two officers were gunned down with an Uzi: "Joe Tamarit and Manuel Martinez, two San Jose, Calif., police officers armed with revolvers, faced a policeman's nightmare when a motel guest fired at them with an Uzi semiautomatic weapon. . . . Tamarit crawled away with bullets in the stomach and shoulder—and a determination that military-style weapons be taken out of the public's hands."[93] In Los Angeles, Detective Thomas C. Williams was murdered with a fully automatic firearm in a calculated hit to prevent him from testifying in an upcoming trial in 1985; an undercover officer, Daniel Pratt, was killed by a gang member with an AR-15 in 1988. As hundreds of police died in the line of duty and many more found themselves surviving AR-15s, AK-47s, and other assault-style weapons, police became increasingly politicized to explicitly support gun control.

San Jose's chief Joseph McNamara soon became an outspoken advocate of gun control, linking it to a militarized war on crime that was escalated by the NRA's policies:

Our cops are out-gunned. Daily, the guys in blue are coming up against semiautomatic handguns and assault rifles capable of firing

15 to 30 rounds of 9mm ammunition in a few seconds. These weapons, made for combat, are easily and legally available in gun shops all over the USA, and they are selling like hot cakes. It's not just bank robbers pointing assault rifles at cops. Dope heads are defended with Uzis, AK-47s and U.S.-made Mack 10s. . . . So when cops ask for more powerful weapons to defend themselves and the public, they're being realistic, not paranoid. The enormous increase in weapons is part of a domestic arms race, the result of an aggressive marketing campaign by gun manufacturers and dealers, aided and abetted by the National Rifle Association. . . . Failure to stop the flow of these guns has led police to replace their traditional six-shot, .38-caliber revolvers with semiautomatic handguns capable of firing up to 15 rounds of .45-caliber or 9mm ammunition. SWAT teams are now armed with automatic military weapons.[94]

By the early 1990s, many police understood their work as an urban war against the superpredators pathologized by DiIulio. In this context, the ban on cop-killer bullets seemed like the perfect legislation to proponents of gun control in the 1980s. Never mind that the very term *cop-killer bullet* was a matter of acute dispute:[95] who could argue against regulating a specialized round of ammunition that jeopardized the police who faced off with urban criminals?

The NRA. The organization opposed a ban on so-called cop-killer bullets, and walked a fine line to ensure that it could maintain an image of being "tough on crime" while also protecting gun rights. One rhetorical way to do this was to emphasize the futility of the ban. For example, retired Phoenix police Sgt. William Costello told attendees at the 1983 NRA Annual Convention, "Armor-piercing ammunition is a fact . . . but 80 percent of police officers are shot with standard ammunition of .38-caliber or less and body armor will stop that."[96]

Given widespread cynicism regarding crime and criminal justice, the NRA was perhaps overly confident that this strategy would prove successful. Instead, it backfired: the NRA's opposition galvanized many police, who in turn reframed gun control as police safety. As one 1984 article notes,

A large part of the NRA's membership comprises policemen, and they are outraged. "Police are not for gun control, never have been and never will be," says Richard Boyd, national president of the Fraternal Order of Police. "But this is an officer-safety issue. I speak for 167,000 police officers, and I can tell you we're going to make it uncomfortable for the NRA."[97]

A couple of police chiefs I interviewed referenced this era as hotly politicized; one admitted, "I was [a member of the NRA] years ago when I was younger, but I left back in the 80s when the issue of cop-killer bullets came up, and the NRA just would not budge on it." This resonates with what the *New York Times* noted in 1983: "Police groups support the [ammunition ban] bill with unusual unanimity, from unions to the conservative International Association of Chiefs of Police."[98]

Even so, the bill was destined to go nowhere fast; political pressures helped ensure that the bill would be pulled off the congressional agenda in 1984, a midterm election year.[99] Nevertheless, news coverage made much of this apparent seismic shift in police attitudes on guns and tied gun control to officer safety. A *New York Times* article noted,

> In the past, law-enforcement officers remained mostly in the background on issues related to gun control. . . . [N]ow, however, the police group [Fraternal Order of Police] is actively opposing those efforts, in a coalition with the National Sheriffs Association, the International Association of Chiefs of Police, the National Organization of Black Law Enforcement Executives, the National Troopers Association and two research and policy groups, the Police Executive Research Forum and the Police Foundation. . . . [E]stablished groups within the gun control lobby such as Handgun Control welcome the police pressures. . . . [T]he police . . . are widely considered part of the conservative, blue-collar middle class who cannot be accused of coddling criminals.[100]

Story after story gloated that the apparent reversal of police was a profound threat for gun rights advocates:

The police this time may have signaled the beginning of the end for the NRA's influence. Nobody can say cops don't have a familiarity with weapons. A lot of officers are sport and target shooters. They are not subject to the kind of slanderous drivel the NRA routinely aims at its opponents. . . . Once cops learn that they've got to get into the battle early and threaten the Honorables in Washington with organized opposition, the NRA's power will be as dead as the 30,000 people who get blasted into oblivion every year with the gun lobby's favorite toys.[101]

By the late 1980s, the NRA's hard-line opposition to gun control emboldened police who spoke out as an increasing presence in Washington, DC, attending congressional hearings to advocate gun control, sometimes in the hundreds and outnumbering the police the NRA assembled to advocate on its behalf. Their testimonies and statements often emphasized warlike descriptions of urban gun violence that jeopardized police. In 1989 testimony to the U.S. Senate Judiciary Committee, LAPD police chief Daryl Gates explicitly justified assault weapons regulation by presenting an urgent account of urban warfare:

My police department has already lost two officers who were killed by assault weapons. . . . I do not want any more officers to be spray-gunned to death by street punks armed with high-tech killing machines.[102]

That Gates would become a key spokesperson for gun control perhaps says less about the liberal leanings of California and more about the particular brand of law enforcement cultivated within the LAPD in the 1980s—and the racial politics of crime at the time more broadly. Gates's support for an assault weapons ban is illuminated by the broader context of the increasingly militarized war on crime: from his perspective, the assault weapons ban worked primarily to advantage and protect the frontline soldiers—the police—in the war on drugs. In this regard, Gates asserted a unified front among police: "These weapons have got to go. Policemen all over America are united on this."[103] Media coverage during the early 1990s buttressed this view, asserting that the California and federal assault weapons bans responded to "Police . . . complain[ts] of being outgunned by drug dealers with Uzis and AR-15s"; a *Time* magazine article from the same year notes that "President [Bush Sr.] was torn between wanting to protect the rights of sportsmen and the lives of police officers."[104]

From this vantage point, the assault weapons ban and other gun laws endorsed by California police in this period were less about gun regulation and more akin to an article in the Police Officer's Bill of Rights that some states had passed during the war on crime:[105] the right not to be outgunned by criminals. Stiffer gun laws were about protecting police and enhancing their firepower as crime fighters in an urban war on crime. This helps explain why, for example, the 1997 Hollywood shootout did not just invigorate calls for gun control; it also created the impetus to widely introduce the AR-style firearm as so-called patrol rifles to California law enforcement to level the playing field.[106] Thus, police entered onto the control side of the gun debate complicit with gun militarism: police need to disarm and overpower the enemy.

Eventually, police support was crucial in passing what had been hailed as watershed gun control: first, an assault weapons ban in California and, next, a federal ban. But unlike the push for gun control in England or Australia (which focused on protecting child victims of a mass shooting) or the mobilization for gun restrictions in Canada (which centered on protecting women),[107] efforts to pass American gun regulations emphasized the police's engagement in urban warfare—which sheds light on why U.S. gun control so often comes with strings attached with regard to the police. Clinton's crime bill not only restricted guns in the hands of civilians; it also provided funds to hire more police officers and created the Office of Community Oriented Policing Services (or, the COPS Office), a program that would ironically expand police militarization in years to come.[108]

Police militarization emerged from a much broader reconfiguration of crime control in American society, reflecting shifts in what police do, with what kind of equipment, and how we understand it. In the 1990s, both gun rights and gun control lobbies struggled to harness the politics of crime to their respective political agendas. Neither the gun rights lobby nor the gun control lobby engineered police militarization, but police militarization nevertheless provided the foundation on which the gun debate took place in that period. Initially, this terrain seemed to advantage the gun control lobby while raising distinctive challenges for the NRA. Even today, the gun control lobby still has the ear of the International Association of Chiefs of Police and plenty of support from urban police chiefs as well as organizations representing African American officers, including the National Black Police Association and the National Organization of Black Law Enforcement Executives (both of which are on a 2014 list of "antigun lobbying organizations" compiled by the NRA).[109]

But this terrain also provided new opportunities for the NRA. By the early 1990s, the NRA understood that it could not assume the allegiance of law enforcement. In the years to come, the NRA reinforced two distinct, but complementary, frames that linked the politics of guns with the politics of the police: gun militarism and gun populism. In doing so, the NRA mobilized the politics of crime to suggest to police that it was in their own interests—professionally and, for some, also personally—to resist gun control.

THE NRA'S "TOUGH ON CRIME" COPS

Starting with Kahr's 1916 call in *Arms and the Man*, the NRA had billed itself throughout the twentieth century as a foe of violent gun criminals. But by the 1980s and into the 1990s, the NRA doubled down on its view that "gun control is not crime control."[110] James Baker, a lobbyist for the NRA, reframed the gun debate on the NRA's terms in this way: "We're at a crossroads. . . . We're going to go down the road of either prohibitive firearms regulations or tough criminal justice provisions."[111] This rhetoric crystallized around two distinctive frames of legitimate violence: gun militarism and gun populism. Reflecting the frame of gun militarism, the "gun control is not crime control"[112] stance implied that crime control, rather than gun control, was the surest way to the aggressive disarmament of violent criminals. Reflecting gun populism, this rhetoric suggested that gun control—conventionally

understood—was incompatible with crime control insofar as gun restrictions stood to disarm the "good guys"—whether private civilians
or public law enforcement—to defend themselves against criminals.
Calling for more prisons, more aggressive gun law enforcement, and
more gun access for law-abiding civilians (including police),[113] the NRA
interwove the frames of gun militarism and gun populism together as
it positioned itself not just as the gun rights lobby but also as the true
"tough on crime" advocate.

Emboldened by the sentiment that gun control is at cross purposes
with crime control, the NRA capitalized on a handful of fiercely committed allies within the law enforcement community—eventually influencing not just the gun lobby but also the police lobby.[114] These allies
helped the NRA pursue a two-pronged lobbying strategy: sway the police lobby from the inside, and build a pro-NRA police organization that
would act as a counterweight to police organizations supportive of gun
control. The San Jose police officer Leroy Pyle would be the key to both.

Leroy Pyle worked under the leadership of Chief Joseph McNamara—
the same Chief McNamara who made a name for himself promoting
gun control from the 1980s on. Unlike McNamara, Pyle supported the
NRA. By the early 1980s, according to an autobiographical essay by
Pyle,[115] he was serving on the NRA's board and pushing for the NRA to
more proactively bring police into the fold. Apparently, he was unim-
pressed by the NRA's efforts at that time, but he continued to work for
the organization. He helped to revamp its training programs and even
appeared in an advertisement that caught the attention of McNamara—
and riled conflict between the two. Given the public personae of both
men, it is perhaps no surprise that Pyle eventually took to publicly criti-
cizing McNamara as "'a phony baloney plastic policeman' who is using
a gun control crusade to cover up his own failures to fight crime."[116]
The conflict, Pyle alleged, escalated: Pyle claimed that McNamara
violated his civil rights as well as broke union rules. Not only did the
NRA provide Pyle with legal funds to sue the department, but he was
also picked to head the new Law Enforcement Alliance of America
(LEAA), which was founded in 1991.[117] As Pyle described it on his personal blog, "After almost 10 years, Wayne LaPierre finally agreed to

support a more political law enforcement organization. . . . Wayne asked if I was interested in forming a coalition of pro-gun cops with a presence in Washington D.C. I assured him that I was more than ready."[118] Pyle resigned from the San Jose Police Department and moved to Washington, DC, to head up the organization. The NRA bankrolled the organization, according to the NRA lobbyist James Baker, "in order to show that there is a great body of law enforcement officers out there that doesn't support the gun control proposals put in the hopper before Congress."[119] In another interview, Baker admitted, "We have been behind the eight ball. . . . [W]e're trying to rectify that."[120] Soon afterward, Pyle was replaced by Jim Fotis, himself an NRA liaison and former police officer from Lynbrook, New York.[121]

LEAA was intended as a "counterweight" to the Fraternal Order of Police (FOP), which by this point was supporting the Brady Bill and the assault weapons ban. (Founded in 1915 to represent the labor interests of police officers, the FOP today represents some 330,000 officers, the largest and most influential organization of its kind.[122] Though it represents police at all ranks, its positions on policies and initiatives are often taken as a barometer of rank-and-file police sentiment.) The FOP, however, was also changing from the inside. By 1995, the gun control proponent and FOP president Dewey Stokes would leave his position, and James Pasco, a friend of the NRA's James Baker, would become executive director. The rebirth of the FOP was imminent. James Pasco got to know James Baker while the former served as the ATF's lobbyist from 1983 to 1995; though Baker says he had no veto power over the ATF, Pasco tells a slightly different story, according to one newspaper account:

> "I'd say 'I need 200 more agents, 100 more inspectors,'" said Pasco, who was ATF's man on Capitol Hill between 1983 and 1995. Pasco guaranteed the new hires would stick to chasing criminals with guns, not the gun owners and collectors who are the bulwark of the NRA's membership. After that, his NRA counterpart, Jim Baker, "would sign off." . . . "I don't think the NRA was interested so much in how big ATF got as they were in what ATF was doing," said Pasco.[123]

Pasco and Baker perhaps forged an uneasy (and unlikely) relationship between the ATF and the NRA. In the years to come, Pasco would work primarily behind the scenes, hidden from the public as head of the FOP. Nevertheless, his few public pronouncements would largely reverse the FOP's stance on gun control from the 1980s. Indicating a profoundly different stance on the politics of crime and gun policy from that previously adopted by the organization, Pasco told the *Wall Street Journal* in 2000: "We have more guns than we've ever had, and the crime rate and gun-crime rate are dropping. That tells me that what is going on can't just be the prevalence of guns."[124] Pasco came out in opposition to a proposed ban on the 5.56 M855 rifle round;[125] he has raised questions about smart guns;[126] and he has "debunked" concerns about deregulating silencers.[127] That said, the FOP under Pasco has not always been in lockstep with the NRA. It supported a renewal of the assault weapons ban in 2004, and Pasco has spoken out in favor of expanded background checks—something that the NRA has endorsed in theory but vehemently opposed in practice.[128] Pasco also disavows any formal link with the NRA's LEAA, telling a *Time* magazine reporter, "If we have ever agreed with them, it's been totally coincidental."[129]

Perhaps FOP's most important feat in the arena of gun policy—and one that the LEAA leader James Fotis counts among his most important accomplishments—was the Law Enforcement Officers Safety Act (LEOSA). LEOSA is a 2004 law that allows active-duty police officers to carry a gun off-duty while outside of their jurisdiction. The law had met resistance in the 1990s; police and policymakers were concerned about the unevenness across police agencies in terms of department policies, rules regarding the use of force, firearms training, and community demographics and crime trends. The surging public consciousness surrounding active shootings and terrorism, however, soon made these concerns less pressing—at least compared to the palpable public approval for preventative and first-response measures. If the American public could tolerate the Transportation Security Administration in airports, it most certainly would embrace off-duty cops carrying weapons they were presumably trained and skilled to deploy. As the congressional hearing on LEOSA revealed of the LEAA and FOP support for the new law,

> LEAA argues that this legislation will "allow tens of thousands of additionally equipped, trained and certified law enforcement officers to continually serve and protect our communities regardless of jurisdiction or duty status at no cost to taxpayers." FOP contends that this legislation will help its members to protect citizens in the wake of a terrorist attack and that it is even more necessary since September 11, 2001.[130]

The NRA's advocacy of this law illustrated an integration of gun militarism and gun populism akin to the organization's "gun control is not crime control" argument. It *expanded* the police's prerogative to fight dangerous criminals, but to do so, it likened off-duty cops to a reserve army of would-be first responders. In doing so, LEOSA shrank not just the rhetorical distance between off-duty police and private armed civilians but also the legal distance between laws that protect police and laws that empower ordinary civilians with respect to self-defense. Indeed, within pro–gun rights communities, LEOSA is sometimes understood as a first step to national concealed carry reciprocity for civilians.[131]

Meanwhile, the NRA has steadily expanded its offerings to public law enforcement. The organization offers a line-of-duty death insurance policy, college scholarships, and small grants to agencies (e.g., the NRA gave the Detroit Police Department a small grant the same year that its police chief James Craig was featured on the NRA's magazine embracing concealed carry). It publishes a *Line of Duty* magazine aimed at police and military. It even sponsored the FOP's annual conference in 2017.[132] Finally, starting in 2016, it called on all of its members to "Back Our Blue" by donating cars to support local law enforcement. As the campaign materials read,

> Our nation's police officers put their lives on the line every day to protect those in need—including the ignorant and ungrateful who direct criticism toward the entire profession. We at the NRA salute

those who wear the badge, especially as they find themselves targeted for undeserved blame.[133]

Similarly, the NRA's broader campaigns—including its *America's Safest
Place* video series—draw linkages between support for gun rights and
support for public law enforcement. Consider the NRA spokesperson
Dana Loesch's narration in her viral "Clenched Fist" video, in which she
describes the threats facing Americans posed by activists on the left:

> They use their media to assassinate real news, and they use their
> schools to teach children that their president is another Hitler. They
> use their movies and singers and comedy shows and award shows to
> repeat their narrative over and over again . . . all to make them
> march, make them protest, make them scream racism and sexism and
> xenophobia and homophobia, to smash windows, burn cars, shut
> down interstates and airports, bully and terrorize the law-abiding.
> Until the only option left is for police to do their jobs and stop the
> madness. And when that happens, they'll use that as an excuse for
> their outrage. . . . The only way we save our country and our free-
> dom is to fight this violence of lies with the clenched fist of truth.[134]

By 2018, the NRA had come full circle: whereas in the 1920s, it
pressed for public law enforcement to become skilled and qualified with
firearms in order to train police for the task of crime fighting, by the
2000s, the NRA had helped shape a legal, political, and cultural landscape in which its agenda aligned with that of the police. Gun rights,
at least the NRA's version of them, were increasingly synonymous with
"Backing Our Blue." And this is why both the FOP[135] and the NRA could
vigorously endorse Trump for president: he represented the populist
stitching together of hard-knuckled policing with gun rights patriotism.
As the "Clenched Fist" video suggests, this populism would be reserved
for those Americans who were not just law-abiding but also law-
respecting, having the due reverence for law enforcement that the riot-
ers, looters, and other tropes of disorderly black and brown bodies
lacked. For the latter, a stance of gun militarism—centered on aggressive disarmament of violent offenders—would instead be embraced.

CONCLUSION

American power has long been distributed among a series of individuals, groups, parties, associations, organizations, and institutions not readily designated as wholly *either* public *or* private.
Think, for instance, of the hybrid public-private roles of the American Bar Association, the American Medical Association, Fannie
Mae, the American Stock Exchange, the American Farm Bureau,
the Federal Reserve, Underwriters Laboratories, the Ad Council,
the American Legion, the American Red Cross, the YMCA, the East
Bay Municipal Utility District, and the National Rifle Association.
—*William J. Novak,* "The Myth of the 'Weak' American State"
(2008)

The NRA is not just a lobbyist for particular laws, policies, and regulations; it is also a broker in legitimate violence. Since the early twentieth century, the NRA has had an enormous influence on the symbolic,
legal, and in some cases material intersection of legitimate violence and
public law enforcement. The NRA was instrumental in making gun proficiency central to public law enforcement. It has advocated for particular kinds of police firepower and, at some points, even provided a stopgap to cash-strapped agencies in need of emergency firepower. The
organization continues to assist police departments with funding for
equipment and training, and to support individual police officers with
Officer of the Year Awards, college support for dependent children of
law enforcement, and line-of-duty death insurance. Furthermore, it has
forged a bond between support for local law enforcement and support
for gun rights: at least according to the NRA's version of gun rights advocacy, to be a proponent of gun rights is to respect and recognize
public law enforcement (and vice versa).

The gun control lobby, for its part, has also participated in buttressing a particular relationship between police and firearms, especially
in the 1980s and early 1990s. Advocating on behalf of police who had
become victims of gun violence, gun control advocates argued that gun
restrictions were needed not just to protect police but also to thicken

the line between police and those they policed. Police embraced gun control in the 1980s and 1990s as a strategy in the war on urban street violence that they thought they were losing; had they been motivated by general concerns about gun violence, they would have said as much about the nonpolice victims of gun violence (who far outnumbered police deaths) as about police killed in the line of duty. Yet, police support for gun control appeared rooted in a view of the world as divided between the good guys (police) and the enemies (drug dealers, gangs, and superpredators). Gun control, as it was framed in this era, stood to protect the former from the latter.

This is the often-overlooked common ground of the gun control and gun rights lobbies in the late twentieth century: both endorsed policies that harshly sanctioned the kinds of gun criminals associated with urban street crime. But where the gun control lobby aimed to further restrict gun access in conjunction with these measures, the NRA sought to otherwise expand gun access. For the NRA to win back the allegiance of the police with that platform, the organization doubled down on "tough on crime" rhetoric and subtly reminded cops that gun control was supported by liberals—and liberals were notoriously soft on crime. They also institutionalized relationships between police and the NRA that could better weather the dicey moments when gun rights appeared to endanger police. Finally, the NRA pushed one step further beyond making friends and spreading a popular message: it made good on its message that gun rights could directly benefit police. This was the genius of LEOSA insofar as it showed that the NRA was willing—as it had been since the early twentieth century—to work on behalf of police to make sure that they had access to, and were trained in, the kind of firepower they felt they needed as police, both on and off duty. The firearm is often a taken-for-granted symbol of American public law enforcement, but its centrality to law enforcement reflects not just the professional ethos of American policing. It also reveals the mighty reach of gun politics in the United States.

CHAPTER 2

THE WAR ON GUNS

Firearms violations should be aggressively used in prosecuting
violent crime. They are generally simple and quick to prove.
The mandatory and enhanced punishments for many firearms
violations can be used as leverage to gain plea bargaining
and cooperation from offenders.
—United States Department of Justice, *Criminal Justice Manual* (2018)

There is a war on guns. Targeting criminal guns, this war on guns reflects a broader U.S. project of crime control that, over the past several
decades, has ramped up the criminal justice system's capacity to proactively police and aggressively punish. This war on guns entails a tangled web of policies, practices, strategies, and sensibilities that all aim
to establish a state—that is, a police—monopoly on legitimate violence.[1]
This war on guns is made possible by the prisms through which urban
gun violence is viewed by the public and by police alike, one that de-
limits gun violence as a particular kind of problem and that racializes
gun offenders as particular kinds of people. It is echoed loudly by gun
rights advocates in the National Rifle Association, within police circles,
and beyond—even by gun control advocates, too.

I expect at least a few readers to bristle at my use of the phrase *war
on guns* to describe gun policy. At one point, Americans declaring a war
on something meant taking it seriously as a foundational threat to the
fabric of society: crime, drugs, terrorism, and so forth. To say that we
have a war on guns, advocates of stronger gun regulations would rightly
object, suggests a level of consternation that does not reflect the ongoing apathy, especially among many politicians, regarding American gun

violence as a social problem. The total number of Americans who have died by guns since the passage of the 1968 Gun Control Act outpaces the cumulative number of American deaths in all wars in U.S. history.[2] Roughly forty thousand Americans die every year from gunshot wounds (in 2017, nearly four in ten were homicides; six in ten were suicides); around one hundred thousand each year are wounded but survive.[3] When medical expenses, lost productivity, and legal costs are taken into account, one estimate put the costs of gun violence at more than $700 per American per year.[4] With these figures as the backdrop, federal inaction on a variety of gun regulations suggests to many not war but surrender.

But although many Americans have favored broad-based gun control in the form of universal background checks or an assault weapons ban, they have received—both in policy and in enforcement—a war on guns. This war on guns encompasses the set of gun policies aimed at urban violence, not the whole of gun control or even gun law enforcement. This war on guns is evident in the late-1990s Project Exile, a national initiative that aggressively enforced federal gun laws by not just prosecuting but also relocating offenders to distant federal prisons (hence *Exile* in the name of the program). It is apparent in the Department of Justice's current Project Safe Neighborhoods program, which the legal scholar Bonita R. Gardner argues targets gun offenses in African American communities while ignoring gun offenses elsewhere.[5] It is likewise visible in "zero-tolerance" gun policies that take the form of sentencing enhancements and mandatory sentencing and that drive an irreconcilable divide between the "good guys with guns" (e.g., the police) and the "bad guys with guns" (e.g., "the violent felons who illegally carry and misuse guns," according to the NRA's praise of Project Exile).[6] And it is also visible in more mundane ways in day-to-day policing: gun violence provides a legally acceptable justification for police to disproportionately stop and frisk people of color. Although these searches rarely find illegal weapons, they provide a pretext for arrests for drug-related and other nonviolent offenses.[7]

The *Washington Post* columnist Radley Balko suggests that racial disparities in drug law enforcement may be dwarfed by those in gun law enforcement.[8] The *Truthout* editor-in-chief Maya Schenwar has questioned the utility of mandatory minimums in the context of gun possession.[9] And the *Jacobin* contributor Daniels Denvir has noted, amid outcry that the United States has no gun control, that "the only kind of gun control we have in the United States is the kind that locks up black people."[10] The statistics are suggestive of something deeply amiss: in 2016, a startling 51.3 percent of those convicted of federal gun crimes (and these are exclusive of violent crimes such as murder, robbery, and so forth) were African American.[11] That's a larger concentration than for any other federal crime—including the crimes of drug trafficking and drug possession.

It is possible that black people are more likely to illegally possess guns; even if rates of unlicensed gun carry are equal, the racial disparities in felony records—1 in 3 black men have felony records, as compared to fewer than 1 in 12 U.S. adults overall[12]—would tip the scales in favor of black criminalization. But more than a century of American criminal justice scholarship—starting with the work of W.E.B. Du Bois[13]—casts serious doubt that, even assuming racial disparities in offending, the institutions charged with transforming an illegal act into a criminal record would not aggravate these disparities. In a viral Twitter thread posted in the aftermath of the Parkland shooting,[14] the sociologist Eve Ewing unraveled how structural racism intersects with gun policy to aggravate, rather than ameliorate, vulnerabilities facing communities of color:

Consider this scenario: two 15-year-olds are in rival sets. They both join because they feel they have to in order to survive, because on the block where they live everyone else is affiliated so people assume they're in a gang anyway. On the way to their school they have to cross several boundaries and territories to get to school because the city closed their old school and they have a long commute. On the way to school these young people meet and each of them thinks the other is a threat. They both shoot. Instantly one is a criminal and one is a victim. Which one is basically a question of chance. Now we have one young person who is going to be incarcerated, which will lead to long term trauma, educational gaps, and problems with employment. And another who is physically harmed, also traumatized, and whose family and friends are traumatized (and maybe retaliate).

Ewing's remarks articulate for gun law enforcement what scholars of drug law enforcement have long known: that under the current configuration of the U.S. criminal justice apparatus, not just crimes but also punishments have dire consequences for individuals, families, and communities.[15] The law professor James Forman Jr. reminds us that "of course, there are good reasons to regard the issues [of drugs and guns] differently . . . but despite such differences, drugs and guns—and our response to them—have commonalities we rarely acknowledge."[16] As Radley Balko notes, "you enforce the gun laws with the institutions you have, not the institutions you want. . . . [W]e can only consider the demonstrated history of how investigators and prosecutors have used . . . discretion [to enforce gun laws], not some idealized prosecutor or ATF investigator that we'd *want* to be in charge."[17]

This chapter unravels the racial politics that undergird the wars—the war on alcohol, the war on drugs, and, I argue, the war on guns[18]—that are disproportionately fought in urban America against black and brown boys and men. Specifically, it examines police chiefs' gun talk in the context of urban gun violence: how they embrace a war on guns, how they understand themselves within it, and how they frame the license and limit of legitimate violence accordingly. This chapter approaches police chiefs as "representative brokers"[19] who must navigate—by virtue of their professional standing—the interface between the cultural conditions within their own police jurisdiction, on the one hand, and the political conditions in the broader U.S. landscape, on the other. In reference to urban violence, police chiefs embrace "tough on crime" policies such as mandatory minimums. They reinforce a "Warrior mindset" that emphasizes aggressive policing and harsh punishment. And they adhere to a particular understanding of legitimate violence—what I call "gun militarism"—as they imagine legitimately armed actors (here, the police) as engaged in a protracted, high-stakes battle to disarm illegitimately armed actors (here, the urban gun criminals). As a racial frame, gun militarism clarifies where and how the battle lines of this war on guns are drawn—and why, at times, these lines break down.

WHAT MAKES A GUN ILLEGAL?

Defining what constitutes an illegal gun, or illegal gun use, is legally, socially, and morally complicated.[20] This is, perhaps, because illegal guns are never just about guns themselves but also about the people wielding them, as evidenced by the lengthy list of attributes that disqualify a person from possessing or purchasing a gun, including a felony record, age, a documented history of severe mental illness, and dependency on illicit substances. When gun rights advocates emphasize that law should regulate the person and not the gun, they are actually tapping into a long history of gun control: though certain guns and accessories have been regulated or banned at particular times in history (see, most notably, the 1934 National Firearms Act, 1986 Firearms Owners Protection Act, and 1994 Public Safety and Recreational Firearms Use Protection Act), gun laws have more often regulated *which* people can do *what* with their guns and *where*.[21]

Historically, race has been central to these delimitations. Early gun laws and gun customs enforced a color line that equated freedom, citizenship, and arms-bearing with whiteness.[22] This trend can be traced all the way to the 1967 Mulford Act, a law introduced by the California Republican legislator Don Mulford. The Second Amendment expert Adam Winkler describes Mulford as having "a history of fighting radicals," with "special contempt for the [Black] Panthers."[23] The law was intended to end the armed patrols of the Black Panthers active in Oakland, California—the heart of Mulford's home district of Alameda County. The Black Panthers were one of many Black Power groups turning to arms in the 1960s; the group embraced the Second Amendment as part of a broader ten-point program to address the twin problems of state brutality and neglect (the Black Panthers' overall plan spanned from gun rights to social services, including providing free lunches and health care for the underserved urban black community).[24] Mulford's law, however, would effectively disarm Black Power, "giv[ing] California an unusually strict set of gun control laws," according to Winkler.[25] At the same time, it largely left untouched hunters as well as the nativist and white supremacist groups operating in the state at the time.[26]

Though the 1967 Mulford Act is often singled out as a standout example of the intersection of gun law and race, its visibility reflects both its audaciousness in drawing a color line with guns and its standing as historical anachronism. For gun policy in the 1960s and afterward, the color line would be predominantly drawn not by using gun laws to target African American "extremists" and "subversives" for disarmament, but by deploying firearms laws as a vehicle of expansive criminalization. "Tough on crime" gun laws would become the unifying mantra across the increasingly polarized gun debate. Such laws included enhanced sentencing and mandatory minimums for those who commit a crime with a firearm as well as while in possession of a firearm; they also included expanding prohibitions on firearms and firearm paraphernalia for those deemed unfit due to a criminal record or other disqualifying status.

Although popular debates about gun policy have often noted the uncanny capacity of the NRA to block federal gun laws, federal gun regulations have been successfully proposed and passed—but under the mantra of "tough on crime" policy rather than "gun control." In 1984, at the behest of NRA-backed President Ronald Reagan, the U.S. Congress enacted the Armed Career Criminal Act; the Act stipulates that repeat offenders who have three or more prior convictions involving violent felonies or drug felonies must serve a *minimum* of 15 years in prison. Shortly thereafter,[27] federal sentencing guidelines expanded the penalties for firearms-involved crime, with 5-, 7-, 10-, and 30-year mandatory minimum sentences for possessing, brandishing, or discharging a firearm during the commission of a crime, as well as 25-year mandatory minimum sentences for subsequent offenses.

Even before these federal laws were changed, states were already busy enhancing punishment for firearms-related offenses, alongside other offenses, during the early decades of the war on crime. For example, in Michigan in the 1970s, the African American mayor of Detroit Coleman Young insisted on clear-cut protection of gun rights for the city's black residents: "I'll be damned if I'll let them collect guns in the city of Detroit while we're surrounded by hostile suburbs and the whole rest of the state . . . where you have vigilantes practicing in the wilderness with automatic weapons."[28] Unwilling to disarm Detroiters, however, he "saw mandatory minimums for gun crimes as a reasonable compromise,"[29] as the law professor James Forman Jr. observed. Michigan passed a two-year mandatory minimum sentencing for crimes committed while in possession of a firearm in 1976. That same year, Arizona passed a law so that "anyone found to have used a firearm while committing robbery, kidnapping, rape, various forms of aggravated assault, or resisting a police officer was no longer eligible for a suspended sentence, probation, parole, or other release from custody before serving a mandatory sentence."[30] In 1978, Arizona further expanded the scope of this sentencing apparatus to include "dangerous" offenses as well as "repeat offenders."

Although the trend toward mandatory minimum sentencing guidelines transformed penal codes across the United States, perhaps the most infamous example of "tough on crime" gun law came from California in the 1990s. Known as the "Use a Gun and You're Done" law, the 1997 measure added respective enhancements of 10 years, 20 years, and 25 years to life for "using" a gun, firing a gun, or killing or seriously injuring another person with a gun. As with federal guidelines, these enhancements were added onto the sentence for the underlying conviction—and were to be served consecutively. Following on the heels of California's "three strikes" law enacted in 1994, it was billed as the most onerous gun law in the nation and passed, according to the *Washington Post*,[31] "with little fanfare or [the] controversy" usually associated with gun-related legislation. A decade later, California's Department of Justice got to work tracking down—and prosecuting—persons illegally in possession of firearms with the Armed Prohibited Persons System. Its database lists individuals who at one time owned firearms but then became prohibited due to a criminal conviction, mental health designation, or other issues. The system makes it bureaucratically possible to prosecute California's Felon with a Firearm law, which stipulates that those convicted of a felony, anyone convicted of specific misdemeanors, and narcotic drug addicts may face additional sentencing, an extended loss of gun rights, and—for legal immigrants—possible deportation if they are found to possess a firearm.

GETTING TOUGH ON GUNS

Police chiefs whom I interviewed in Arizona, California, and Michigan remain committed to "getting tough on guns." According to the vast majority of interviewed chiefs across the different political and legal contexts of Arizona, California, and Michigan, they wanted more, and more drastic, enforcement with respect to gun policy. They wanted severe punishment, including mandatory minimum sentencing and sentencing enhancements, to ensure that gun criminals are disarmed and incarcerated. One California chief told me that his "top priority . . . would probably be the administration of justice and punishment. Put teeth in the existing laws. And direct the majority of resources at *that*." Another California chief sardonically echoed this. "How about: let's enforce the laws! 99 percent of the time, if someone is arrested, they have ten different gun violations! But we've weakened the punishment. It's just a farce." Two Michigan chiefs also agreed: "We need to enforce the laws we have and the courts should be held accountable. But we have no money, so people reoffend, they get probation, and this happens multiple times"; "If someone is caught with an illegal gun, they should be punished. They are the ones who should be severely punished and incarcerated, because if they are carrying illegally, that's eventually going to lead to a shooting, and then a homicide." And an Arizona chief even referenced the myth of El Salvador's punitive drunk driving laws to make a similar point: "Look at San Salvador. If you get a DUI, and you are caught, you are killed, there's a sign posted about you. It's brutal—and I'm not advocating that, but I think we need to start prosecuting the shit out of criminals, and I think that would do a lot to take care of gun crime. You know, none of this, 'my mommy beat me.'" Though the chief is wrong about El Salvador (the country ended the death penalty for everything but military crimes decades ago), this "tough on crime" sensibility was consistent across the vast majority of police chiefs with regard to gun policy.

Chiefs did not embrace "tough on crime" policies unilaterally or unthinkingly; for example, when conversation strayed into the topics of drug law enforcement or immigration, for example, chiefs were more ambivalent about the efficacy of such approaches.[32] One chief from Michigan noted, "I am a fan of mandatory minimums . . . even if it can be too punitive at times. Now . . . I don't think someone should be going to prison forever for drug convictions. But firearms, I think, are completely different than drugs. Guns are about public safety, and the mandatory minimums are about incapacitation." Likewise, a California chief saw the best "tough on crime" policies as targeted toward violent offenders, not drug offenders: "I am all in favor of enhancements for violence. You should go to jail. I don't care about subsistence dealers. Violent people is where we should focus. It's the people who hurt people—put them on an island, parachute them in food, and let them figure the rest of it out." And an Arizona chief chimed in: "I would not necessarily say that for all crimes, but for violent crime in particular, I think mandatory minimums are a good thing." Guns were "different," these chiefs and others across Arizona, Michigan, and California noted, because guns made possible irreversible and unmeasurable damage, loss of life, and trauma.

In asserting the unique exigencies of gun law enforcement, chiefs recognized a core finding regarding the criminogenic effects of guns: the instrumentality effect,[33] which holds that the weapon, above and beyond the intentions of its user, affects the outcome of an act of violence. This is why gun availability tracks gun homicides, but not other homicides; why armed robberies committed with firearms are more likely to escalate to homicide than other kinds of robberies; and why lethality rates are correlated with ammunition calibers.[34] These consequences of guns warranted a severe response from the criminal justice system.

Chiefs' sentiments are expressions of punitiveness, but they are also expressions of exasperation at the broader system of criminal justice of which police chiefs are a part—and which they must navigate on *its* terms, not theirs.[35] Amid concerns about the lethal consequences of

guns, police chiefs' support for mandatory minimums, sentencing enhancements, and gun policies was also rooted in misgivings about the
criminal justice system's efficacy in punishing offenders.[36] Chiefs described a "revolving door" of criminal justice, frustrated that their efforts are deemed futile by lenient judges, inadequate prison space, and
prosecutors interested only in "winnable" cases. Chiefs offered that
"what it comes down to is, it is very hard to get to prison" (Arizona);
they regretted that "you have felonies turned into misdemeanors turned
into infractions—all through plea bargaining" (California); they won-
dered "why we always plea down the gun crime" (Arizona); they lamented that "if the court system would just enforce [gun laws] and put
people away so that if they have a gun or use a gun they never see the
light of day—well, that's what I'd prefer" (California). One Michigan
chief, who policed an African American–majority jurisdiction, expressed his frustration by detailing how plea bargaining had created a
library of absurd offenses, including "attempted CCW [concealed carrying of a weapon]":

> I am all for mandatory minimums. So, take this offense: attempted
> CCW. Do you know what that is? How do you "attempt" CCW? Well,
> I will tell you what it is. You have your first HYTA [a conviction that
> is expunged due to age-related eligibility]. Then you have your sec-
> ond HYTA. Then you have a plea down, from CCW to attempted CCW.
> And then you have a CCW. And then only on the fifth time do you
> have the mandatory minimums kicking in, and the convictions go
> federal.

In this excerpt, this chief references Michigan's HYTA program as an
illuminating point of frustration. The Holmes Youthful Trainee Act,
which was enacted in 1927, was intended to allow youths facing criminal convictions avoid a permanent criminal record. A holdover from
when American criminal justice was characterized by rehabilitative justice,[37] HYTA has come to signal a criminal justice system weak on
juvenile justice in an era of "tough on crime" sensibilities.

Although Arizona, California, and Michigan chiefs were largely cyn-
ical about the broader criminal justice system, California chiefs raised

an additional grievance—California legislators. California police chiefs were particularly chagrined about the rollback of the war on crime that California legislators were attempting in the aftermath of the U.S. Supreme Court's 2011 decision in *Brown v. Plata*. (The U.S. Supreme Court found that prison conditions in California violated the Eighth Amendment and mandated that the state must reduce its prison population to 137.5 percent of capacity within two years.) Though the case represents a powerful symbolic critique of inhumane and unconstitutional conditions within California prisons,[38] the reforms undertaken in response have largely shifted the burden of incarceration from the state prisons to county jails, localizing and fragmenting a supervised population in order to comply with the Supreme Court mandate—a strategy known as "realignment."

Realignment and other reforms have failed to dismantle mass incarceration, as the legal scholars Keramet Reiter and Natalie Pifer note,[39] but they did spark a backlash among Californians in favor of a renewed "tough on crime" approach to punishment. At the time of my interviews, one recent reform in particular—Proposition 47[10]—caught the ire of many chiefs. The proposition reduced a variety of felonies to misdemeanors, including certain crimes involving drug possession and stolen property worth $950 or less. Chiefs were quick to point out that that included virtually all stolen firearms—an oversight that would eventually be addressed through Proposition 63, passed in November 2016. At the time of my interviews, though, chiefs used Prop 47 as an occasion to argue that the state's "tough on crime" policies had led to historically low crime rates and to assert their apprehension regarding California's recent penal changes. As one California chief pointedly noted, "I think we are going backwards. In terms of sentencing, we now have a number of felonies that we have turned into misdemeanors. And we see property crimes sky rocketing, significantly increasing. And I think the same thing will happen if we do that for violent crime. So it's not so much about punishment, but about what works. Look at the stats: when we put people behind bars, we keep crime lower."

Criminologists have found limited support for this chief's assertion; the number of people imprisoned in the 1990s did have an effect on crime rates—as did changes in policing and demographic shifts, though criminologists remain unable to explain the totality of the dramatic drop in crime the United States experienced from the 1990s onward.[41] But mass incarceration also imposed heavy costs on those incarcerated, their families, their communities, and taxpayers. These costs have become the subject of sustained public debate due to public intellectuals like the legal scholar Michelle Alexander, author of *The New Jim Crow*, as well as growing criticism from political leaders on the left and right alike.[42] Accordingly, public opinion and public policy—especially with regard to drug law enforcement—have started to shift away from their "tough on crime" antecedents. In contrast, gun law enforcement largely remains under the mantra of "tough on crime" politics, both within and outside of law enforcement circles. As one chief admitted with regard to California's Armed Prohibited Persons System, which focused on felons in possession of firearms, "it was easier to get people behind that mission because everybody—whether it's the Brady Campaign, the NRA—everybody wants people who shouldn't have guns to not have them. So that was our focus." The criminalization of armed felons, this chief seemed to imply, was a crucial rallying point for uniting foes across the gun debate and creating politically feasible gun policy. This maneuver reflected the persistence of punitive sentiments among the American public with respect to gun law; it also spoke to the ethos of U.S. police agencies tasked with enforcing it.

THE WARRIOR

There is an elective affinity between "tough on crime" gun policies and the police subcultures that characterize American public law enforcement. Police subculture is the topic of a deep body of scholarship; scholars[43] who have worked alongside urban police—often as researchers, but at other times as police recruits themselves—have documented that police embrace a subculture that emphasizes a crime-fighting mission; a desire for action and excitement; an us-versus-them mentality; the glorification of (crime-fighting) violence; suspiciousness and cynicism (toward criminals and toward the criminal justice system); social iso-

lation and strong in-group loyalty (what the policing scholar P.A.J. Waddington calls "defensive solidarity");[44] and authoritarian conservatism.
Police subculture provides police—from patrol officers to chiefs—with
stories to interpret their own engagement in the world of police work,
values to understand their moral standing within that world, and cultural tools to navigate the unique and intractable tasks that go along
with policing.[45] Likewise, police subculture helps explain the social
organization of police work; as the policing scholar Peter Manning
argues,[46] police work is best understood as a drama—one centered on
law enforcement projecting their crime-fighter image to the broader
public, to the individuals they police, and even to themselves. Finally,
police subculture helps explain how policing produces disparities and
inequalities despite formal adherence to equality and fairness: ideas
about what is suspect are shaped by race[47] through implicit biases linking blackness to criminality, which in turn shape how police make big
and small decisions that add up to major racial disparities in policing
outcomes.[48]

The Warrior is a foreboding presence in the context of contemporary
police subculture. The former officer and legal scholar Seth Stoughton
notes that "within law enforcement, few things are more venerated
than the concept of the Warrior."[49] He describes the Warrior as "a sim-
plified attempt to provide an ethical framework for an inherently violent job"[50] that "refers to a deep-bone commitment to survive a bad situation no matter the odds or difficulty, to not give up even when it is
mentally and physically easier to do so."[51] The Warrior reinforces the
necessity of law enforcement as the key barrier between order and
chaos (i.e., the "thin blue line").[52] It acknowledges the exclusivity of
the law enforcement profession—not everyone is morally equipped to
face the kinds of violence that police officers must accept as the price
of admission to their chosen profession. It allows officers, furthermore,
"psychological protection" from any cognitive dissonance that arises
from the gap between how they understand themselves and the reality
of the actions they both respond to and must undertake as part of police work.[53] It offers practical leverage to officers who "are frequently
reminded that their single most important goal every day is simply to

make it home at the end of their shift . . . [and] that every aspect of policing is intensely dangerous."[54] And finally, the Warrior is appealing to people beyond law enforcement, from "tough on crime" politicians across the political spectrum to ordinary people who want the assurance of a robust police force ready and able to address issues of law and order in ways that they themselves cannot or will not— whether morally or legally—undertake.

The Warrior became an ascendant paradigm of policing in the context of the urban crack epidemic of the 1980s; the epidemic's "unprecedented carnage" helped to indelibly connect drugs, violence, and urban America in the minds of both the public and the police.[55] Pantomiming previous eras of American crime fighting, the threat of violence was conflated with, and co-constituted by, blackness,[56] but this time, the specter of urban disorder justified an unprecedentedly militarized response from law enforcement. As the legal scholar James Forman Jr. notes, "the fight against crack helped to enshrine the notion that police must be [W]arriors, aggressive and armored, working ghetto corners as an army might patrol enemy territory."[57] Indeed, the criminologists David Ramey and Trent Steidley found that an increased population of racial minorities is associated with increases in the amount of military equipment transferred through the 1033 Program set up to offload surplus goods from the Department of Defense to local police departments.[58]

The celebration of the Warrior has dovetailed with the proliferation of militarized equipment,[59] ramping up crime fighting as a hypermasculine mission.[60] As the police militarization scholar Peter Kraska describes his fieldwork, "the 'military special operations' culture— characterized by a distinct technowarrior garb, heavy weaponry, sophisticated technology, hypermasculinity, and dangerous function— was nothing less than intoxicating for its participants."[61] The Warrior's overemphasis on danger in police work and the encouragement that police approach every individual and interaction as potentially lethal "because everyone they meet may have a plan to kill *them*"[62] amplifies an already intense valorization of masculinity within policing. Writing more than three decades ago, the ethnographer and police expert Jennifer Hunt finds that police "construct their world in terms of a binary system of oppositional categories with masculine and feminine significance," associating "crime-fighting" with "particular masculine skills and personality attributes" such that "the street cop . . . is a brave and aggressive soldier who has mastered the art of violence."[63] Likewise, the sociolegal scholar Stephen Herbert analyzes the "hard-charger" masculinity that frames aggressive police work as courageous and heroic: "Many police officers reinforce a robust form of masculinity, which encourages them to aggressively pursue 'bad guys.' . . . [O]fficers remind each other that the danger of their job requires a brave and often aggressive response. . . . Policing is mythologized as a test of agility, strength and tenacity."[64] Reflecting a style of masculinity as much as a style of policing, the Warrior encourages police to approach their interactions with civilians as masculinity contests;[65] devalue certain tasks—such as paperwork—as "feminine";[66] imagine the jurisdictions they police as military grids to be dominated;[67] and embrace firearms as both practical and symbolic evidence of their willingness to face danger.[68]

In my interviews, one police chief in particular illustrated the Warrior. A white man nearing retirement, the chief had worked for nearly four decades in a high-crime African American–majority city; we met in his office, a large suite that overlooked the city he policed. When I asked him how he first decided to go into law enforcement, he responded with sarcasm: "Because I want to help people!" After some stilted laughter, he added: "Because I want to catch bad guys! Lock 'em up!" In a matter of seconds, the chief juxtaposed two overarching ideals of police work: the helpful public servant and the hard-charging Warrior. Sarcastically dismissing the former as naive, the chief implicates a set of desires that have populated classic cop dramas such as *Dirty Harry*, *Magnum Force*, and *The Enforcer*. In these valiant, and edgy, films, police use of force is depicted not just as the reestablishment of justice. It is also portrayed as something that police seek out as a test of grit, or what the historian Richard Slotkin calls "the myth of regeneration through violence."[69] Drawing a line between "cops" and "police officers," this chief echoes Herbert's and Hunt's observations that police work is valorized through its association with a masculine ethos of crime fighting:[70]

> There are police officers, and there are cops. The police officer, they will be there at roll call. They'll answer the calls, they will file the reports. They will write their tickets. But when their 8 hours is up, they go home. And that's it. That's what they do. A cop: he gets to work, and he starts reading the reports of what happened on the last shift. He gets into his car, and if he stops someone, he's not writing a ticket. He's saying you fit that description. He's looking for the car involved in the robbery. He's jumpy, he's ready to stop a felony, to get the bad guy. He's expecting that. He's not just there to write a ticket—he's gritty, and he has the edge. He goes the extra mile. And he has the dream.

In this excerpt, this chief explicitly endorses going "the extra mile" to profile suspects ("he's not writing a ticket. He's saying you fit that description"). This could be understood as a nod to racial profiling; throughout the interview the chief recognizes and recuperates the racial politics of urban violence. He refers to statistics regarding the disproportionate representation of African Americans among gun offenders and prison inmates. He suggests that black men are less likely to become cops because "a lot of the black men smoke and can't pass a drug test." And noting that "we don't have social programs to deal with the fallout," he pathologizes the black family, referencing a column by the conservative African American economist Walter E. Williams titled "The True Black Tragedy."[71]

This chief's references to black marginalization served to substantiate and celebrate a particular rendition of high-drama police work—one that required the stakes of urban violence for its appeal. To illustrate, this chief told me about what he called "the dream." The dream, he explained, reveals the anxieties of the "real" cop: in the "dream," the officer can't find his gun; he (as this chief tells it, it is always a "he") can't draw his gun; his trigger finger is weak; there is just a click where there should be a boom when the trigger is finally forced back. The dream, I realized, was a crucial illustration of the intertwining of gun violence and police identity: by conjuring a stylized rendition of urban gun violence (and to the exclusion of other kinds of gun violence, such as domestic violence, active shootings, and negligent shootings), this chief and others could articulate the Warrior's appeal through the drama of gritty crime fighting.

Other chiefs likewise articulated the Warrior as they reminisced about their early days on street patrol. One white chief discussed policing in 1980s Detroit: "Those were the good old days. . . . There was a lot of action—catching bad guys. It was legitimate police work." Throughout the interview, the chief struggled with the politics of race, by turns wondering whether slavery was a "fatal birth defect" dooming the viability of the United States, bemoaning the "breakdown of the nuclear family," emphasizing black men's "disproportionate" involvement in gun crime as a reflection of "core family values," and wagering that his own upbringing as white but poor helped him understand the plight of Detroiters better than other police. Alongside these ruminations, he recalled one experience while on patrol:

> I got a call for a carjacking. And when you get into the hang of things, you get a sense of how things go down, so maybe a carjacking happens on one street, and you know to go straight over to another block nearby. It turns out there is a driver, a passenger, and two kids in the back seat. One kid in the back, a thirteen-year-old, pulls out a gun that looks like it has a fourteen-foot barrel. I know it was just a gun, but it looked like the biggest thing I have ever seen. I pulled out my gun and just shot—I didn't see a kid, I just saw a cannon right in my face. And the only reason that kid didn't die was because I was using "city council" rounds at the time, with limited penetration. They were frangible rounds.

This chief was notably silent on the racial details of this stop, but the tropes surrounding urban crime and law enforcement's role in combatting it appear to nevertheless shape how he framed his own experiences of gun violence. The thirteen-year-old Detroit boy is literally reduced to weaponry ("I didn't see a kid, I just saw a cannon right in my face"), and he casually dismisses the precariousness of life and death in Detroit: "the only reason that kid didn't die was because I was using 'city council' rounds." But his story could have been told differently: the chief could have emphasized his relief at having had "less lethal" rounds so that both the boy and the chief were able to leave the incident unscathed. Instead, this story of a close encounter with gun violence communicated a particular understanding of policing as a high-stakes drama that tests the perspicacity of police officers as they face off with firearms.

But police chiefs' stories about, and insights into, urban gun violence did not just communicate how they saw themselves; they also communicated how they understood the people they policed.

THE URBAN GUN CRIMINAL

For decades since the inception of the war on crime in the 1960s, urban gun violence has been popularly associated with the criminal propensity of racialized boys and men figured as hyperviolent aggressors: thugs, gangbangers, drug dealers, and superpredators. These tropes of urban criminality circulate on television screens, in tabloid headlines, in movie theaters, and on social media feeds. They populate fictionalized dramas and documentary accounts alike of crime in the United States. They appear in the stump speeches of politicians looking to galvanize voters through fear of crime. And they animate how those people professionally charged with addressing problems of crime and justice in the United States—such as police chiefs—understand and explain their work. Scholars of criminalization have overwhelmingly shown that these tropes reflect and reinforce racial distinctions regarding blameworthiness and criminality.[72] The race scholars Michael Omi and Howard Winant understand such tropes as "racial code words,"[73] or putatively race-neutral terms that nevertheless communicate implicitly racialized expectations and presumptions. Racial code words animate color-blind racism: though color blindness rejects explicit racial prejudice and animus, racial code words allow color blindness to sustain systems of racial domination by minimizing the grim consequences of racial inequality, oppression, and discrimination as the results of individuals' bad behavior and moral laxity.[74]

Police chiefs across Arizona, California, and Michigan—even chiefs who did not have direct experience with urban gun violence—spontaneously referenced popular tropes of urban criminality: "the drug dealers that drive through from Detroit" (Michigan chief); "the gangbangers who still have their Roscoes [guns] in LA" (California chief); and the "gang members in Chicago" (Arizona chief). As one California chief explained, "I am not worried about the people who just want an assault weapon for the hell of it, or a military guy who had an M16 and wants one because it reminds him of his old gun. I'm worried about the gangsters who bring in guns [to California] and then they get into the hands of people who have hatred for America." Here, the "gangster" is seen as assisting "people who have hatred for America" (that is, terrorists),[75] while the person "who just wants an assault weapon for the hell of it" and the "military guy" are figured as harmless, lawful gun owners. A Michigan chief similarly explained: "The urban terrorists are gang members." A California chief shared his perceptions of illegal gun owners: "I just think about all the guns that are illegally owned. Gangsters, people on probation, illegal immigrants." And an Arizona chief maintained that it was largely "gangbangers and crooks" who take advantage of loopholes in existing gun laws.

More rarely, chiefs explicitly acknowledged racial disparities related to gun violence, throwing their hands up at a problem they can see but do not feel capable of fixing. For example, one chief noted:

> A couple years ago, we had 19 shootings in 18 days. It was really bad. And they were all arrested, they are all doing time. But the reality is, you know, they might be doing 7 years, 10 years, but eventually—whether if it's in a few years' time or longer—they are going to come back to the community and they are going to go back into the same violence. And I get it: I get that there's a lot going on, the fact that they are all African American, but I'm not trying to solve the world's problem. I'm just trying to deal with the fact that 10 out of 12 of them will shoot someone else when they come out.

Reducing complex problems of racial inequality—as this chief noted, "there's a lot going on, the fact that they are all African American"— to singular acts of criminality produced a simple, and putatively color-blind, line between "good guys" and "bad guys." This chief's exasperation rightly acknowledged the difficulties in solving urban gun violence; accordingly, he resigned himself to redefining this problem in narrower terms that aligned with his professional capacities as a police officer: "I'm just trying to deal with the fact that 10 out of 12 of them will shoot someone else when they come out."

Other chiefs attempted to get a handle on the problem of urban gun violence by emphasizing that it was contained, both in the sense of being relegated to particular cities or parts of cities, and in the sense of involving a tight, racialized network of perpetrators and victims. As one chief told me about gun violence in his Michigan jurisdiction,

> It's very concentrated among a network of people. Let me show you a picture. [He grabs a picture that shows homicide victims; it's three rows of several faces. Two white men in the middle, one African American woman, and the rest black men. He puts his fingers on the two white men to cover them.] Besides those two, they are all the same: black men who are between 18 and 24. [He does not acknowledge the African American woman.] It's gang-related, but it's local gangs. It's organic. It's not Chicago or Detroit gangs. It will happen when people are playing dice or what have you. So, one homicide victim—he was shot at 6 am and it was the third time he was shot. The guy who shot him then goes and kills himself. And it was because they had words, one of them accused the other of cheating at dice, and that's it.

This construction of gun violence minimized it as a broad issue of public safety by confining its effects to relatively small circles of boys and young men of color and developing police strategies to isolate gun violence to particular settings and contain the "spillover." Similarly, a California chief in a high-crime area naturalized this violence by appealing to the demographics of the city, "We have gang issues, and that's connected to us having a low-income community and a high minority rate; we are 70 percent Hispanic. So that goes sort of hand in hand. Our crime rates have dropped about 25 percent, but here the gun violence is still people shooting people!" Another California chief in a jurisdiction that bordered a high-crime area likewise used the language of containment: "We are concerned with making sure that the gang violence does not spill over. As we say, we like to keep our enemies on the other side of the gate." This language reflects a presumption, as the sociologist Nikki Jones notes, "regarding the value placed on black life . . . : violence is only a problem when it spills *outside* of the Black community."[76]

This construction also minimized gun violence by blurring the lines between perpetrators and victims. Emphasizing that an incident can be "classified as gang-related if it is a gang member killing another gang member" (according to one chief), chiefs at times separately tallied homicides in non-gang-related and gang-related categories as they explained their city's terrain of gun violence, and they refrained from labeling those who die in gang violence as "victims." As one chief told me, "I would say that gun violence is my number one concern. . . . 90 percent of it is targeted. It's people who are involved in a criminal lifestyle." Another chief noted, "Usually these kinds of cases are gang on gang cases that involve people getting physical and then it escalating to a weapon."

Note that these sentiments *do* reflect the empirical reality that urban gun violence is concentrated—in terms of both perpetrators and victims—in small circles of boys and men of color,[77] and initiatives that have used a blend of policing strategies and community support networks to target "at-risk" individuals have meaningfully reduced categories of gun crime (see, for example, the Boston Miracle).[78] Constructing urban gun violence as a localized issue of "bad people" from "bad places" doing "bad things," however, chiefs reflected not just empirical trends with respect to gun violence perpetration and victimization. They also forwarded a moral claim about those involved in urban gun violence: that they are, by definition, involved in a "criminal lifestyle" rather than community members and fellow citizens.

THE CRIME OF SELF-DEFENSE?

As Ewing and other scholars of crime and criminalization remind us, the victims and perpetrators of gun violence are often distinguished not by moral standing but by the exigencies of circumstance. Likewise, the distance between criminal violence and defensive violence can be excruciatingly small. Imagine someone who has grown up in a violence-saturated, economically depressed neighborhood. They decide it makes sense to involve themselves in small-time drug deals. This, however, exposes them to even more risks of violent victimization. Without a felony record or any other disqualifier, they purchase a handgun for self-defense—and, eventually, find themselves in a situation when they need to use it: someone violently assaults them. Could this be self-defense? Or is it necessarily criminal violence? Does it matter if the assaulter knew the victim through the latter's criminal activity? If so, how?

Given that the police chiefs I interviewed were broadly supportive of gun rights, I almost always posed to police chiefs a question that pushed their embrace of self-defense: does a drug dealer have the right to self-defense? In Michigan, California, and Arizona, most chiefs answered in the negative. As one chief in California reasoned:

> It's not self-defense—any death incident to the commission of a felony in California is a felony murder. That's the felony murder rule. There are some cases, where you have someone say, I was getting mugged! Well, then you drill down and realize, that's the what but that's not really the why [i.e., there was a criminal element going on].

An Arizona chief agreed:

> It's felony murder. I believe so. It would be illegal—what they were doing. If they hadn't done all of the illegal things leading up to that, there would have been no shooting.

Felony murder refers to a criminal homicide that results from the commission of a felony: it makes a person criminally liable for murder if a co-conspirator kills someone, or if a death is a reasonably foreseeable consequence in the commission of a violent felony. As a legal term, *felony murder* defines the circumstances in which a suspect can be held responsible not just for the underlying felony but also for murder. States vary in terms of their felony murder doctrines. California has a long-standing legal culture of felony murder;[79] in Michigan, felony murder was abolished by the Michigan Supreme Court in 1980; and Arizona retains felony murder by statute, but it does not inform the state's legal culture to the same extent as in California.

These state-level differences mapped onto cleavages among chiefs: chiefs in California were most likely to see self-defense as revocable, whereas Michigan chiefs were most ambivalent about rendering self-defense a crime. These differences also revealed that felony murder is not just a legal category but also a moral category that exceeds its legal parameters: broadening the felony murder rule, many chiefs, especially in California, adhered to a one-drop rule of criminal involvement, whereby drug dealing, gangbanging, and other activities associated with urban crime indicated both criminal depravity and legal and moral exclusion from the right to self-defense. One California chief even explained a case in which defendants were held criminally liable for a homicide that resulted from self-defense by their victim. When asked whether his jurisdiction has had any justifiable homicides (the legal term for self-defense homicides), he responded by explaining,

> We've had them. We had one with a jewelry store where the merchant was armed, and shot back [on a group of armed robbers]. One of the guys died in the front of the store in the parking lot, and we tracked them [the rest of the robbers] down and charged them with felony murder.

Given my pledge to police chiefs that I maintain their anonymity, I could not determine the veracity of this story, or its outcome, but the charge of felony murder in such circumstances would be unusual. Nevertheless, the felony murder doctrine allows this chief to align himself—legally and morally—with an armed citizen defending a jewelry business. Not unlike mandatory minimums and sentencing enhancements, self-defense in this story operates as an additional means of criminalizing the attacker, above and beyond the underlying felony.

As another example, one Michigan chief ruminated about the legal and moral gaps between self-defense law and the felony murder doctrine (recall that Michigan has abolished its felony murder doctrine): "I do think they should be charged if they are involved in illegal acts. I think they forfeit the right. But we had one case where a guy was getting beat up by a drug dealer. It was some kind of deal gone bad. Well, the son, who was not to my knowledge involved in any kind of illegal activity, gets a gun and shoots the guy because he sees his father getting beaten. And he kills the drug dealer. And that guy wasn't charged. And that's a tough one, because he wasn't really involved, but it happened because of drug dealing." The moral standing of the killing in this case presents the chief with a "tough one" insofar as the perpetrator cannot be straightforwardly categorized as either a "bad guy with a gun" or as a "good guy with a gun." On the one hand, the proximity of the son to illegal activity rendered him suspect, and his actions were intended to protect his father, who was involved in criminal activity. On the other hand, he played the part of a "good guy with a gun" by acting in defense of his father and killing a drug dealer—not an otherwise innocent civilian. Even as the chief insists on the general rule that those "involved in illegal acts . . . forfeit the right" to self-defense, the chief accedes to the prosecutor's decision not to charge in this "tough" case.

As these examples illustrate, the politics of urban crime predisposes police chiefs—and, for that matter, the public—to imagine gun law, and gun criminals, with particular frames designating boys and men of color as suspected criminals. But not all police chiefs unwittingly reproduced these frames. Navigating circumstances not of their choosing, with moral compasses and everyday experiences at odds with popular cultural frames, some police chiefs questioned the criminalization of self-defense—as well as its racial foundations.

Consider one chief who policed a rural area in California's Central Valley; despite their bucolic veneer, small rural towns such as this

chief's often harbor a fair share of criminal activity. Pro-gun in his
sensibilities, this chief wrestled with one incident involving a violent
encounter between a "gangbanger" and "a wannabe gang member."
He set the stage: "There was a gang member at a party, and he was
just beating up people. He took this one kid, and just threw him
against the wall and was just beating and beating and beating him
against a light. Well, this kid took out a buck knife and was waving it
around and slit everyone. One guy actually died. . . . Another guy
survived. This guy with the knife: he was no angel; he was a wannabe gang member. And I wanted to arrest him for homicide." The
story could have ended there as yet another example of felony murder, but the chief went on: "The detective had more common sense
than I did, who saw it as self-defense. And I think that was right, that
was the right call. That guy went to the Marines." Again, the story
could have ended there: a kid given a second chance turns straight.
But: "He came back and ended up getting a [concealed pistol license]
and getting into another shooting and killing a gang member, and
then was arrested for homicide. But that was still deemed self-
defense." Here, the chief moves from sympathetic to exasperated; he
admits that he understands the reasoning behind the man's desire for
a concealed pistol license: "He said, 'These gang members want re-
taliation.' And I think that's a credible threat." The chief continues:
"But then what does he do? Put himself into a situation where he
knows there will be gang members. . . . I would not have issued [him
a concealed pistol license] because I know that he was associated
with a gang." At this point, the chief reiterates a point widespread
among many police chiefs: that criminal involvement—including
criminal association—can, and even should, put people in liminal
spaces where their rights are de facto suspended. But then this chief
catches himself yet again: "But you have to review every case.
Because his brother was a gang member, and he looked up to him.
Now, he's [the brother] had a stellar career—because someone gave
him a chance. . . . So it's human nature—and you have to think about
that. And again, I really agree with that saying: guns don't kill,
people kill." Rather than embracing a one-size-fits-all "tough on

crime" sentiment on gun law enforcement, this chief tries to shine light on the long shadow of racialized tropes of criminality such as gang-bangers': he recognizes that people *can* change (even as they often do not), that officers can be wrong (even as they struggle to do the right thing), and that the law does not provide a clear "how-to" guide in dealing with the real-life problems of policing. Ultimately, he settles on a stance borrowed from pro–gun rights rhetoric—"guns don't kill; people kill"—to tie up these tangled strands.

Across Arizona, California, and Michigan, a meaningful minority of chiefs were likewise openly flummoxed by racial profiling and racial disparities, explicitly recognizing that armed people of color are too often profiled as threats. One California chief who endorsed concealed carry for civilians noted, "Racial profiling is real. That's a reality. . . . [That's why] there needs to be *crystal clear rules* on how law enforcement engage armed civilians, and we should be able to check your ID, whether you are open carry or concealed carry, and we should have a right to hold on to your weapon as long as we need to." An Arizona chief explained his broad support for civilian gun carry and his personal reluctance to use force by referencing Philando Castile as tragically avoidable: "the guy in Minnesota—he was just trying to get his insurance out, and then the officer is shooting. There is no way I'd be going for my gun in that case." Finally, one California chief, largely ambivalent about gun policy itself, nevertheless linked guns to the politics of race in a clear-cut manner: "You have that corrosive racism. Look at [Johannes] Mehserle [a Bay Area Rapid Transit officer who killed the unarmed twenty-two-year-old Oscar Grant], look at his face after that shooting. Or the guy [officer] in Minnesota. Listen to him. They're afraid. And they don't even know how afraid they are! Totally uncomfortable. . . . You can just imagine what the [officer] thought in Minnesota, the guy says, 'I have a gun permit,' and the police officer hears 'Gun! Black man with a gun!' and thinks, 'gotta shoot!' It's like a Richard Pryor joke: 'Shoot the black man with a gun!'" These chiefs resisted—in different ways, and to different degrees—the racial tropes that mark guns in the hands of black and brown hands as inexorable threats to public safety, public order, and police power, bucking police *and popular* sensibilities alike.

Most chiefs embraced, to some degree, gun rights and the right to self-defense. Looking at the question of self-defense from the racial lens of urban gun crime, however, revealed the racial fault lines in demarcating the moral and legal boundaries of self-defense. Race shapes the terrain of legitimate violence. Through the color-blind lens of criminality, racial tropes of urban crime provide cues for demarcating what does and does not count—morally and legally—as legitimate violence. Some chiefs could see the racial contours of this terrain—and oftentimes, these chiefs did so not *despite* but *because of* their embrace of gun rights. Accordingly, they could name race as a visible dynamic shaping legitimate violence, not just as exercised by armed private civilians but also as exercised by police.

CONCLUSION

"Black Man with a Gun." "Driving while Black." "Walking while Black." "Breathing while Black." Or simply, "Criminal Black Man."[80] Each of these phrases describes how the structural[81] condition of blackness inflects the otherwise ordinary stuff of everyday life: the "strange experience"—in W.E.B. Du Bois's words—of "being a problem."[82] Accordingly, the public and private lives of African Americans[83] have been shaped by an awareness that their presence and their actions— whether clothing, body language, words, glances, or simply skin color— may render them unduly suspect and therefore endangered.

These everyday sensibilities are rooted in structural realities. Police are disproportionately likely to stop African Americans for reasons such as a broken tail light.[84] Once stopped, police are more likely to use respectful language with white drivers than with African American drivers,[85] and police are also more likely to search and ticket African American and Latinx drivers.[86] Arrest rates are also racially disparate, especially for possession offenses: racial minorities are disproportionately likely to be arrested for drug-related offenses, but this difference cannot be explained by differences in drug offending, nondrug offending, or more general crime rates.[87] Police shootings may represent a small percentage of overall stops, but they represent a rather large number in terms of the absolute number of deaths; so while police conduct tens of thousands of stops every day,[88] roughly one thousand people are killed by police in the United States per year, based on crowd-sourced data from the *Washington Post* and *The Guardian*. People of color are disproportionately represented among those killed by police. According to an analysis of 2011–2014 data by the anthropologist Cody Ross, unarmed African Americans are 3.49 times more likely to be shot than unarmed whites, holding crime rates constant.[89]

Most of the scholarship, public debate, and punditry regarding racial disparities in policing in particular and criminal justice more broadly has focused on the war on drugs. This chapter aims to start a similar conversation regarding the racial politics of gun law enforcement. Although the police and the public overwhelmingly question "tough on crime" policies for addressing drug crime and drug addiction, the war on guns enjoys broad approval. Among the police chiefs I interviewed, support for "tough on crime" gun laws is bound up with a broader understanding of legitimate violence (gun militarism) and allegiance to a particular police identity (the Warrior). Gun militarism envisions a distribution of legitimate violence that emphasizes police firepower and that marshals racialized imageries of the "bad guy with a gun"—gangbangers, drug dealers, and superpredators—to justify this aggressive gun law enforcement. This suggests a state monopoly on violence even stronger than that envisioned by the classical sociologist Max Weber,[90] who saw states monopolizing not legitimate violence itself so much as the prerogative to define the limits of legitimate violence. Perhaps, then, U.S. policing can be understood as "Weber with a Vengeance," where the racial politics of crime and crime control combine with a militarized police force to ramp up the potential for escalated violence, antagonize police-civilian relations, and transform the police-citizen relationship into one of soldier-enemy combatant.

But alongside gun militarism and the Warriors who animate it, there is another strain of policing, one that represents a distinct politics of race and that elicits a different distribution in legitimate violence across state and society: gun populism. In order to understand gun populism, we must understand not just the politics of black criminality but also the power of white innocence in relation to a racialized threat that emerged at the turn of the twenty-first century: the active shooting.

CHAPTER 3
NEVER OFF DUTY

Perhaps now America would wake up to the dimensions of this
challenge if it could happen in a place like Littleton.
—President Bill Clinton, remarks on the attack at Columbine High School
in Littleton, Colorado (April 20, 1999)

On April 20, 1999, two students entered Columbine High School with
guns and bombs. When the bombs failed to detonate, they used their
guns to kill thirteen people before turning the guns on themselves.
Though school shootings were not a new phenomenon in the United
States, the almost-live broadcasting of the Columbine carnage brought
it chillingly close to Americans who were otherwise insulated—or who
thought themselves to be insulated—from gun violence. As Dave Cullen remarked, "Much of the country was watching the standoff unfold.
None of the earlier school shootings had been televised; few American
tragedies had."[1] A full 68 percent of Americans reported that they
closely followed the story that year.[2]

But the tragedy was staggering not just because of the nearly live
coverage. As the media scholar Cynthia Willis-Chun notes, "The violence at Columbine High was all the more shocking because it defied
American assumptions about both whiteness and middle-class-ness."[3]
The massacre at Columbine pierced the association across urban schools,
drugs, and guns that naturalized poor, racialized communities as violent. It revealed the safety, security, and serenity of "normal" schools
like middle-class, suburban Columbine High as fragile and flimsy. It
also disrupted the commonplace tropes of gun perpetrators—both killers were white, middle-class teenage boys.

Columbine didn't just rattle the off-guard American public—it also shook the police. Believing that they were responding to a hostage standoff, patrol officers arriving on the scene focused on securing the perimeter and providing aid to survivors who trickled out of the school building. They followed decades of police convention—known as "contain-and-wait"—that relegated hostage situations to specially trained SWAT teams. Writing for *PoliceOne* in 1997, just two years before the massacre, the Indianapolis police officer Robert L. Snow celebrated SWAT as "one of law enforcement's greatest assets . . . [as] teams of highly trained, well-equipped specialists who have a continuum of choices to use when confronting a high-risk incident."[4] He distinguished SWAT specifically in relation to mass shootings like the 1966 Bell Tower shooting, which occurred on the campus of the University of Texas, Austin, on August 1 and left eighteen dead (including the perpetrator) and thirty-one injured.[5]

Associated with no-knock raids and aggressive war-on-drugs policing, SWAT often conjures up a show of excessive force, unrestrained by policy or procedure, against black and brown suspects. But in the white, middle-class setting of Columbine High School, the fatal flaws in police response turned out to be measured restraint and meticulous adherence to protocol. Patrol officers waited forty-five minutes for the SWAT unit to arrive as shots were being fired inside the building, and then they waited another three hours as the SWAT team methodically searched the school building: this is what their training and protocol told them to do. Dave Sanders, a coach and teacher, was shot as he tried to warn students of the attack; he slowly bled to death as the SWAT unit roamed the building.[6] Years later, a group of police practitioners would summarize: "The law enforcement profession had conditioned the patrol function to fail in an active shooter situation like Columbine. . . . [W]hat training was provided reinforced the concept of containment and calling for SWAT teams to handle critical situations."[7] Indeed, on the ten-year anniversary of Columbine, the Associated Press ran a story about the impact of the mass shooting on police training and tactics. Headlined by Fox News as "Shoot First: Columbine High School Massacre Transformed US Police Tactics,"[8] the article outlined the new police sensibilities about the phenomenon of the "active shooter": with a gunman killing a person every fifteen seconds in an active shooting event, police now "rush toward gunfire and step over bodies and bleeding victims, if necessary, to stop the gunman—the active shooter—first." In contrast to the strategies employed at Columbine, "it's been a complete turnaround" according to the Commission on Accreditation for Law Enforcement Agencies.

This chapter examines how police have grappled with the threat of active shootings. It focuses on interviews with police chiefs, and it unpacks the social construction of gun violence in predominantly white, suburban and rural communities. In contrast to the aggressive enforcement described in the context of urban gun violence, police chiefs articulated a sense of shame and devastation at failing to adequately respond to active shootings, and they embraced a particular policing mindset—the Guardian—centered on proactive protection rather than aggressive enforcement. Wrestling with active shootings as a policing problem, chiefs invested their guns with distinctive emotions, swapping the Warrior's eagerness to confront danger for the Guardian's anxious worry about responding with inadequate speed and firepower. Police chiefs forwarded a brand of hybrid masculinity[9] that blended "hardness and violence, plus compassion and care,"[10] allowing them to adopt the stance of a benevolent protector rather than aggressive enforcer. And in doing so, they did not just remix masculinity; they also remade the boundary between state and society, blurring their public obligations and private duties to protect as they understood their guns, especially off-duty, to be vehicles of public safety and personal protection alike.

THE TERROR OF ACTIVE SHOOTINGS

The FBI defines an active shooter as "an individual actively engaged in killing or attempting to kill people in a populated area." According to a 2018 analysis by the *Washington Post*, since the Bell Tower massacre on August 1, 1966, 1,135 Americans have been killed in active shootings.[11] Though active shootings comprise a relatively small proportion of annual firearms deaths, they receive disproportionate coverage compared to other kinds of gun violence. In their study of media coverage of gun violence from 1997 to 2012, the public health scholar Emma McGinty and her colleagues found that most coverage occurred in the context of mass shootings.[12]

The heightened public attention to active shootings is often attributed to the demographics of their victims. These shootings disproportionately involve white victims as compared to other kinds of gun crime. However, they far from exclusively affect white communities. The urban planning scholar Patrick Adler's analysis of Stanford's Mass Shootings in America database suggests that just over 30 percent of active shootings take place in communities that are more than 80 percent white; 42.4 percent take place in communities with populations less than 64 percent white. Writing for *CityLab*, the social scientist Richard Florida and the journalist Alastair Boone note, "In fact, the burden of mass shootings has fallen slightly heavier on communities that have a higher share of African Americans, on average. While African Americans make up 12.6 percent of the U.S. population on the whole, they make up 17 percent of the population in communities that experienced mass shootings."[13]

The racial and gender contours of active shootings suggest that active shootings signal a fundamentally different moral economy of criminality and innocence as compared to urban gun crime. This difference was evident in how police chiefs talked about active shootings: they emphasized the unambiguous moral status of victims as innocent, and they understood active shootings as an acutely pervasive, but simultaneously "out of place," threat. The more I listened to police chiefs, the more I came to understand that they understood active shootings as more than just acts of gun violence. To the majority of chiefs, active shootings were acts akin to terrorism.

The sociologist Austin Turk writes that "terrorism is not a given in the real world but is instead an interpretation of events and their presumed causes;"[14] the media scholar David Altheide describes terrorism as a "condition and state of affairs."[15] Elevating the urgency of active shootings, chiefs routinely referenced active shootings as central to this new-felt "condition and state of affairs," especially as they explained shifts in their off-duty gun carry habits. They collapsed active shootings under the broad umbrella of "terrorism," connecting "9/11," "assassinations" of police, "domestic terrorism," and active shootings as they name-dropped places associated with gun violence (e.g., "San Bernardino, Orlando, Sandy Hook" and "Dallas, Newtown, Orlando"). On the one hand, this conflation of terrorism and active shootings reinforced police chiefs' standing as crime fighters,[16] reflecting both the increasing expectation that law enforcement should be involved in antiterrorist activities[17] and the resonance between the war on crime and the war on terror as sets of political claims and policing strategies.[18] On the other hand, chiefs reinforced a racial politics of gun violence centered on white victimhood as they framed active shootings as terrorism. By referencing perpetrators of a variety of racial backgrounds and framing their actions as terrorism, police chiefs subtly sidestepped the empirical reality that white men are disproportionately represented as perpetrators of active shootings.[19]

Reinforcing the sense that active shootings represent a seemingly new, urgent, and increasing threat, police explained their newfound awareness of gun-violence-cum-terrorism. These three chiefs, for example, recognized that active shootings had shaped not just their awareness of gun violence but also their off-duty gun carrying habits:

You know, since 2001, 9/11 was a major trigger. And just last year you had assassinations in Dallas and Baton Rouge. And so those are the things that make a big splash. . . . I have everyday awareness and practice situational awareness. I understand that this stuff can happen anytime, anywhere.

I used to not carry as much, but now in the last five years, I'm carrying a lot more. It's the terrorism, the domestic terrorism, the climate for law enforcement.

It's really been the last ten years that I've been carrying more. . . . [M]ass shootings had a role. It just seems that as you experience more, and you read more, you have more of an obligation to protect. And it's just common sense. You could seriously help people.

Active shootings shaped how police chiefs understood suburban and rural space and the policing problems endemic to these spaces. Active shootings scrambled the racial politics of policing gun violence, upending sensibilities about where gun violence should or should not take place. While the war on crime (and its subsidiary war on guns) has focused largely on containing crime within urban spaces marked as poor, disorderly, and dangerous, active shootings have represented a different kind of penetrating threat, one that bucked containment to urban space and instead unsettles white space. For example, these three chiefs illustrated how the threat of otherwise rare acts of violence could mushroom into a cloud of ever-present danger as they reflected on the spatial politics of active shootings:

> You never know where and when someone will start shooting, and you can't outrun a bullet. So you have these things happening in the theater, schools, Best Buy, where some nut job just snaps. I do think about that.

> Active shootings—I don't like to call them school shootings because they can also be a workplace and other places—those are up. I read the intelligence bulletins, and it's happening at the national level, but that doesn't mean it can't happen here.

> Something can happen in the strangest places. I wouldn't go to church without a gun.

The church, the school, the workplace: none of these are necessarily "strange" places with respect to violence, except by virtue of their racial and class marking. In other words, they are the public equivalents to the private sanctuary of the white picket fence: places that "should" be peaceful and serene. Reflecting this marking of space, one chief told me the 2012 movie theater shooting in Aurora, Colorado, had particularly affected him because it exposed these newfound vulnerabilities:

> Aurora: it seemed commonplace. It wasn't a school. This is a movie theater where there is no security; people buy a ticket, and they go in. They let their guard down. They are sitting and eating their Red

Vines and popcorn, and they are vulnerable. They lose consciousness of place and time.

As such, active shootings disrupted a social geography of violence that neatly designated certain spaces as "safe" and others as "dangerous." Accordingly, chiefs understood active shootings to be inherently uncontrollable and foreign to the spaces in which they emerge—that is, terrorism. Accordingly, this threat to unexpected places and unexpected victims led chiefs to see active shootings as an urgent problem, even as they recognized their rarity.

POLICING MENTAL HEALTH

Active shootings do not just scramble the racial politics of gun violence with respect to where gun violence takes place and whom it victimizes. They also scramble the racial politics of who perpetrates gun violence—and why.

Active shootings are more likely to involve white male perpetrators than other kinds of gun violence.[20] The criminologists James Alan Fox and Jack Levin found that non-Hispanic whites represented 69.9 percent of mass killers,[21] while the dataset compiled by Mark Follman, Gavin Aronson, and Deanna Pan for *Mother Jones* shows that white boys and men have perpetrated 57 percent of mass shootings.[22] The politics of white masculinity have shaped coverage of these tragedies over time: before the Columbine massacre, school shootings were typically portrayed in mainstream media as involving black and brown perpetrators in marginalized, "inner city" schools, and these tragedies were typically treated as clear-cut cases of criminality. Today, however, as the sociologists Scott Duxbury, Laura Frizzell, and Sadé Lindsay find in coverage of active shooters,[23] white perpetrators are more likely to be framed in terms of mental illness, even though the vast majority of people with serious mental illnesses are nonviolent and are more likely to be the victims than the perpetrators of violence.[24]

Framing the perpetrators of active shootings as suffering from mental illness helps to repair the community bonds that these tragedies rattle by emphasizing them "as [individual] aberrations, anomalies within society, or psychopaths who represent the antithesis of mainstream America."[25] The designation of active shootings as terrorism thus dovetails with the social construction of active shootings as a problem of mental illness rather than gun violence. Both highlight the unambiguous moral status of victims; both emphasize victims as "normal kids" in "normal places" doing "normal things" (to paraphrase); and both therefore resisted any narrative impulse to "blame the victim." Both the "terrorism" and "mental illness" designations, furthermore, help make sense of active shootings by individualizing the blameworthiness of the perpetrators and treating it as fundamentally foreign to the social contexts in which it occurs. This perhaps explains why police chiefs labeled white shooters by turns as "terrorists," "mentally unstable," and even "evil": each of these designations situated the killers as outside of the communities that they terrorized.

But these designations also situated active shooting perpetrators as outside the purview of law enforcement, too—as mental health problems rather than policing problems. Historically, mental illness has long been used to pathologize forms of survival and protest among African Americans: the physician Samuel A. Cartwright made a racist wager that runaway slaves were merely exhibiting signs of a mental illness, drapetomania, while displays of Black Power in the 1960s were often popularly diagnosed as symptoms of psychotic illness. In *The Protest Psychosis,* the medical scholar Jonathan Metzl unravels the suturing of antiracist protest and mental illness to explain why, in the mid-twentieth century, schizophrenia transformed from a disease disproportionately affecting whites to one that disproportionately affects African Americans.[26] In the contemporary context of gun crime, however, the racialization of mental illness has taken a markedly different form: mental illness–associated gun crime is now popularly associated with gun violence perpetrated by whites, whereas black-involved gun crime is subsumed under the auspices of criminality, even when issues of mental illness are evidently in play.[27]

Situated beyond the long shadow of black criminality, then, mental illness–related gun crime elicited a less punitive, and more rehabilitative, approach with more second chances for redemption among the police chiefs I interviewed. Police chiefs' near-unanimous embrace of a war on guns in the form of enhanced sentencing and mandatory minimums (see chapter 2) was matched by an equally vigorous call for a softer side of this war in the form of mental health services and enhanced background checks. From Arizona to California to Michigan, police chiefs overwhelmingly depicted the intersection of mental health and guns as one of the most urgent, but also vexing, criminal justice issues.[28] One Arizona chief called for "comprehensive mental health background checks, and the ability to correlate it with firearms checks. Criminal background checks are not enough." A California chief reasoned, "Mental health: we all agree that that's a problem. I don't understand why we try to build consensus, instead of working where there already is consensus." A Michigan chief adamantly noted, "Mental health, that's my top concern . . . and we are 100 percent dropping the ball."

Many (though not all) police chiefs saw the background check system itself as fundamentally flawed, with lackluster interstate data sharing and poor protocols on data integrity. But several chiefs worried about more than just shoddy bureaucracy; they saw the flawed U.S. background checks system as indicative of a broader breakdown, marked by a broken mental health system. As one Michigan chief said, "We don't deal with mental health, like we don't deal with anything. Think of all the places [mental health facilities] we've closed, too. In Ypsilanti, there used to be a huge mental health facility. Hundreds of people were there. Where are all these people? Nothing is being done. And it's not hard for someone with mental health issues to get a gun." This chief is right: mental health services have dramatically shrunk in the past few decades, and prisons and jails have turned into de facto mental health facilities—so much so that *The Atlantic* could declare in 2015 that "America's Largest Mental Health Hospital Is a Jail."[29]

In sharp contrast with their Warrior sensibilities surrounding urban crime, police chiefs resented—rather than relished—running into danger in the context of mental health crises. They begrudged that their call to duty had expanded to require them to also act as mental health care professionals. Chiefs from Arizona, California, and Michigan disliked that police are now charged with addressing problems that other sectors of society have shirked. One Arizona chief saw this as a broad trend that burdened police: "Most of the US's problems land in the laps of police—whether it's homelessness, mental illness, gun violence, substance." Similarly, one California chief bemoaned the use of force against people experiencing a mental health crisis: "One of the things that just really bothers me is that I hate to use force against the mentally ill. It bugs me and bothers me when officers are forced to do it. And so when there is a 5150 [California dispatcher code for a mental health call], I tell my officers to call dispatch and ask for the Crisis Intervention Team. And they are like, 'Why? We don't have one.' And I say, because I want it recorded." Faced with a broken system, this chief turned bureaucracy into resistance: a paper trail documenting society's moral abdication toward mental health.

Make no mistake, then: police chiefs want policies to address mental health–related gun violence—these were often cited as police chiefs' top priorities alongside the "tough on crime" gun laws described in chapter 2. But they saw these brands of gun policy as a fundamentally different kind of project than those targeting the urban gun offender; *this* project prioritized mental health services rather than law enforcement. As such, calling for gun policies in the form of enhanced background checks, mental health services, and social supports to address active shootings not only echoed public opinion broadly in support of these initiatives; it also freed up police to do the "real" work of law enforcement.

Advocating mental health supports they believed would ameliorate the threat of active shootings and gun violence more generally, chiefs vehemently insisted that they were not mental health professionals. But as I learned while listening to them describe their encounters—both real and imagined—with active shootings, neither did they understand themselves as Warriors vis-à-vis urban and suburban gun violence. Instead, they saw themselves as Guardians.

THE GUARDIAN

One Michigan chief I interviewed had spent his entire career policing rural jurisdictions. He explained that he is the only police officer in his family, and when asked why he joined public law enforcement, he earnestly smiled: "I will give you a cheesy answer: I wanted to help people." When the interview turned to combating gun violence, this earnest desire took on enhanced urgency. The chief referenced the 2015 Charleston church shooting in which a self-identified white supremacist killed nine black churchgoers at a historically black church:

> You know people say, "Oh, this guy is racist or whatever in Charleston." No, it's just evil. It's evil killing good people. And the evil is getting stronger and stronger, and the good is being made to look evil, and that's why we need to be superheroes.

Sidestepping the much-publicized racial motivations of this mass killing, this chief makes sense of this active shooting by appealing to a color-blind discourse of good and evil.[30] The chief concludes that such killings are "just evil," which in turn compels him to embrace a particular understanding of himself—as a "superhero." Framing police as "superheroes," this chief and others adopted a distinctive brand of policing—the Guardian—in response to active shootings.

The emergence of the Guardian reflects shifts in recent years[31] as police practitioners, policymakers, and politicians have promoted it as an alternative to the Warrior. The former sheriff Sue Rahr and the criminal justice scholar Stephen Rice juxtapose these two mindsets by reminding police that they are not soldiers: "The soldier's primary mission is that of a warrior: to conquer. The rules of engagement are decided before the battle. The police officer's mission is that of a guardian: to protect."[32] Likewise, one rural Arizona chief summarized this shift,

> There's [been a] switch [to] the Guardian mindset. . . . We are here to protect the public, their rights, and . . . we need to do whatever we have to [to] do that. So, we're not just investigating, we are

protecting—and that is whether we're talking about a shooting, terrorism. We are now expected to do more.

In this chief's and in Rahr and Rice's framings, the Guardian is charged with a moral obligation to protect innocent lives, grounding police work not in dominating others (as in the Warrior) but in protecting others. Distinguishing these two mindsets can be tricky; after all, as Seth Stoughton reminds us, the Warrior may likewise be motivated by ideals of "honor, duty, resolve, and the willingness to engage in righteous violence."[33] For this reason, the Warrior and the Guardian are perhaps better understood not as mutually exclusive ways of approaching police work but rather as distinctive stances on policing that can be mobilized for different kinds of policing problems.

Listening to police chiefs, I learned that not just their thoughts on gun violence *but also their understandings of their own police guns* were key to unraveling the distinctions between the Warrior and Guardian as police experience these mindsets and the emotive worlds they entail. I expected—and found—that in the context of the Warrior mindset, guns are deployed as a means of evoking aggression, empowerment, and hostility vis à vis criminal aggressors as described in chapter 2. What I didn't expect was the very different purpose that they served for the Guardian: to *avoid* feelings of guilt, shame, and devastation at being unable to protect an innocent.

Shame was central to how the Columbine massacre and other active shootings haunted the police chiefs I interviewed. Judging from my interviews almost two decades after the Columbine shooting, the sense of collective failure regarding the police response to that active shooting has remained palpable. One white, middle-aged chief oversaw public law enforcement in a former mining town in Arizona, but before that, he had patrolled a neighboring community to Littleton in suburban Denver. He explained,

> I was in a neighboring community in Colorado when Columbine happened. And you know, that really impacted us. We felt like failures. We thought: how could we have allowed this to have happened? Here, we waited outside while kids were being killed. And that was really

> our attitude—we were failures. . . . And I would say that in Colorado, we found it offensive that some people went to gun control. Because we felt like we let society down.

Though this chief spoke of intense feelings of responsibility for the police response to Columbine, he was not present at the high school that day. Nevertheless, he uses "we" as he discusses the feelings of failure in the aftermath of Columbine: the police response at Columbine was a failure of the law enforcement community writ large, and he was personally aggrieved by the loss of life ("Here, we waited outside while kids were being killed"). This was not the mere mistakes of the individual officers on the scene that day ("bad apples," as debates on officer misconduct in the context of urban policing often reference); rather, the police response at Columbine is understood as a failure of police to stay true to their core mission of protection. In the words of this chief, "We really are the only first responders. We have to treat every situation that way." This takeaway suggests that police should see themselves not as specialized experts but as first responders, ready and willing to engage whatever threat may come their way—and wherever and whenever it may come.

If the "dream" haunted chiefs with respect to tropes of urban gun violence (as described in chapter 2), then a different kind of nightmare disturbed chiefs with respect to active shootings: not being able to intervene to "run to the threat," even if that meant "not stopping to help the people who needed our help." As another Arizona chief noted,

> That [the Columbine massacre] was a watershed moment in terms of active shooting. That was when we were all retrained to intervene— and trained to step over the dead bodies to run to the threat. And the hardest part there was not stopping to help the people who needed our help who we were stepping over.

In this nightmare, perpetrators all but vanish into an amorphous threat; victims—whether dead and stepped over or screaming and helpless— are central to how police understand these encounters.

This nightmare takes place not in the high-crime imaginary of the urban streets, but in the most unassuming spaces—what one chief called, as noted earlier, "the strangest of places." And whereas the "dream" that haunts police in the context of urban law enforcement involves a gun that refuses to shoot, this nightmare revolves around a police officer—oftentimes off-duty—who finds himself unwittingly unarmed. As three chiefs illustrate:

> I could not live with myself if I was in a situation where I could save lives, and I wasn't able to [because I was not carrying my firearm off-duty]. I can't imagine being at a public shooting and not having the tools [e.g., a firearm].

> If you have an ability to carry a gun, it is your responsibility to do and intervene should there be an attack. Say I'm in a movie theater, and there's a shooting, and I am there, but I can't do anything because I don't have a gun? I would feel devastated. Ashamed. Guilty. I would feel like all of those lives lost were on me. And it would ruin me forever.

> Shame on us if we are called to this, and we are able to save a life, but because we were unprepared we didn't. It would break my heart. . . . More than any other thought, I carry a gun because of that.

Although other chiefs did not share the former Colorado chief's close encounter, they often articulated unprompted fears of impotence amid the threat of active shootings. Surprisingly, even the handful of chiefs who told me they rarely carried off-duty also expressed this moral imperative: "I would feel stupid if something happened, and I was walking around without my gun. . . . I feel responsible for my community"; "I am worried that I'll be out and about and need one and wish I had one on me. . . . I need to be able to do something."

Active shootings appeared to have transformed the emotive attachment of police chiefs to their guns. By emphasizing feelings like embarrassment, shame, devastation, and guilt, chiefs focused less on courageous crime fighting against suspected criminals and more on the sense of failure, particularly with respect to victims, that would come with an underwhelming response to active shooter situations. Guns *evoked* feelings of aggression, empowerment, and hostility in the context of urban gun violence, but in the context of active shootings, guns seemed to help police chiefs engage in a different kind of emotional labor. Their practical usefulness notwithstanding, guns also helped police chiefs *avoid* feelings of guilt, shame, and devastation with respect to active shootings. In such contexts, these chiefs seemed less concerned with the thrill of the chase; they were not emphasizing trouble as a means to prove their police chops. Instead, they were anxious about how trouble might find them—in places where and times when they least expected it and would be caught off guard.

Accordingly, rather than the overt hypermasculinity of the Warrior, these chiefs embraced a hybrid masculinity—one that integrated "hardness and violence" in the service of "compassion and care."[34] Chiefs' sense of duty vis-à-vis active shootings echoed Iris Marion Young's observation regarding "masculinist protection": namely, that violence is not just a vehicle of aggressive domination among men but also a means of asserting "good men's" utility to their families and communities as protectors.[35] Amid the threat of active shootings, chiefs from Arizona, California, and Michigan did emphasize a masculine imperative to courageously face danger; however, under the Guardian mindset, this urgency is centered on protection of innocent victims, especially children,[36] rather than enforcement against suspected criminals (e.g., "catch the bad guys! Lock 'em up!") as under the Warrior.

FROM POLICE PREROGATIVES TO CIVIC DUTIES

Police have always been attached to their off-duty guns, but the threat of active shootings—now framed as terrorism—has provided a renewed emphasis on off-duty carry, both among police and among policymakers looking to bring a "see something, say something, do something" approach to counterterrorism to its logical conclusion. As one chief noted,

I would say there's been a significant shift in the last 10 years [in terms of carrying off duty]. You know, more things are happening—shootings, that sort of thing. And so I just think it's more and more important to be able to engage. If I weren't able to engage because I didn't have a weapon—I would be overwhelmed with guilt. You know, and it used to be the case that police couldn't carry out of state—that changed under Bush 43 [President George W. Bush]. But I went to the FBI training in DC, and we weren't allowed to carry a firearm. And the directors of that program told us—you could follow the rules and not carry, but then you'd be the only people in DC without guns. [Interviewer: So you carried anyway?] I carried anyway. I wouldn't want to be without it.

Throughout the history of modern policing, police have largely embraced off-duty carry,[37] even as they have recoiled at the requirement that they carry off duty as an uncompensated extension of their professional duties beyond working hours. In other words, police have long wanted the *option* to carry, just not the requirement. But up until 2004, police were constrained from doing so. That year, the U.S. Congress passed the Law Enforcement Officers Safety Act (LEOSA), referenced by the chief above. (See chapter 1 for a more in-depth discussion of this law and its passage.) The new law cleared the way for police—both active and retired—to conceal carry their firearms anywhere in the United States. Its proponents pointed out that the law would "allow tens of thousands of additionally equipped, trained and certified law enforcement officers to continually serve and protect our communities regardless of jurisdiction or duty status at no cost to taxpayers" and that "this legislation will help its members to protect citizens in the wake of a terrorist attack and that it is even more necessary since September 11, 2001." As Glen Hoyer, a retired law enforcement officer and the director of the NRA's Law Enforcement Division, told Officer.com in 2010, "You've got a tremendous amount of law enforcement experience in a retired officer." Indeed, LEOSA was supported by the NRA, the Fraternal Order of Police, and the Law Enforcement Alliance of

America; the Police Executive Research Forum and the International Association of Chiefs of Police opposed the legislation.

In the aftermath of this law, the police chiefs I interviewed told me that they rarely traveled within-state or flew across the United States without their guns. This represents an interesting reversal in the historical consolidation of public law enforcement as wielders of legitimate violence. Modern public law enforcement grew out of ad hoc citizens' militias taking a variety of forms (see chapter 1), but LEOSA rekindles the militia sensibilities of public law enforcement, blending the police role with the armed citizen and conflating a gun carried for professional reasons (i.e., law enforcement) with a gun carried for personal reasons (i.e., self-defense).

This blending was evident in my conversations with police chiefs: when it came to their off-duty carrying habits, they often slipped between their prerogatives as public law enforcement agents and their prerogatives as private armed civilians. One chief told me, "I carry more often than before. . . . Oddly enough, I was just talking about this with my wife, and we were talking about going to church, and we go to church up near Lansing. And I will carry my gun to church. And part of that is the obligation to protect. ISIS. My biggest concern is to be able to proactively protect my family." Another chief explained, "I don't want to be caught in the middle of some movie theater where someone is shooting—I'm going to be that person that does something. . . . [T]here are lots of examples where people are unarmed, and here you have someone shooting for the hell of it. So I'm not going to be one of those guys. I am going to protect my family and stop—or at least try to stop it."

Police chiefs could easily move between these two scripts—the obligation to protect one's community, the obligation to protect one's family—because the same brand of masculinist protection undergirds both. Indeed, the views of these chiefs echoed the men who carry guns as a means of asserting a masculine duty to protect themselves, their families, and even their communities. As I found in my earlier research on gun carriers, they often embraced a citizen-protector model of gun carrying as a civic duty centered on the willingness to use lethal force to protect innocent life.[38] Blurring the lines between police guns and private guns allowed police chiefs to tap into broader sensibilities about guns as defensive tools, drawing on pro-gun sensibilities to blend—and in doing so, buttress—public and private prerogatives alike. This blurring is not merely symbolic; recently, a Florida court ruled that the state's Stand Your Ground law also applies to police.[39] As we will see in chapter 4, this blurring has also recast how police understand and interface with private armed civilians.

CONCLUSION

On February 14, 2018, an armed assassin entered a high school in Parkland, Florida, and killed seventeen students and teachers. It was a police officer's nightmare—and not only because of the terrible tragedy itself. Soon after the shooting, reports leaked that the school resource officer named Scot Peterson—a Broward County sheriff's deputy—had been on site during the shooting, but had joined fellow officers behind cover as shots rang out and students were murdered. In contrast to police killings of unarmed African American boys and men, which often elicit silence, police were openly condemnatory. Coral Gables police, who arrived on the scene later and immediately entered the building, were shocked and dismayed at the deputy's actions. The sheriff reported that he was "devastated, sick to my stomach."

The officer broke protocol. But he also broke rank with the Guardian mindset that organizes how police understand, and imagine they would respond to, active shootings. In the aftermath, Broward County officials changed policy to codify expectations for police tasked with responding to active shootings: police now "shall" intervene.[40] By January 2019, the Marjory Stoneman Douglas High School Safety Commission issued its nearly five-hundred-page report.[41] The commission members, nearly half of whom were law enforcement or former law enforcement, recommended enhanced prevention, better law enforcement response mechanisms, and increased opportunities for teachers to be armed in the classroom. Together, they noted, such measures would enhance the possibility that first responders would either identify threats before they can escalate into lethal violence—or stop them as soon as they do. And in June 2019, Peterson was charged with child neglect, culpable negligence, and perjury—what the *New York Times* described as "an unusual instance of law enforcement officers being held criminally liable for not protecting the public."[42]

As Egon Bittner famously noted, "the role of the police is best understood as a mechanism for the distribution of non-negotiable coercive force employed in accordance with the dictates of an intuitive grasp of situational exigencies. . . . [T]he role of the police is to address all sorts of human problems when and insofar as their solutions do or may possibly require the use of force at the point of their occurrence."[43] The gap between the reality of police encountering gun violence and/or using their own guns in the line of duty (which is rare compared to the thousands of stops that police conduct every year) and its persistent possibility means that police guns are pregnant with anxieties and hopes, dreams and nightmares. If police are troubled by anxieties about the impotence of their guns amid the specter of urban gun crime (and indeed, my interviews with police chiefs suggest that they are), they are also troubled by fears and frustrations surrounding their guns in the context of active shootings represented by flash points like Sandy Hook, Orlando, San Bernardino, Las Vegas, Parkland, and dozens of others.

But the meanings attached to police guns—and to their identities as police—are strikingly different across these two contexts. Regarding gun violence associated with urban contexts, police chiefs construct themselves as aggressively courageous Warriors pitted against gun violence associated with black and brown gangbangers, drug dealers, and superpredators. However, regarding gun violence associated with rural and suburban contexts, white victims, and white perpetrators, police chiefs embrace the Guardian mindset: they reframe gun violence as terrorism, revamp their own police duties as first responders, and understand police failure in terms of cowardice not in *apprehending* criminals but rather in *saving* victims.

Policing, in other words, is not reducible to the Warrior brand. Rather than a mere *lack* of gun militarism, active shootings ignite renewed focus on police capacities as *protectors*. Juxtaposed with chapter 2, this chapter shows that the racial politics of innocence and blameworthiness, in intersection with a masculine prerogative to protect, bifurcates how police understand gun violence—and themselves as law enforcement. Rather than splitting police into mutually exclusive groups of Warriors and Guardians, these mindsets represent different toolkits[44] that police can bring to understanding the problems they police, which is why the majority of police see themselves as *both* enforcers *and* protectors, according to a recent Pew survey of law enforcement.[45] Thus, though they may wield the same guns across urban, suburban, and rural contexts, police chiefs affixed their guns with different emotions as they confronted different kinds of gun violence. Active shootings provide an opening for police chiefs to bring a populist sentiment to policing and, in the process, deepen their own affinity with the politics of gun rights—both for themselves and, as we shall see, for law-abiding civilians.

CHAPTER 4

WHEN THE GOVERNMENT DOESN'T COME KNOCKING

On January 12, 2017, Arizona Department of Public Safety trooper Ed Andersson responded to early-morning calls that someone was shooting at cars near the desert town of Tonopah. He arrived at the scene and found an injured woman and an overturned car. He wanted to help her, but before he could, he was shot in the shoulder and then beaten. Andersson remembers thinking: "As much as I fought, I probably couldn't have gone on anymore."[1]

Enter a white man in his mid-forties named Thomas Yoxall. A local outlet described Yoxall as "a journeyman plumber, a college drop-out, a convicted felon and a tough guy whom his friends liked because he was an intimidating enforcer." Over the decade and a half leading up to his intervention to save Andersson, Yoxall had turned his life around, according to popular news accounts. He got off of probation; he volunteered with children with developmental disabilities; he successfully petitioned to have his felony conviction expunged. With his rights restored, he became an avid gun owner and took up shooting with a crew of current and former law enforcement and military members.[2]

Yoxall had been on his way to Disneyland when he saw Andersson's car race up behind him; he thought he was about to start his vacation with a speeding ticket. But as the police car passed him and exited to the shooting scene, Yoxall soon realized the situation was much direr. He decided to interrupt his road trip when he saw the trooper struggling. He yelled, "Do you need assistance?" Andersson responded, "Help me!"[3]

Yoxall intervened, killing the suspect-shooter with his firearm. His account exemplifies the logic of the citizen-protector[4]—someone who sees the use of lethal force to protect innocent life as a central civic duty in the contemporary U.S. context. *AZCentral* summarized: "Yoxall said he had no choice but to stop. Throughout his life, he had always seen himself in the role of a protector. This incident validated that notion." He said he couldn't "fathom" that dozens of cars drove by the scene but neither stopped nor called 911.[5] Officer Andersson remarked, "I probably wouldn't be here" had Yoxall not intervened; "I get to see my grandkids grow up, my daughters get married eventually. . . . [H]e did a fabulous thing."

The suspect-shooter—a Mexican man named Leonard Penuelas-Escobar[6]—was rarely mentioned in news reports at any length, except as a setup to the uncannily heroic actions of Yoxall. Glossing over Penuelas-Escobar and his background[7] to instead focus on Yoxall and the drama of the citizen-who-saves-a-cop-with-a-gun, pro-gun venues, local press, and even mainstream national outlets were celebratory. CNN declared, "Good Samaritan with a gun saves wounded cop."[8] A Phoenix-area ABC affiliate summarized: "Arizona trooper ambushed: Good Samaritan says God put him there to save the trooper."[9] These outlets seemed to agree, Yoxall had passed the ultimate test for a good guy with a gun: he rescued a cop in distress.

This chapter analyzes gun populism as a distinct form of gun talk, whereby police understand private armed civilians as productive of social order alongside institutionalized law enforcement. As the police's and public's responses to Yoxall's actions suggest, police are not as invested in a strict monopoly on legitimate violence as accounts of gun militarism might suggest. Instead, they tend to accommodate the reality—and accept the broad benefits—of a widely armed populace, sympathizing with legal gun carriers and even understanding them as productive of social order.

Gun populism clarifies what gun militarism cannot explain. It illuminates, for example, why the police and the public seemed relatively unconcerned with vilifying Penuelas-Escobar, even though his biography could have easily amplified a moral panic surrounding undocumented migrants. Gun populism likewise helps explain why the police and the public would so eagerly embrace Yoxall—who, but for the expungement of his felony record, would have been criminalized by mere possession of the very gun that was now widely celebrated. Under gun populism, focus shifts away from denigrating the racialized criminals and toward commending the law-abiding citizens for their heroic actions. And as my interviews suggested, this color-blind language of lawfulness produces not calls for harsh punishment (as under gun militarism) but calls for empathy and even impunity, as police see the "good guys with guns" (which, at times, include themselves) unduly hampered by misguided gun policy. Though this color-blind language of lawfulness does not exclusively benefit white, middle-class, rural and suburban Americans, it is implicitly crafted in their image as police chiefs bespeak gun populism in terms of the capacity of law-abiding Americans to serve as fellow guarantors of social order.

GUN POPULISM

Populism is a contested concept: Is it a political ideology, or merely a vessel for other ideologies? Is it inherently right-wing, or can populism carry left-wing ideologies as well? And is "populist government" a contradiction in terms (because populism is fundamentally an outsider's rhetoric)? Scholars of populism define it as a repertoire that justifies particular political claims and arrangements according to an antipluralist construction of "the people" that is rallied against cultural, economic, and/or political "elites."[10] Accordingly, populism has been productively used to make sense of emergent political movements and the rhetoric of political claims, especially by outside political contenders.

The term *gun populism* reveals how populism can be mobilized to legitimize particular kinds of state-society arrangements. A brand of gun talk voiced by police chiefs across Arizona, California, and Michigan, gun populism blurs the lines around police prerogatives versus private use of force, often in an effort to protect "the people" from threats from below (e.g., political, economic, and cultural threats posed by marginalized or subordinate groups) and above (e.g., political elites in the federal government as well as economic and cultural elites). Unlike gun militarism, which deepens the divide between police and private civil-

ians, gun populism emphasizes police as working *with* those they police on the terrain of legitimate violence.

Historical accounts and popular portrayals of policing have been inflected with populist sensibilities at various points in U.S. history.[11]
Gun populism was anticipated in the seventeenth century, when
whites—by virtue of their skin color—were effectively deputized to
stop, question, and apprehend people of African descent;[12] in the eighteenth century, when slave patrols comprised deputized citizens who
at times worked alongside newly institutionalized law enforcement
agencies;[13] in the organized white supremacist organizations that
lynched and terrorized people of color—including African Americans,
Chinese Americans, and Mexican Americans—from the nineteenth
century into the twentieth century, at times with the implicit permission if not the active collusion of local law enforcement;[14] and under
the color-blind mantra of "crime control" in the form of neighborhood
watch groups in the late twentieth century and beyond.[15]

Today, I find that gun populism is reflected in the willingness of
public law enforcement to align themselves with legally gun-owning
Americans, who are often, though not exclusively, marked as white
middle-class men. As with gun militarism, gun populism is a form of
gun talk that allows police chiefs to endorse, and justify, a distinctive
arrangement of legitimate violence, one shaped by the specific contexts
in which police encounter gun policy. But under gun populism, the line
between defensive violence and police force blurs, and this blurred
line makes it all the easier for police not just to imagine *themselves* as
armed citizens (see chapter 3) but also to imagine armed citizens *as
policing agents*.

Like gun militarism, gun populism was evident in each of the states
I studied, but unlike gun militarism, populist gun talk varied across
the states. Rather than monolithic, it was reflective of the distinctive
state gun laws and localized gun cultures at work in Arizona, California, and Michigan. In California, the state with the strictest gun laws,
police chiefs endorsed a more limited understanding of self-defense, but
they were particularly vocal about legislative attempts to regulate guns,
and saw themselves—in alliance with putatively law-abiding gun

owners—as unduly regulated by what they saw as legislators' ignorant and ill-fated attempts to address gun violence. In Michigan, the state with a permissive but bureaucratic set of gun laws, police chiefs endorsed gun rights as a means of addressing the limitations of police in the fight against crime—a form of gun populism that I call "crime fighting by proxy." In Arizona, the state with the most lenient gun laws, chiefs took this one step further, endorsing a brand of "co-policing" in which armed citizens were seen as useful to policing, not just in the sense of providing protection in the *absence* of police but also *in support* of police. Across Arizona, California, and Michigan, police chiefs aligned themselves with armed civilians in somewhat different keys of gun populism. Overall, they reveal a terrain of legitimate violence distinct from gun militarism—one in which armed civilians are imagined not as a threat but as a possible benefit to law enforcement.

GUN POPULISM IN CALIFORNIA: ANTI-ELITISM

In a 2013 white paper, the California Police Chiefs Association (Cal-Chiefs) noted, "California has some of the strictest firearms regulations in the nation. These regulations have served law-abiding Californians well and clearly have not interfered with firearms ownership by responsible Californians." A handful of California police chiefs I interviewed echoed this take on gun regulation by vigorously endorsing the gamut of California's gun laws aimed at limiting, if not eradicating, civilian access to guns. Despite some variation, however, most chiefs throughout California voiced confusion, conflict, and cynicism with regard to gun regulation. Discussing the politics behind the 2013 Cal-Chiefs white paper on gun policy, a chief who had sat on CalChiefs' executive board remarked,

> There was such a fight. . . . [We considered] restricting magazine capacity, urging the Feds to do more on background checks, dealing with ghost guns, strengthening the background checks, expanding the time for waiting to purchase a gun. . . . And there was a major, major divide among California police chiefs. . . . We strive to have

best practices—and that's what we wanted to do with firearms. But nothing I ever experienced was as divisive as the issue of firearms among police chiefs. . . . Some chiefs left the organization. They quit because they said CalChiefs was too restrictive.

Despite CalChiefs' general embrace of gun regulation, according to this chief, firearms constituted one of the most "contentious" issues facing the organization.

My interviews with California chiefs revealed that California's uniquely restrictive gun policies had not deepened police consensus in favor of gun control. Instead, the politics of guns in California seemed to have generated skepticism among chiefs, who appear to increasingly sympathize with armed civilians as they become more alienated from legislators. Among many California chiefs was a distinct strain of gun populism: anti-elitism.

Whereas gun policy provided California police chiefs in the 1980s and 1990s with an opportunity to assert police prerogatives vis-à-vis unlawfully armed criminals and to embrace gun militarism (see chapters 1 and 2), gun policy today *also* provides an opportunity for police chiefs to assert their prerogatives vis-à-vis what they see as misguided policymakers, or what the law and society scholar Anjuli Verma labels as "counterfeit experts."[16] Police chiefs—even chiefs sympathetic to the overall project of gun regulation—expressed nearly unanimous apprehension regarding California policymakers. One chief referenced an ill-fated urge among politicians to "do something" in the aftermath of gun tragedies: "After [the mass shooting in] San Bernardino, you just see all these politicians grasping at straws so they can show that they did something." Others showed outright disdain for politicians: "And you know—a lot of legislators just answer to the people who elect them. A lot of them couldn't even pass a civil exam. Most Americans couldn't."

California chiefs reasoned that because "politicians . . . don't know how [law enforcement] works intricately," they "put law enforcement in a bind." Chiefs cited the sheer number of gun laws as leading to contradictory, complex laws that they found unenforceable, even in well-funded agencies.[17] Rather than emboldening police chiefs and committing them to the project of gun regulation, California gun policy had the *opposite* effect by encouraging cynicism. As one California chief commented,

> What I think needs to be done is wipe the books clean. So much of it is piecemeal, and most officers don't even know the law at the entry level—they rely on cheat sheets or senior officers. And we are doing the best we can—and you know, we'll arrest people and then do the research—and then release or charge on the arrest. . . . It's like you need to be a specialist to regurgitate the law. . . . We have 60,000 or so statutes—we are inundated. Then there's about 500 to 700 new laws per year. So really, what are we doing? And why?

This chief resonated with others who described California gun laws as "an enforcement nightmare [that] practically [requires] a law degree to understand the 115-plus pages on ARs [assault weapons]" and that "mak[es] our lives miserable." Fed up with the complexities of California gun laws (and California laws in general), this chief makes the sweeping statement that the state's regulatory apparatus needs to be erased and rewritten from the ground up. Until that happens, however, he maintains that police "do the best we can."

Other chiefs likewise threw up their hands at what they saw as the intricate absurdities of California's gun laws, at times even sympathizing with officers who underenforced California gun laws. As one chief reasoned,

> You'll have the farmer who doesn't realize he has high-capacity magazines and the law changed, and he can't have them. Well, he really doesn't know. And so you have officers who see that, and they might not bother enforcing it. Because we're in triage mode. We have to think about what's worth it.

Such grievances are best appreciated within California's broader policy environment. Whereas criminal justice actors, especially California's prison guard union, played a key role in pushing forward a "tough on crime" agenda in the early 1990s,[18] police chiefs found themselves at odds with new policies introduced in the mid-2010s meant to rein in carceral spending in California and compel the state to comply with Eighth Amendment standards prohibiting "cruel and unusual punishment," as discussed in chapter 2.[19] Two initiatives in particular—realignment of prison inmates into county jails (AB109)[20] and reduced sentencing for certain crimes (Proposition 47)[21]—have created much debate about and public criticism of California's carceral apparatus. Although these initiatives have failed to fundamentally change the state's appetite for punishment, they created a terrain of politics in which chiefs became particularly invested in and incensed about the local and state ramifications of what they saw as a rollback of a largely successful war on crime. One chief explained that California's push toward decriminalization and decarceration appeared "incongruent" with California's elaborate gun laws:

> I have been very vocal on this, and I will tell you exactly what I told Governor Brown. . . . I find it very incongruent that in a state where you are pushing for more gun control laws that we would also be deemphasizing criminal gun behavior.

This chief, who had unique access to Governor Brown by virtue of his leadership position within the law enforcement community, directly mobilized California gun politics to communicate his opposition to California's rollback of the state's war on crime. Another chief succinctly described the politics of California crime control as "asinine":

> They [legislators] don't know what they are doing if they think any of that [e.g., banning assault weapons] has an effect on crime. . . . [I]f you really want to do something, start locking people up. . . . Because, either it's going to make people think twice, and if it doesn't, who gives a shit? Because at least they are off the street for those ten years! Now, I'm on my soapbox, but in California, we have more than enough freaking laws! But it's all these liberals who just want to keep people out of jail. It is asinine!

Though they vehemently supported "tough on crime" gun laws such as mandatory minimums and sentencing enhancement (see chapter 2), chiefs saw many of California's gun control laws as misguided, and even hypocritical, policies in a state that has increasingly gone "soft" on crime.[22] Within a policy environment that had largely veered toward rethinking mass incarceration, gun policy thus allowed California police chiefs to participate in a status competition[23] among criminal justice stakeholders by asserting their moral high ground with respect to the policymakers. The willingness of California police chiefs to speak to me about their "politically incorrect" (to quote one chief) thoughts on guns was likely a reflection of this frustration: I provided a forum for chiefs to anonymously air sentiments that they could otherwise utter only behind closed doors.

But California's legal apparatus not only troubled police chiefs as *enforcers* of gun laws; it also implicated police themselves as *objects* of gun law enforcement. Although the regulation of guns usually sparks a conversation about private civilian access, California's gun laws also shape police's relationship with their own guns. In California, firearms restrictions such as waiting periods, weapons bans, and ammunition regulations typically, but not always, have included explicit police exemptions for on-duty, off-duty, and/or retired police. But several chiefs worried that gun bills proposed by California lawmakers too often fail to clarify exemptions for police. One chief recounts an early debate over Los Angeles city's local magazine ban:

> The way it was originally written made no sense. It would have been illegal for officers from other places to go into LA city. It would have made it so that reserve officers couldn't go in. They exempted LA police, but there were all these other issues. And retired cops who have to qualify every year, they would have also been affected.

Likewise, in 2016, the California Police Chiefs Association publicly opposed Proposition 63, which lays out a background check system for ammunition purchases. Arguing that "Proposition 63 complicates current law with one that is costlier and seriously flawed,"[24] the CalChiefs president at the time, Ken Corney, cited specific concerns regarding how the proposition would complicate ammunition purchases by police departments.

This stake in California gun laws also extends to very personal concerns about gun access. One chief noted that his lack of "passion" about guns reflects the less limiting gun restrictions he experiences as a police officer:

If I couldn't carry [a gun by virtue of being a police officer], I would be a lot more passionate about this [gun rights]. I'd feel like I'm being prevented from protecting my family, and people know that cops don't show up. . . . [I]n the streets, there are not as many rules, and people may need that [i.e., to carry a gun]. Street cops may see it that way, too, and I don't necessarily disagree.

Echoing pro-gun discourse that circulates among gun carriers,[25] this chief cites police inadequacy to explain a need to carry a firearm.[26] His statement is suggestive of how gun policy itself shapes police attachment to firearms: accustomed to carrying a firearm, this chief asserts that he would be politically galvanized if he could no longer carry.

Other chiefs suggested that police *are* affected by California's gun laws, especially when they retire and must relinquish some of the gun access they enjoyed—and became accustomed to—as active police. Consider California's assault weapons ban. The Roberti-Roos Assault Weapons Control Act of 1989, revamped in 1999, bans assault weapons in California. As originally written in 1999, both active and retired "peace officers" were exempt from possession restrictions; in 2002, a U.S. Appeals Court upheld the assault weapons ban but struck down the clause regarding retired police. Today, active "peace officers" in nineteen different California agencies are eligible to purchase and possess otherwise banned weapons, but they must give up these guns once they retire. One chief explained,

It makes no sense—police have their own personal AR's and carry them when they are on duty, but as soon as they stop being cops they have to turn them back in. But they are their personal guns. It doesn't make any sense.

Another chief likewise revealed his personal grievances with California gun laws. When I asked him what he'd like to change with California gun laws, he responded with a very personal request that reflected how his status as active-duty law enforcement made him acutely attuned to California gun laws,

> I'm worried that when I leave law enforcement, because I live in California . . . I won't be able to buy what I want to buy. Because right now I can buy anything.

My interviews with Arizona chiefs suggested that some retired California police even go so far as to leave the state after they retire to relocate to more gun-lenient pastures. One Arizona chief in a rural spot observed,

> This area is full of cops from California. They all come here because they don't want to have to deal with California gun laws—and California in general—so they move here, or Montana. We have so many retired cops in this area!

California police chiefs, on the whole, articulated a specific brand of gun populism: anti-elitism. They defined themselves in contrast to lawmakers and legislators who overwhelmed police with intricate gun laws that are ineffective in stopping criminals but, as they saw it, negatively affected law-abiding gun owners, including police themselves. Allowing police exemptions for guns while active duty did not deepen police consensus in favor of gun control; instead, it compelled some police to empathize with armed, law-abiding civilians. California police chiefs thus suggest that police are not simply street-level bureaucrats "making" public policy on the ground.[27] Rather, gun laws transform police into political actors as they negotiate—whether symbolically or materially—the distribution of legitimate violence within and beyond the state. In contrast to their endorsement of mandatory minimums and their embrace of gun militarism, California police chiefs express gun populism *both* to voice discontent regarding particular gun policies and the legislators who penned them *and also* to acknowledge a constituency of lawful Americans productive of public safety, whether police or civilians.

Amid California's restrictive gun laws, police chiefs blurred the lines between themselves and civilians as *gun owners*. But in Michigan and Arizona, where gun laws are less restrictive in terms of both gun possession and gun use, police chiefs blurred the line between themselves and civilians as *gun users*—and imagined a much more proactive, and even collaborative, role for armed private civilians in the pursuit of social order.

CRIME FIGHTING BY PROXY: GUN POPULISM IN MICHIGAN

In June 2014, the Detroit police chief James Craig appeared on the cover of the National Rifle Association's magazine *America's First Freedom* with the cover line: "We're not advocating violence. We're advocates of not being victims." An African American chief who had worked in jurisdictions as different as Los Angeles, California; Portland, Maine; and Cincinnati, Ohio, before returning to Detroit, Craig saw the desirability of concealed carry among Detroiters as a simple calculus: crime victims do not have time to wait for police in a violence-prone city lacking in police resources. As an African American "big city" police chief, Craig's perspective may seem unusual, but he was far from an outlier across the state. Michigan chiefs echoed Chief Craig; one white rural police chief, who had started his career in Detroit, openly "applauded" him, saying, "Chief James Craig really embraces concealed carry, and I think that's courageous. I applaud him because he says a lot of things that other chiefs wouldn't say."

In line with Chief Craig's public statements, most chiefs in Michigan saw licensed concealed gun carry among private civilians as a form of crime fighting by proxy: insistent that even the most well-resourced police cannot protect all victims at all times, Michigan chiefs said they were comfortable with self-defense by private civilians as part of their overall crime-fighting mission.

Among most Michigan chiefs and across majority–African American and majority-white jurisdictions, licensed gun carriers were imagined as enhancing personal protection—even serving as a stopgap to police limitations. For example, these chiefs of majority-white areas empha-sized the "ridiculous" presumption that police are adequate protection from criminal endangerment:

> I believe that citizens need to be able to protect themselves. We can-not protect them—we just can't. It's impossible. Here we have the fastest response times, and that's partly a result of the population layout. But our police officers: they are true police. They put them-selves in danger. They relish it! True police officers. They get there in two minutes. How much damage can you do in two minutes? The government cannot save people from danger. That is just ridiculous. So people should be allowed to defend themselves.

> I say fight back with everything you have. You have innocent vic-tims who comply, and they still get shot! There was this guy who got carjacked right on 8 Mile [in Detroit]. And he did everything they wanted him to. He got out of the car; he gave them everything. All the witnesses who saw it said he complied. Yes, he did it all, but they still shot him in the chest.

Both of these chiefs emphasize the concealed pistol license as an individual-level stopgap for crime fighting in the absence of police, evoking an almost frontierlike mentality to insist that individuals are on their own when faced with a threat.

Likewise, a chief of a majority–African American jurisdiction main-tained that "crime prevention is the sole responsibility of the people. Police facilitate it. . . . But it is the people who have allowed this to per-meate their neighborhood." He explained:

> That fits in with the idea that it's unrealistic to think of a police of-ficer on every corner. There was a[n African American] woman, a nurse who had a CPL [concealed pistol license]. And she was walking out of the street, and she shoots and defends herself. She—I don't want to say eliminated—she stopped the threat. And she has an absolute right to do that.

This chief seamlessly flows from police jurisdiction to self-defense, suggesting that concealed carry "fits in" at the intersection where police prerogatives meet community responsibility.

Although today's chiefs by and large told me that they were comfortable with licensed concealed carry, Michigan's police had not always endorsed licensed concealed carry in the state, especially before the passage of the new "shall-issue" law that required that *all* qualified applicants be granted a license (before 2001, licenses were given on a discretionary basis only to those who could demonstrate to a gun board that they had "good cause" to carry a gun). On the eve of the implementation of the state's broadened concealed carry law, some law enforcement officials joined gun control groups in opposing the law, and the incoming Wayne County prosecutor Michael Duggan and Governor Jennifer Granholm garnered the support of some law enforcement in an unsuccessful drive to block the law's implementation.[28] A decade and a half later, police chiefs recalled the period as fraught with uncertainty and dismay. One chief noted, "There were the fearmongers at the beginning. . . . I was mildly concerned at the time, but nothing came to fruition." Another offered, "When the law changed, my personal belief was that we were going to have tons of problems. I was shocked that we didn't. I really thought it was a bad idea." One more chief noted, "It meant more training with officers so that they could understand what to expect with the new law." But then he went on: "The people who are carrying illegally, well, they are going to do it regardless, so that didn't change."

As these excerpts intimate, chiefs in Michigan learned to incorporate and accommodate the new laws governing concealed carry into their practical understandings of policing and public safety. From talking to Michigan chiefs, I learned that the concealed carry licensing process did not just vet would-be gun carriers; it also allowed police chiefs to deploy the gun license as a color-blind indicator of good character and moral standing. Accordingly, Michigan chiefs alluded to a distinct moral calculus regarding gun carry and gun carriers, something that might be termed "system exposure."[29] Emphasizing the training requirements and background check process, police chiefs viewed a civilian's willingness to undergo "the process" to obtain a concealed pistol license as a key marker in itself of moral fitness to carry a gun. In this way, the concealed carry licensing process shapes how police chiefs draw lines between lawful civilians and criminal suspects, and how police come to be more comfortable with a well-armed populace. One chief summarizes this transformation by drawing a parallel between police badges and gun carry licenses: "In 2001 [when the state's new concealed carry law was first implemented], it was a little unnerving. But you grow into it. I mean, you go into a room with armed people, and it's unnerving, but then you see their badges or licenses, you know that because of that, they have training—or at least that's what you presume."

System exposure eased police chiefs' discomfort with a system they knew to be fallible. Consider one police chief who explained, "No bureaucracy is perfect. Human error is possible, and we're always vulnerable to that. But it's not likely. And a criminal isn't looking for permission for illegal activities." Realistic that "no bureaucracy is perfect," he settles his uneasiness by averring that a civilian's willingness to "look for permission" distinguishes them from the criminal gun carrier. Other chiefs made similar statements. One chief remarked, "If people are even willing to approach the system, they are probably citizens who are responsible." Another maintained, "I don't care if people carry if they go through the process. They are probably responsible, and if they aren't, it's drinking at the bar, not shooting up a daycare." This suggestion that concealed carriers are "probably responsible" is revealing: even if they fail to live up to responsible gun ownership, they are still fundamentally different from the imagined criminal who is "shooting up a daycare."

Chiefs' ability to see gun carriers as proxy crime fighters therefore depended on their comfort with the credentialing process these gun carriers underwent to receive a concealed pistol license. One chief reasoned:

[Interviewer: What do you think about civilians carrying guns?]

That's a hard one. Because it depends on the citizen, and we have to get it right in terms of how we screen citizens. I don't know if we have the answers. But when we get it right, we have a well-trained citizen who is armed and familiar with the operation of a firearm, they understand firearms safety, and they can save lives and help people in a situation that needs that. On the other hand, if training is not adequate, if people just do the bare minimum—and then plus you have mental issues—well, they can hurt people.

With the disclaimer that civilians need to be vetted, chiefs understood concealed carry as a mechanism of crime fighting.

Opting out of the controversial and often highly technical debates about whether "more guns" mean "more crime" or "less crime,"[30] most chiefs saw concealed carry as having little impact on crime one way or another; as one Michigan chief bluntly noted, "Ultimately, the people with [legal] guns aren't the fucking problem!" At the same time, they did see concealed carry as an invaluable proxy for police at the *individual* level. And some chiefs did insist that concealed carry *reduced* crime. These two chiefs clarified that they felt safer with more guns in the hands of civilians:

> I'm in support of it, provided there is the proper training and background, yes. I have no problem with it at all. [Interviewer: Do you feel more safe, less safe, or about the same knowing that people in Michigan are carrying guns?] More safe.

> Really, when was the last time you heard of a mass shooting in Michigan? There are so many guns everywhere. . . . I firmly believe that the reason why we don't have mass shootings is because people don't know who is carrying.

Among the majority of Michigan chiefs I interviewed, the licensing process served as a positive credentialing procedure to divide would-be gun carriers into "good guys with guns" versus criminals by virtue of their willingness to undergo "the process." In this way, Michigan police chiefs articulated a populist vision of order maintenance, one in which ordinary armed citizens ("the people") are crucial ingredients of social order.

But if, as the political scientist Jan-Werner Müller notes,[31] "the people" of populist thought represent a narrow, antipluralist subset of the political community, then it is the concealed pistol licensing process that does the color-blind work of narrowing down this community of "good guys with guns." Just like the negative "mark" of a criminal record,[32] this sorting reflects a color-blind sensibility sheathed in a language of law abidance versus criminality. The vetting process itself reproduces racial disparities in access to legitimate violence by virtue of its reliance on criminal justice records: while concealed pistol licenses are granted to all qualifying applicants, men of color are disproportionately likely to be disqualified because they are disproportionately likely to have felony records[33] and other kinds of contact with the criminal justice system that bar them from obtaining a concealed pistol license.[34] As chapter 5 will describe in more detail, the loosening of concealed pistol licensing laws in states such as Michigan has obscured the historical color line distinguishing legal and illegal gun access by reframing gun access around lawfulness and legality—but the color line in gun access nevertheless persists. The concealed pistol license also functions as a color-blind device by reproducing the politics of respectability for those gun carriers of color who qualify. The emphasis on training and responsibility—against the backdrop of criminal record vetting—allowed police chiefs to cast the armed civilian[35] in terms of a color-blind embrace of "respectable" racial minorities.[36] Accordingly, police chiefs celebrated gun carriers of color who used guns in self-defense—such as the armed nurse described by the Michigan chief above—as examples of the color-blind appeal of gun carry, even as the police killings of lawfully armed African Americans such as Philando Castile and Emantic Bradford Jr. (as well as the analysis I will present in chapter 5) suggest that the privileges attached to such licenses are *not* color-blind in practice.

In Michigan, concealed licensing laws have set up a vetting process that buttresses a color-blind line between "good guys with guns" and "bad guys with guns," allowing hundreds of thousands of civilians in the state to legally carry guns.[37] Often expressing comfort with the idea of licensed concealed carry, Michigan's police chiefs have largely accommodated the state's gun laws by embracing a populist stance on gun carry best characterized as "crime fighting by proxy." But police chiefs could also adapt to gun-rich contexts in which no such vetting process exists, such as Arizona, and as they adapted, they embraced a more entrenched version of gun populism.

CO-POLICING: GUN POPULISM IN ARIZONA

In 2010, Arizona removed the permitting requirement to carry a firearm concealed; an individual who can lawfully own a pistol can also carry it openly or, provided they are over twenty-one years old, concealed without a special license.[38] Despite the state's reputation as a Second Amendment haven, however, Arizona police chiefs do not unilaterally embrace the state's unprecedentedly deregulated gun policy environment. Concerns—about gun training, gun safety, poorly coordinated police databases, and other gun law enforcement tools that Arizona police lack—often surfaced among Arizona chiefs. As one chief noted with chagrin, "Just about anyone can carry a firearm—why? Why does that make sense? . . . That's not the 'true' Arizona. The true Arizona cares about firearms safety."

These concerns, however, generally did not rise to the antagonistic tenor exhibited by California chiefs with respect to that state's restrictive gun laws; Arizona chiefs were guarded in expressing misgivings about Arizona gun laws, at times scratching their heads as to why Arizona's gun laws did not cause more problems—and even offered solutions—for public law enforcement. Against the backdrop of a generally pro-police legislature and pro-gun populace, police chiefs (whether willingly or begrudgingly) say they have adapted to Arizona's gun laws, asserting a distinct brand of gun populism—co-policing—as they see armed private civilians as potentially productive of public safety.[39]

Chiefs with long careers in Arizona provided a glimpse into the different worlds of gun regulation in Arizona over the past several decades. As one chief commented,

> In the 1970s, it was very strict. You could not have a gun concealed. . . . If it's in your glove compartment, that's concealed, and that wasn't allowed. Now . . . you can have it anywhere. . . . I can say

that at the time [when permitted concealed carry was legalized], law enforcement was not happy. They did not support going to concealed carry permits. Because they saw it as putting us in danger. It was really a safety issue for us.

This chief initially appeared to vindicate what many advocates for enhanced gun restrictions warned about loosening gun laws: more guns mean less officer safety.[40] I probed further: "How would you say that [this change] affected police then?"

It really raised our awareness, so now we always say, "Watch the hands!" If someone has their hands in their pockets, we say take your hands out of your pockets, because now we assume everyone is armed. The mindset definitely changed. We adapted. We accepted that that's the law—and that's the case with all laws. That happens all the time. And so as far as affecting officer safety, I don't think so, I don't think assaults on officers went up because of that exact law. Now, we are seeing a rise in assaults on officers, but I think that is just because we [American society] are more violent.

According to this chief, although police "were not happy," they responded not with legal cynicism surrounding the law but by "adapting." Experiencing the impact of gun laws on officer safety as overblown, this chief resisted attributing violence against police to laxer gun laws ("Now, we are seeing a rise in assaults on officers, but I think that is just because we are more violent").

Other chiefs also expressed ambivalence: on the one hand, they maintained apprehension about the removal of regulatory mechanisms in Arizona, but on the other hand, they experienced little fallout in terms of safety as a result. Consider these two chiefs:

I don't think it's a good thing. Now, it has not come to fruition. I have not experienced any fallout from getting rid of the training. But still, I don't think it's a good thing to get rid of the training. Because you should be formally trained in the law and the handling of a gun.

Anecdotally, I think the lack of incidents involving the mishandling of guns means that it isn't that much of an issue. Now, are there people who have guns within a mile of here that I'd be concerned given their level of training? Sure, but they haven't posed an issue.

Arizona police chiefs found a variety of ways to downplay the risks of policing a heavily armed population. For example, they focused on the tactical aspects of interfacing with a widely and well-armed general public. One chief maintained that he was a better cop when he assumed everyone was armed; comparing his experiences in Arizona with his brief time in California, he found he appreciated the Arizona approach:

> You know, when I was a deputy [in Arizona], every tactic we had was based around the idea that every car had a gun—and that 90 percent of those guns were legal. So in my view, our approach was smarter and safer. I'm just talking about the mechanics of the stop. . . . In California, everyone assumed that [occupants of] cars weren't armed, but that's not the case at all. The truth was, you have just as many guns in California, except 90 percent of them are illegal! Now, of course, that's partly because of California law. You make one small little error in transporting the gun, and you are illegal. . . . So what ends up happening [in California] is that first, you approach the car less tactically. Then you scan, look, you don't see anything that maybe raises the flag that there's a gun—and then your tactics get even worse!

In this chief's view, a greater number of legal guns did not endanger but instead enhanced police safety insofar as guns become an ever-present weight on an officer's mind, compelling officers to approach vehicles more tactically.

As with California and Michigan, such attitudes must be contextualized within Arizona's broader policy environment; amid few grievances about the general direction of Arizona criminal justice policy, police chiefs offered that they generally encountered a police-friendly environment. One chief notes, "We are a very pro-cop state, so I would say [legislators] are open [to listening to police]." Another agrees that "Arizona is a very law enforcement friendly state, it's conservative."

Arizona chiefs thus adopted a pragmatic stance that allowed them to emphasize how police might benefit from a widely armed citizenry. Navigating the practical consequences of an armed citizenry, different chiefs provided different renderings of how armed civilians could serve as what one chief described as an "asset to public safety." Amid the assumption that Arizonans had a "reputation for being sharpshooters," as one chief told me, police chiefs entertained the idea that Arizona gun laws had, indeed, deterred violence:

> Here, everyone has a gun. And I don't know if there is a correlation, but it certainly seems like there could be a connection because we don't have the level of gun violence here. You know, think about it: if you go to rob a store, there's a good chance the store owner is armed. And there is a good chance everyone else in there is armed, too!

Illustrating the costs of gun control, chiefs referenced gun violence in big cities—especially Chicago—as a counterpoint to Arizona. As one chief wagered, "Look at places with strict gun laws—like Chicago!" Another chief reasoned, "Well the places with the strictest gun control—Chicago, New York City—they also have the highest murder rate. Now, places where it's more lax? Phoenix is the sixth or seventh largest city—and our homicide rate is really low." But New York City's murder rate has dropped dramatically since the early 1990s—and is one of the lowest among major U.S. cities.[41] Likewise, the designation of "strictest gun control" is loose; Chicago does *not* have the strictest gun control (California's gun laws are stricter, for example).[42] Of course, historically, these cities have—and, in Chicago's case, continue to have—elevated murder rates, and they most certainly have stricter gun controls than in Arizona. Further, these cities are associated not just with gun violence in general but with a particular *kind* of gun violence: urban gun violence associated with boys and men of color (see chapter 2).

Arizona gun violence rates rank it in the top third of states.[43] But when police chiefs embraced gun carry among private civilians as a prosocial activity, they often emphasized specific, relatable instances of civilian gun use rather than rely on broader trends in crime. This is reminiscent of the legal scholars Dan Kahan and Donald Braman's cultural theory of risk,[44] which argues that the risks ascribed to guns are filtered through people's cultural orientations; rather than crime rates, chiefs' understandings of guns as productive of public safety were situated within their hands-on, intimate understanding of police work. For example, chiefs regularly referenced examples of civilians assisting officers, including the widely covered Department of Public Safety (DPS) incident in 2017 that opened this chapter. In that incident, the armed civilian Thomas Yoxall used his firearm to kill an assailant, assisting the Arizona DPS officer Ed Andersson, who had been shot. One chief described this and another incident to illustrate that "these sorts of things happen a lot":

> There's this great video of a crazy big guy who is beating a police officer. And you have this African American guy who comes up, and he's armed, and to alert the officer, he just yells at the guy—stop, get off, or I'm going to shoot. Well, the guy stopped, and this guy laid down his gun. It was done perfectly. And then you have the DPS incident [involving Officer Andersson and the armed private civilian Yoxall]. So I think those sorts of things happen a lot. I would say I would feel more comfortable if more good people were armed. . . . Because if you think about the shootings that have happened in malls, in schools, if someone with training and experience with the weapon would have been there, they could have stopped that bloodshed. And that's okay in my book!

Although this chief does not racialize the "crazy big guy" or the "police officer," his deliberate racial marking of "this African American guy" as a "good guy with a gun" suggests *both* the noteworthiness of an armed African American man playing the role of the "good guy" (thus reinforcing the implicit whiteness of the "good guy with a gun" trope) *and* the greater porousness of this category with respect to race for "respectable" people of color rendered so by the defensive uses of their guns.[45]

In a similar vein, another chief squarely placed gun carriers as part and parcel of a generalized duty to police. As a school resource officer, this chief had encountered the active shooter who would massacre a public constituent meeting held by then–U.S. Representative Gabrielle Giffords in 2011 in Tucson, Arizona, killing six people and leaving more than a dozen wounded. I queried the chief about his thoughts on the response, at this active shooting, of concealed carriers such as Joe Zamudio, who ran out of a nearby business to help disarm the shooter as the shooter was reloading his firearm.[46] The chief responded with sardonic humor: "I was mad they didn't shoot him!" His response reiterated the blurred lines, discussed in chapter 3, between police and private armed civilians as first responders to active shootings. He continued:

> But they saw him reloading, and they knew: *that's my opening.* That's education, and that's a bystander doing a good job by deciding he is not going to fire. It all comes down to education, and if they can provide back up with education. I'm all for people taking on a life of responsibility. I'm just two eyes! But if I have eight eyes? It's much easier to see everything. And if civilians call 911, and then they can handle an attack?

I interrupted him to ask what, then, he thought about Stand Your Ground laws.

> We love it. Carjackings in Tucson: we were having one a day. And suddenly, you try to carjack and you get shot in the face? Well, my goodness! They started to come down.

Likewise elaborating on armed private civilians as first responders alongside police, another Arizona chief expressed a similar, if more generic, sentiment, expanding the paradigm of community policing to include armed civilians:

> Yes, I'm okay with people having weapons. And I would say, the more good people with guns, the more chance you have to stop the bad guys. . . . [My feelings have] changed since I started. I think there was something about police carrying a gun, that it brought certain benefits, like—oh, I was one of the few! And everyone else had to apply for a permit. . . . [But lately] I've really thought a lot about community policing. And that we can't do it all ourselves. And maybe that's stretching it to include guns, but that's where I'm going to stretch it.

This chief is particularly striking insofar as he links his shifting relationship to his own gun with his shifting sensibilities regarding armed civilians amid the perceived limitations of police. No longer seeing himself as "one of the few," he now sees armed civilians as a necessary stopgap, given that police "can't do it all [themselves]."

Even Arizona chiefs apprehensive about armed civilians still found themselves endorsing civilian intervention in some instances, given the realities of policing remote, resource-poor jurisdictions, on the one hand, and the unpredictability of police work more generally, on the other hand. One chief admitted, "My concern is if someone is a concealed carrier, I don't know him—is it a bad guy? A good guy? And in that case, the situation really dictates." Nevertheless, he noted,

> I would say—if an officer needs help? And they know that it will be an hour for anyone to get there and that's with their lights and sirens going off? And then there's a responsible citizen that would help? Well, I would say that that would be welcomed. Because we just don't have the manpower.

Thus, with "everyone" armed—indeed, even "grandma may be carrying a gun!" according to one chief—police chiefs learned to see guns as productive of social order, downplaying gun violence in the state in favor of embracing local gun laws. As such, police chiefs acclimated to Arizona's gun laws, framing their concerns in terms of a populist sensibility of co-policing that integrated armed civilians into the pursuit of public safety.

FROM POPULISM TO IMPUNITY

If gun militarism intensified zero-tolerance, hard-line criminalization, gun populism appeared to foster the opposite: discretion, caution, even impunity. In addition to blurring the lines between police and civilians as armed protectors, gun populism echoed libertarian and conservative concerns about government overreach and overcriminalization.[47] Such concerns were loudest in California with respect to gun possession; they could also be heard in Michigan and, to a lesser extent, in Arizona.

As mentioned earlier, California chiefs articulated uneasiness about state laws that criminalized the "wrong" people but let those whom they saw as hardened criminals off easy. One chief I interviewed had worked extensively with California's Armed Prohibited Persons System (recall from chapter 2 that the system is a database of individuals who at one time owned firearms but then became prohibited possessors). The chief explained his take on California's gun laws: "It's more restrictions, it's more difficult for the manufacturer, and that's our business plan for gun control." Sensing ambivalence, I asked whether he supported this "business plan." "Good question," he said, and paused for several long moments before responding in full:

> I don't know. I don't personally have a problem in terms of banning those guns. And it works. Because manufacturers are opting out [of the California market].

> [Interviewer: So why the long pause?]

> Well, it goes back to: How far are we going to take it? Now, if you have a magazine that has more than ten rounds, you are a criminal. And you could have someone who moves from out of state . . . but as it says on the Department of Justice's website: ignorance of the law is not a defense! I've just dealt with so many people who just didn't know. They didn't even know to register. . . . [S]o that's [what] gives me pause.

This chief's hesitancy contrasts with his—and other chiefs'—broad endorsement of "tough on crime" gun laws. Pivoting the target of gun laws from urban gun criminals to people who "just didn't know," this chief becomes stuck on recognizing the criminalizing reach of California's gun laws.

Other chiefs were more explicit in their opposition to California's gun laws, rooting their criticism in how these laws, as they saw it, unfairly and even unconstitutionally criminalize gun owners. One chief bemoaned that these laws "punished the whole class" for the misdeeds of a Johnny-come-lately (e.g., "If Johnny is late, punish the whole class? But we do exactly that with these [gun] laws"); another California chief lamented that "harsh gun bans" are forced on "the masses" while criminals enjoy leniency. And still another chief said that these laws threaten to "creat[e] the propensity to act outside of the law for people who would have otherwise been law-abiding but who are now criminals." These sentiments suggest cracks in the so-called Blue Wall that shrouds police work and keeps police subculture insular. Instead of advocating that police maintain exclusive access to firearms (as gun militarism might suggest), chiefs see gun restrictions from the perspective of gun populism as unduly harming the people they police.

But not all people fall under the purview of the police's concerns.

As I listened closely to police chiefs as they described their worries about overzealous gun laws, I saw a pattern: the "normal people" (in the words of one chief) who many chiefs saw as unduly bearing the regulatory brunt of California gun laws were designated with tropes associated with white, middle-class status. Chiefs used archetypes—the "rancher with a gun," the "teacher with a gun," the "farmer"[48]—to describe such gun owners. The "teacher" evokes public service; the "farmer" and the "rancher" evoke Thomas Jefferson's yeoman republicanism, which lionized early white settlers as "real" Americans by virtue of their ethic of self-sufficiency and self-reliance.[49] Typecast by an implicit work ethic, they each represent mainstream, "salt-of-the-earth" sorts. These tropes contrast starkly with those tropes—the gangbanger, the drug dealer, the superpredator—associated with urban gun criminals, as discussed in chapter 2. And these "salt-of-the-earth" tropes elicit a different response from chiefs with respect to gun law. Whereas the urban gun criminal warranted aggressive laws amid an enforcement apparatus that was too often too lenient toward criminals, the "normal people" who found themselves on the wrong side of unnecessarily onerous regulations deserved, if not the benefit of the doubt, at least the benefit of mutual commiseration.

To illustrate, consider three chiefs who voiced concerns about mandatory minimums:

> I think everything should be done on a case-by-case basis—or at least, that you should have the ability to consider special circumstances. Because you box people in with generic laws. Let's say you have a nineteen-year-old kid that jumps into his dad's truck. He's going to work, he's late, gets pulled over, and then he's found with his dad's gun in the car because his dad didn't take it out, and now he is facing five years, and so he's going to plead that down. [Michigan]

> I think people need to be evaluated as individuals, in their individual circumstances, and yes, that can be time-consuming, and that's why people fall back on the mandatory minimums. But Arizona— [consider] our DUI laws. In those cases, you have to serve the minimum. So you have a career criminal who is basically a turd, and they get the same sentence as someone who never committed any crime, and who is drunk because their father just died, they just went to the wake, they decided to get hammered, and now they are driving home. We treat everyone the same, but they are not the same. I strongly believe that crimes committed in the heat of passion are different than crimes that are planned—but they could both involve a gun! [Arizona]

> Well, that's where I come up with a little bit of a problem—I have had issues with—say you have a guy who is arrested and convicted for a white-collar felony. But now he's a taxpaying family person, you know, not that that is the only thing that's important, but I'm trying—[Interviewer: To paint a picture?]—Yes! It would be someone like you and me! And so maybe this person has a hiccup when

they were younger, they made a mistake—and so now he can't go hunting, you know, something that doesn't have anything to do with a gun crime—but he's banned. Because he's on that [Armed and] Prohibited Persons list. So I see that as a problem, because then someone else can steal a gun, and what do we do? I write a ticket. [California]

Each of these more nuanced takes on mandatory minimums reproduces a similar reasoning—that certain criminals must bear the force of the law, but the law should not be onerous for the "taxpaying family person . . . like you and me," the hapless nineteen-year-old trying to get to work on time, or the grieving son coming home from his father's wake. Each of these imagined gun offenders operates outside of the purview of tropes of black criminality; the politics of respectability—cued through explicit tropes of hardworking, taxpaying, family-focused people—exempts these gun offenders from the category of "hardened" criminal and instead puts them in the category of people who made an understandable mistake. These chiefs' words suggest the significance of racial ideologies linking not blackness and criminality but whiteness and innocence: Although a handful of chiefs explicitly extended this greater care to gang members (recall, for example, the discussion of felony murder in chapter 2), by and large chiefs afforded greater impunity to gun owners marked as white, middle-class Americans. Such moral improvisation produced zones of exculpatory discretion for those deemed by police as—to paraphrase the legal scholars Stephen Maynard-Moody and Michael Musheno writing on frontline decision making[50]—"deserving a break."

Though loudest in California, chiefs raised resonant concerns in the other states I studied. In Michigan, chief after chief expressed profound ambivalence regarding gun prohibitions related to restraining orders[51] due to domestic violence. Their legal cynicism wasn't entirely surprising or unique; police chiefs across Arizona, California, and Michigan described restraining orders as "just a piece of paper."[52] What was striking about Michigan chiefs' ambivalence, as compared to California and Arizona chiefs, was not their exasperation at the legal process but rather their frequent concerns about "vindictive" (in the words of two Michigan chiefs) girlfriends, wives, and exes who used restraining orders to manipulate men and, sometimes, other women. For example, one chief expressed his ambivalence by noting,

> I think the [restraining orders] are a good thing. Now, let's say there's a boyfriend and girlfriend fighting, and there's a police report, she says its physical abuse. Is it made up? Could be, and the guy is going to jail if he has a gun. And he might not even know he has [a restraining order]! So too many take them out too easily, but I don't want someone to be denied a [restraining order].

Another Michigan chief asserted, "I think it would be naive to not believe that a [restraining order] can be taken out as a tool, for example, in child custody or something." And yet another Michigan chief summarized: "It doesn't happen as much now, but you'll still have times where the guy breaks up, and you have two girls fighting over the guy for a while—and one girl will take a [restraining order] out on the other girl. It's just foolish!"

The more I listened to Michigan chiefs vent their concerns about restraining orders, the more I realized that this was not just a matter of protocol; much like California chiefs' concerns about overzealous gun regulations in that state, this was personal, but unlike California chiefs (or Arizona chiefs, for that matter), Michigan chiefs were uniquely affected by state-specific laws related to gun prohibitions under restraining orders. In California, police work is exempted from these orders, and restraining orders in Arizona do not trigger gun seizures, but in Michigan, police under restraining orders lose their guns, which means they cannot work patrol. To illustrate, consider this chief's concerns regarding restraining orders that require that a person relinquish his or her guns:

> It's a remedy if there is a presumption of guilt. . . . But there's a big issue with my guys [police officers]. If a police officer gets a [restraining order on him], he can't do his job [because he can't have a firearm]. He's suspended, and even if he gets it dismissed, it is impossi-

ble to recover from the stigma and the financial losses. So, you have to watch out. There was this one guy who started dating this hot woman; he brought her to our after-work drinks. Turns out this woman had been in a few car accidents, and that's how they started dating. I had to talk a lot of sense into the guy. Like, do you realize that guys can be blacklisted and [passed] over for promotions and just generally ostracized because they end up getting all caught up with women on the lookout for men they can use?

This chief alludes to stereotypes of women as conniving Jezebels,[53] on the "lookout" for vulnerable police who can be used for their personal gain. Another Michigan chief similarly emphasized the impact of restraining orders on police in particular, emphasizing the harm that a restraining order can wreak on an officer's job while doing little more than "giv[ing] people a false sense of security":

There are people who take out [restraining orders] because they are vindictive, and judges are quick to issue them, and they have the ability to do great harm—let's say an officer is having a divorce, and the wife takes out a [restraining order] on him. Then he can't even work [because he can't be around guns]. It also gives people a false sense of security. Because if someone really wants to do you harm, a [restraining order] is not going to stop them.

Michigan police chiefs' concerns about restraining orders circled back to legal gun carriers, especially worries about the fairness of seizing guns amid the specter of the vindictive spouse. One Michigan chief explained,

That's [gun restrictions related to restraining orders] tough. I know people who have had a [restraining order].

[Interviewer: In law enforcement?]

No! If you are in law enforcement and you get a [restraining order], that's goodbye job! But in the general public, there are people who get into an argument. Say John Q. Public. He gets in an argument with a wife, and he's loud, and she's afraid, and so she takes out a [restraining order]. But John Q. Public is a CPL [concealed pistol license] holder! And now his gun is taken away.

As this chief reveals, though Michigan chiefs widely and straightforwardly embraced aggressively enforcement of gun laws against the "bad guys with a gun" (see chapter 2), they seemed more ambivalent (e.g., "it's tough") regarding enforcement against the putatively "good guys with a gun" (in this excerpt, John Q. Public, the concealed pistol license holder). Another Michigan chief told me he found unfair the federal gun regulations banning those convicted of domestic violence assault from possessing firearms because "it was applied ex post facto."[54] Accordingly, though he was aware of at least one hunter in his jurisdiction with such a conviction, "he [the hunter] has not suffered that consequence. He's kept on hunting. I think he's continued to own a gun. He's technically in violation, and so that's not right. But the Constitution forbids ex post facto punishment." Each of these examples suggests that Michigan chiefs, like California chiefs, find themselves entangled with gun laws in ways that not only *blur* the distinctions between them and armed private civilians but also make them hesitant about the gun laws themselves—leading one chief, in this final case, to appeal to constitutional principles to knowingly underenforce the law.

Reflective of Arizona's lenient gun laws, chiefs found fewer opportunities to bemoan overzealously restrictive gun laws (as in California) or lament the possibility of being disarmed by restraining orders (as in Michigan). But a politics of impunity was visible in how Arizona as well as California and Michigan chiefs tended to address open carriers (who wear their guns visibly) and sovereign citizens (who do not recognize the authority of the federal government or local police). Although police chiefs held a range of attitudes on open carry and "constitutional types" (in the words of one chief) and many vehemently opposed open carry,[55] most chiefs saw them less as a public safety threat and more as a threat to the delicate balance between gun rights and gun safety insofar as they unnecessarily made people "feel uncomfortable." As one Michigan chief narrated a hypothetical encounter with an open carrier: "We get calls about two or three times a year about it. And I have to explain [to people], 'It's legal.' I know it's legal, and it's fine. But it's not about me. It's about the people who aren't comfortable. And is it worth it to make people uncomfortable?"

This reasoning is striking for a number of reasons, not least because police violence against black and brown people often *also* starts with discomfort: as in widely covered incidents in Philadelphia,[56] Oakland,[57] and elsewhere, a white passerby calls police to report a "suspicious" or "out of place" person of color, which then instigates a chain of events that may result in harassment, detainment, arrest, or violence. But in the case of open carriers and sovereign citizens (who are disproportionately, though not exclusively, armed white men), police chiefs show a propensity to disengage, instead opting to inform the public that uncomfortable actions are, in fact, entirely legal. In a handful of cases, police chiefs told me about specific nonconfrontational approaches they had taken to open carriers and sovereign citizens. For example, one chief in Michigan told me,

> [A while back], there was a guy who came in and wanted to have an open carry meeting in the library. The librarian, who was really smart, asked, "When?" [The open carrier] was dumbfounded, because his point was not to have a meeting; he just wanted her to say no. [After that,] the city manager said, let's set a policy. But I said, no, let's just have two cops there, and let them have their meeting. Because once you set a policy, that is a whole other can of worms: a formal policy would be worse because these groups are highly organized. They can fight you, and my job is to take care of this city. We have to figure out how not to get caught in their bag of tricks. Be sophisticated, and don't let them trap you.

Rather than taking a "law and order" approach to open carriers, this chief takes a more subtle, nuanced approach, aimed at neutralizing open carriers and the discomfort they pose rather than entangling them in the legal system. Likewise, an Arizona chief in a rural, predominantly white town told me how he coached his officers to address sovereign citizens:

Most people don't give us any hassle [but] we have a few of the "constitutionalist types." They'll have no plates, no driver's license, and they don't recognize our authority. They only recognize the authority of the elected sheriffs, not the police. So I tell my officers, don't be confrontational, don't get into a debate, because you are not going to win a debate with them! Just be polite, do your job, and if they want to argue the ticket, they can take it up with us later. Be cordial and professional.

In the case of open carriers, sovereign citizens, and "constitutional types," police chiefs described nimble interpersonal know-how aimed at subduing a potentially volatile situation—and these included the police chiefs who found themselves frustrated, irritated, and even angered by these gun-wielders. The chief in this excerpt describes a highly professionalized approach of deescalation—exactly how police stops should unfold. It starkly contrasts with how high-profile police killings of black boys and men have unfolded. For boys and men of color, the "furtive movements" of lawful gun owners or even the admission of being lawfully armed, such as in Philando Castile's case, have resulted in split-second decisions, quick trigger-pulls, and, ultimately, death. Likewise, the seemingly straightforward offense of illegal gun possession indicates dramatically different misdeeds across different racial frames of violence. In the context of the gangbanger, drug-dealer, and superpredator, the illegally possessed gun reflected yet another indicator of criminal depravity (see chapter 2). But for the farmer, the teacher, or the rancher, illegal gun possession both constituted a potentially forgivable mistake on the part of the gun-offending individual and cast doubt on the legitimacy of gun law itself. Alongside gun militarism, gun populism thus reminds us that at the intersection of gun politics and the politics of the police lie *both* power to criminalize some people *as well as* the prerogative to treat others with impunity. Gun populism—and the blurred lines it entails between police and certain civilians—captures the broader imageries of legitimate violence that naturalize this disparate politics of impunity.

THE LIMITS OF GUN POPULISM

Though most chiefs embraced populist sentiments with regard to gun law and policy, chiefs were not hard-line gun rights proponents. Nearly all chiefs wanted to retain some form of vetting for gun carriers, and police chiefs generally supported—albeit with caveats—a variety of gun regulations. Chiefs, furthermore, switched scripts between gun populism and gun militarism. They might embrace a populist stance with regard to some gun policies (e.g., licensed concealed carry), but eschew it with regard to others (e.g., open carry), and embrace gun militarism with regard to still others (e.g., mandatory minimums). As distinct brands of gun talk, gun populism and gun militarism coexisted, and chiefs invoked and tailored them to make sense of particular instances of gun uses and gun users.

Some chiefs, however, rejected gun rights on principle. They were a handful who outright questioned the Second Amendment, breaking with the political necessity that police show at least some willingness to enforce the laws of the land, including the U.S. Constitution. Though they policed in wealthy low-crime areas, in rural high-crime areas, and in sleepy tourist towns, these chiefs were few and far between. They were aware that they were in the minority, and they were downright perturbed by their colleagues. As one chief told me, "Cops don't make sense. The street cop: he doesn't want any gun control. He doesn't want crooks to have guns, either. But he doesn't see that wide access means crooks will have guns."

Some were uncomfortable with guns, seeing even police as too dependent on guns as a "necessary evil" and opining that they wished they could get rid of all guns—including even their own. These few chiefs disliked guns, and they rarely carried their own off-duty. One chief in particular saw himself as coming from a different era; one of the oldest police chiefs I interviewed, he bemoaned that the world had changed, and American gun culture was no longer recognizable to him. He preferred, as he told me, the way "the Canadians do it." And true to form, this chief carried his own gun only under one circumstance: when he traveled to remote areas where bears might pose a threat.

Others, however, were just as committed to carrying off-duty as their pro-gun counterparts, but they doubted the efficacy of private civilians intervening. As one California chief who policed an ultrawealthy suburb noted,

> I think it's [concealed carry for civilians] crazy. I think it is a bad idea for civilians to arm themselves. You know, sometimes people will occasionally tell me they want to get a gun—and I try to talk them out of it. Here's what I say. . . . If you have a gun for defense, you better be shooting to kill if someone is doing something that calls for a gun. And the average citizen has just not thought that through. So I tell them they need to have a serious sit-down and think of the consequences—not just legal. The moral, psychological consequences. And if they are still absolutely convinced, I tell them—buy a dog. Get a bullhorn. Get an alarm system. Stay away from guns!

This chief reasons that private civilians are morally and psychologically unprepared for engaging in armed self-defense. Nor are they equipped to navigate the moral and psychological consequences if they do engage in armed self-defense—consequences that are too easily enabled by the presence of an impulsively acquired firearm. Unlike gun populism, which blurs the distinctions between police and the civilians they police, this sentiment extends the "us-them" logic of gun militarism, though without the racialized overpolicing often attached to it. Given the internal weakness and even turpitude of civilians, an armed citizen is "crazy" to this chief.

Although a minority of police chiefs assertively separated themselves from private civilians with regard to access to firearms, most of the police chiefs I interviewed did not draw such clear lines.[58] Police chiefs on the whole appear to have absorbed (even if, at times, begrudgingly) the gun-wielding citizen-protector,[59] not as a threat to public law enforcement's purview, but as a boon to public safety, seeing armed private civilians as buttressing, rather than undermining, public law enforcement.

CONCLUSION

Throughout the history of public law enforcement, police have known that the actions and reactions of civilians are critical factors in determining the course of public safety. This is why police popularized the emergency call—dialing 911—as an act of public-safety-making in the early twentieth century. It is also why police have encouraged civilians to join together in neighborhood watch groups since the 1970s. And finally, it is why police today want civilians to be observant—"see something, say something"—so they can serve as citizen-witnesses if circumstances warrant. The story of twentieth-century police professionalization has been a story of cultivating these bonds between police and civilians, often in ways that situate police as the experts in crime fighting. But with the increase in gun carry by private civilians, the normalization of legal guns in everyday life, and the changing understandings regarding gun violence as a social phenomenon, police are confronting new questions: in what contexts, and with what kinds of justification, is private legitimate violence appropriate and even appealing with respect to the maintenance of public safety?

Gun populism helps us unravel how and why mainstream gun rights sensibilities resonate with police as law enforcers. Under gun populism, police may undermine the state's monopoly on legitimate violence as they tout their alienation from legislators (as in California) or emphasize their alignment with legally armed civilians (as in Arizona and Michigan). As I found, police may take on these stances not to undermine police legitimacy but to enhance it. Police chiefs' embrace of pro-gun discourse revealed that this discourse provides, perhaps paradoxically, a mechanism for police to justify *state* behavior (i.e., if civilians are justified in owning assault weapons, shouldn't police also be justified?). In this way, police may well benefit from the politics of *private* self-defense by deriving from it a justificatory gun talk regarding *state* use of violence.

As a brand of gun talk, gun populism makes sense within a particular policy and social context: where police are willing to—or, at least, have accepted that the policy and cultural environments require them to—selectively embrace legitimate violence of certain private civilians alongside their own. Accordingly, police chiefs across Arizona, California, and Michigan voiced three distinct versions of gun populism, each sensitive to the state-level policy regime in which it was embedded: "anti-elitism" in gun-restrictive California, "crime fighting by proxy" in gun-permissive Michigan, and "co-policing" in gun-lax Arizona. Across all three states, chiefs embraced a color-blind rhetoric that emphasized gun owners and gun carriers as mainstream Americans who reflected the virtues associated with white, middle-class respectability. They often illustrated their stylized understandings of "good guys with guns" by alluding to law-abiding, hardworking, and reputable typecasts—the teacher, the rancher, the taxpayer, and the family person, for example.

Not all police chiefs embraced these sentiments, and not all who did embraced them with equal enthusiasm. But the vast majority of police chiefs I interviewed voiced, to some degree, gun populism as a means of recognizing the category of "good guys with guns" to include not just police but also private civilians.

CHAPTER 5

LEGALLY ARMED BUT PRESUMED DANGEROUS

In mid-fall a few years ago, Frank Swift[1] was called to the Wayne County gun board, located in the heart of Detroit. An African American man who appeared to be in his late sixties, he had previously obtained a concealed pistol license years earlier; he had filed a renewal application and expected to receive the updated license by mail. Instead, he received a notice that his application had been denied due to blemishes on his criminal record.

Between the time that his first concealed pistol license was issued and he applied for a renewal, he had had no run-ins with law enforcement and no arrests. But in that intervening time, his record took on a life of its own. Interstate databases were compared and compiled; new arrests were added. He was informed by Wayne County gun board administrators that his file had been "updated." It now included two out-of-state arrests—but no convictions—from the 1960s in Birmingham, Alabama. As he stood at the podium, hearing the panel of law enforcement officials lay out the details of his case, he was flummoxed. The grounds for one of the arrests was made up on the spot by the arresting officer, he recalled; it was, after all, Birmingham, Alabama, in the 1960s. He professed no recollection of the other arrest. Motivated to renew his license, he entered a maddening labyrinth of bureaucracy and paperwork: after being told to clear the arrests, he went back to Birmingham, but police there claimed that they did not keep records that far back and provided him with no additional documentation. That wasn't enough for the gun board. He was instructed to go back to Alabama: if he couldn't get documentation of the arrests being cleared, then he needed to document the nonexistence of the documentation of the arrests being cleared.

The Kafka-esque maze that Frank Swift faced as he attempted to renew his concealed pistol license reveals that gun law enforcement—and its racially disparate impacts—cannot be fully captured by acts of police detention, arrest, and violence, as consequentially life-changing as these acts are. Policing the Second Amendment is not just about *who dies* by the (lawful) gun—as the police killings of Philando Castile, Emantic Bradford Jr., and others reveal regarding the unlivable space that lawfully armed men of color inhabit—but also how people such as Frank Swift are differentially compelled to *live* by the gun. Through gun law enforcement, police and other administrators have the power to profoundly shape the social, cultural, and even legal norms and expectations attached to the practice of gun carrying for those private civilians who choose to engage in it legally.[2]

This chapter focuses on gun regulation *in action* in order to unravel how gun *talk* translates into *practice*. It pivots to the "gatekeeper brokers"[3] of legitimate violence: those officials who make the fine-grained decisions regarding how legitimate violence (in the form of the capacity to lawfully carry a firearm) has devolved from the state to private actors. It focuses on decisions related to concealed carry licensing. In contrast to the "may-issue" licensing system that prevailed across American states until the 1970s, today most states issue concealed pistol licenses under a "shall-issue" system that minimizes the discretionary authority of licensing officials in favor of statutory requirements.[4] Instead of requiring claimants to demonstrate need, shall-issue systems require state administrators to demonstrate disqualification. From the outside, these licensing regimes appear legally designed to minimize bias. But whether these licensing regimes are as nondiscretionary as they purport—or, better put, *how* discretion takes shape in these regimes—is an open question that has largely been unanswerable. This is because the vast majority of the decision-making with respect to gun licensing is closed to the public, journalists, and researchers: gun licensing decisions are generally not open to public scrutiny, and records on gun licensing are often unavailable to the public due to exemptions from Freedom of Information Act (FOIA) requests.

Until recently, one exception was Michigan. Up to 2015, Michigan held public gun board meetings, where people like Mr. Swift could appeal decisions involving denied, revoked, or suspended gun carry licenses. Staffed largely by officials drawn from active or retired public law enforcement, these now-defunct boards were charged with issuing, denying, revoking, and suspending licenses to conceal carry a firearm. The public gun board meetings I attended in Michigan in Oakland County and Wayne County provided a rare look into how decisions are made in the context of gun licensing,[5] showing how police struggled to make sense of, and enforce, gun law on the ground.

Gun populism and gun militarism served as guiding frames for gun board decisions about the distribution of legitimate violence across state and society. My observations of gun board meetings in two counties one lower-income, predominantly African American urban county (Wayne County) and one middle- to upper-income, predominantly white suburban county (Oakland County)—reveal that more is at stake in gun licensing regimes than merely enforcing statutes. Comprised almost entirely of white, middle-aged men with former or current law enforcement experience, these gun boards tasked claimants—themselves overwhelmingly African American—with clearing or cleaning their records. Gun board members lectured African Americans (as compared to white claimants) regarding their behavior during police stops, their intimate relationships, and their financial responsibilities to their families. And they often used stereotypes of black masculinity such as the Thug and the Deadbeat Dad—what sociologists call "controlling images"—to discipline would-be gun carriers of color.[6] In doing so, they mobilized the concealed pistol license to bridge gun militarism and gun populism, punitively disciplining African American men (in line with gun militarism) and devolving responsibility to these men for protecting themselves and their families (in line with gun populism).

Although policymakers, politicians, and pundits across the gun debate may argue about whether gun laws should fundamentally be geared at policing guns (e.g., bans on assault weapons) versus policing people (e.g., criminalization of gun use), this chapter suggests that this may be a false binary. In a context where gun carrying has become increasingly commonplace,[7] where police largely support licensed gun carry, and where the politics of legitimate violence is saturated with the politics of race, guns themselves are the vehicle through which people are disparately policed.

PROCEDURAL PAINS

Rachel Simpson, an African American woman in her forties, walked up to the podium in the large auditorium that housed the Wayne County gun board. Not long before, she had learned that her gun carry license had been suspended; she was informed that she had an outstanding warrant for an arrest issued by the Detroit Police Department. Unsure of the warrant, Ms. Simpson assumed it was for an incident that occurred in 2001; as she explained, it was the only time she can remember having a run-in with the police. She brought her paperwork for that charge, which she asserted had been dropped. Her paperwork lacked a case number, however, so the gun board sent her back to the issuing court. As they explained, "There's no case number, so there's no way for us to know it is the same case." Flummoxed, the woman asked for the case number for the warrant that concerned the gun board so she could follow up with the court. The gun board refused: "We can't give you that. We can give you the date." The woman at this point appeared visibly deflated. In a seeming snap decision, however, one of the five gun board members that day opted to give her the case number anyway, sending her off to track down—and clear—her record.

Ms. Simpson's case highlights how the gun board functions as a mechanism to compel claimants not just to comply with the law but also to confront their records[8] and either clear them (if the records are accurate and charges are outstanding) or clean them (if the records are erroneous). Individuals were routinely called to the gun board for a wide array of offenses, including unpaid parking tickets, outstanding arrests ranging from disorderly conduct to attempted homicide, unpaid child support, and other offenses. This reflects broader trends in net-widening[9] surveillance and recordkeeping as well as racialized policing.[10]

This racial disparity in gun board cases is evident in the gun board meetings I observed: though only roughly 43 percent of Wayne County's concealed pistol license holders were African Americans, 72 percent of individuals called before the gun board were African American, and a full 80 percent of claimants called to the gun board because of charges more than twenty years old were African American. In wealthier Oakland County, this racial disparity was even wider.

The majority of gun board cases involved records-related issues— low-level "blemishes"—rather than major infractions flagging acute public safety concerns. In place of overt punishment, the very *process of obtaining*[11] a gun license via these administrative channels served as a vehicle of discipline for roughly four in ten claimants. (See appendix A for more details on these gun boards, and additional data on the breakdown of cases and claimants.)

Records lay at the center of these *procedural pains*, a term[12] that highlights how paperwork and bureaucratic hurdles are deployed as a penal mechanism. As I observed, a basic premise of decision-making in gun board is that records, however erroneous or incomplete, are the gold standard of the decision-making process, and gun board members placed the onus of addressing "wrongful representation"[13] on claimants. As one gun board member told a claimant, "It's your record, your responsibility!" Gun boards' demand for paperwork devolved responsibility for accurate records from state agents to the claimant. Combined with the selective withholding of information,[14] this effectively discouraged claimants from pursuing their licenses, though without official denial or revocation. Procedural pains explain why African American claimants disproportionately appeared at gun boards: not only are they more likely than whites to have contact with the criminal justice system,[15] but by virtue of the demographic concentration of African Americans in urban areas, they are also more likely to face the consequences of urban decline in the form of scantily funded, inadequately trained, and/or poorly interfacing public agencies,[16] which can exacerbate difficulties in maintaining accurate public records.

Paperwork served as a key vehicle for statutory requirements to come alive as disciplinary techniques. As mechanisms to ration administrative goods[17] as well as deliver symbolic services by way of referring clients to other offices,[18] paperwork requirements do not simply reflect a set of binding rules. They also serve as a game of maneuvers.[19] Cases at gun boards were routinely marked for "reschedule," pending additional paperwork to be painstakingly amassed by claimants prior to another appearance. In Wayne County, claimants were routinely referred to a single officer at a specific police precinct; presumably, this officer reliably knew how to issue the proper paperwork and remove outstanding warrants and arrests from the electronic records system, a task easily encumbered by bureaucratic mishaps.[20] Gun board members unilaterally demanded the "the yellow paper" from this particular officer and grimaced at other-colored paperwork. For those claimants with nonviolent felony records, the gun board sometimes walked them through the expungement process in what appeared to be sincere attempts to help applicants clear their records. At other times, however, the gun board took "refuge in regulations"[21] and strategically "threw the book" (colloquially speaking) at applicants who asked too many questions by simply referring them to other offices or giving them false hopes, as I observed in a couple of cases, that their records could be cleared or expunged.

Clearing one's record was easier said than done.[22] One claimant, an African American woman who appeared to be in her forties, was denied a license because of an arrest related to a drug felony. Instead of acquiring "the yellow paper" preferred by the gun board, the woman appeared with a clearance letter from a police precinct that simply stated that the arrest was not in the system:

GUN BOARD ADMINISTRATOR #1: The clearance letter doesn't help.

GUN BOARD ADMINISTRATOR #2: That's why we gave you *specific* instructions.

CLAIMANT: But it never even made it to court. I've been *everywhere*. I've been to four or five police departments, and they told me it doesn't exist . . .

GUN BOARD ADMINISTRATOR #2: Then get a letter that says that!

CLAIMANT: No one will give me that letter! I got the runaround.

GUN BOARD ADMINISTRATOR #2: It's *your* arrest, you have to take care of it!

GUN BOARD ADMINISTRATOR #3: Go back to Central [Processing] and get a letter that the arrest was discharged.

The incident was visibly frustrating to everyone involved; gun board members were themselves often agitated by the meshing of gun rules with criminal records.

Though rare, these frustrations sometimes led gun board members to argue *against* the protocol of relying on records. In one case, an African American man in his forties was denied a license because of two active warrants. As soon as the claimant reached the podium, one of the gun board administrators stood up from his chair, visibly unnerved: "They cancelled one of the warrants, but not the other. But they are the *same case*, same name, everything. And he has the dismissal paperwork. It is my recommendation that he is approved." Thanks to the claimant's due diligence of bringing dismissal paperwork, this gun board administrator convinced the others to approve the license, but the claimant was nevertheless given a helpfully stern warning: "You need to keep your paperwork with you at *all times*. Do *not* lose it." Because the case still had not been removed from the electronic records database, the apparent outstanding warrant could endanger him if police, even in a routine traffic stop, became aware that he was armed. The case perhaps reflects law-enforcement-cum-administrators' own legal cynicism.[23] But it also reveals that gun law enforcement is motivated not just by the *letter* of the law but also the *spirit* of the law.[24] Administrators were aware of both the promises and the pitfalls of overreliance on records, and counseled claimants accordingly. Furthermore, the case reveals that gun rights—far from "absolute"—are embedded in local understandings and practices. As the law and society scholar Alec Ewald writes of administrative restrictions on firearms ownership, "Ultimately, it is not clear that there is a 'black-letter law' answer" to the question of firearms possession. Instead, "the legality of firearms possession—that is, the status of an individual's federal constitutional right" revolves around "the practices and shared understandings of local legal interpreters" that themselves reflect "legal ambiguity and uncertainty."[25]

Claimants at gun board experienced procedural pains associated with having to account for records that were erroneous or incomplete. But these procedural pains also affected claimants more concretely through the loss of goods, services, and security that claimants and administrators alike associated with gun licensing. Repeated gun board visits cost them time and lost wages (claimants at times protested that they could not afford to take off work to continue coming to gun board). The loss of, or inability to obtain, a gun license could impose tangible costs on claimants, too.

Consider the case of an African American man in his thirties who was called to gun board. As a security guard, his employment was tied to his gun license. A veteran who had served in Afghanistan, he came to gun board in his military uniform, perhaps to compel administrators to ask about his service (a tactic that appears to have been successful). He recollected the offense that led him to the gun board: "I blew a 0.03 [blood alcohol content] while carrying. . . . I take complete responsibility for this. I'm not trying to say I'm not responsible. But I work security." One of the gun board administrators interrupted him to ask, "Where?" The claimant continued, "At Guardian Alarm. I've lost a ton of money. I went down from $12 an hour armed to $8 an hour. It's putting stress on me and my wife." Looking at the claimant's military uniform, the gun board administrator remarked that because the ticketing officer wrote up the offense as a civil infraction, it was up to the discretion of the gun board whether to revoke his license. Pondering the decision, the administrator moved the conversation in an unexpected direction: "Why are you a security guard?" The claimant replied, "I'm going to school." The gun board administrator offered, "You can get $18 an hour here [at the Sheriff's Department]. Go online . . . we're hiring." Another gun board member jumped in, "We need about 60 to 70 people . . . right now. You can make $42K to $47K—and we top out at $62K." The claimant, apparently stunned to be given a job lead, muttered, "That's a good life."

The claimant's financially motivated desire for a gun license revealed that gun licenses do not just *reflect* a person's record but also *constitute part of that record*.[26] Inverting the "mark" of a criminal record,[27] a gun license credentialed this claimant as a skilled employee to security companies *as well as* to the very state agents tasked with licensing him to carry a firearm. The racial politics of respectability seemed to interact with the gun board administrators' localized understandings of gun rights; presenting himself as a responsible gun owner willing to wield firearms on behalf of state interests (as embodied by his military uniform) and to better himself and his family socioeconomically (as evidenced by his stated plan to fund a college degree with his security guard work), this claimant distanced himself from stereotypes of black men as criminal or lazy. The board reinstated his gun carry license.

This claimant's dependence on his gun carry license for higher income was not uncommon. More commonly, though, employment needs related to gun carry revolved around jobs viewed as "dangerous." These included jobs in liquor establishments, delivery jobs, and jobs requiring the handling of large amounts of money, especially at night. Likewise, license seekers tried to demonstrate that their life situations called for heightened security measures in order to convince gun board members of their legitimate need for a firearm. Gun board members at times took an understanding tone toward claimants who had been repeated victims or who lived in areas recognized as crime-ridden. Even those claimants brought in on attempted homicide charges sometimes found a sympathetic ear with the gun board, who viewed their actions as examples of self-defense and, therefore, as evidence of their exposure to crime. This sympathetic sensibility among gun board officials resonates with gun populism. In line with both the valorization of victims' rights[28] and a general public willingness to treat criminals (that is, those against whom licensees presumably use their firearms) swiftly and harshly,[29] gun board administrators were at times willing to overlook blemishes for gun carriers who, by virtue of their employment status or need for a firearm, could present themselves to gun boards as respectable and responsible.

On the way to a gun license, then, claimants often experienced a records "runaround" that landed them in bureaucratic and moral entanglements they were compelled to unravel in order to carry a firearm legally. With more criminal justice contact than whites, African Americans disproportionately experienced this runaround. But African Americans were not just more likely to be called to gun board to address paperwork. Once they arrived there, they were subject to a distinct kind of processing as compared to their white peers—one that punished and disciplined claimants of color, especially African American men, according to controlling images of black criminality. As my observations revealed, this treatment reflected both gun militarism and gun populism. On the one hand, gun boards at times extended gun militarism by revoking the gun licenses of claimants of color as a way to supplement the shortcomings of the criminal justice system, mobilizing the gun license in the service of criminalization. On the other hand, gun boards enacted an apprehensive brand of gun populism as they issued licenses to gun carriers of color by communicating to them the racialized terms on which their licenses were issued—and could be revoked.

THE LONG ARM OF THE LAW

Midway through the morning session at a Wayne County gun board meeting, a gun board member opened a file folder and called for Jerome Brown, an African American man who appeared to be in his forties. Mr. Brown arose from his chair and walked down the stairs. Arriving at the podium at the front of the auditorium, he stated his name and then quickly spelled it out. The administrator read the details of his case, "Mr. Brown, you were denied a [gun license] application because of an active Third Circuit Friend of Court Warrant." Due to unpaid child support, a warrant for his arrest had been issued.[30] The administrator continued, "You appeared in September, at which point you were arrested." Reviewing my fieldnotes, I realized that Mr. Brown must have been one of the two arrests I witnessed that month; Mr. Brown had already appeared before gun board and had already been *arrested* at gun board. The administrator queried further, "Then your warrant was cleared. How much did you pay?" He responded, "$2,500. I paid the full amount after I got arrested." Paperwork in order, he was approved for a license to carry a gun concealed. His case was the only one I observed in which someone arrested at gun board returned with the proper paperwork and a cleared record and was ultimately approved for a license. Nevertheless, it highlighted the capacity of administrators to funnel, or threaten to funnel, individuals into the criminal justice system based on their criminal records.

Statutorily, administrators *must* deny licenses pending resolution of certain outstanding issues. But if these issues involve warrants, then gun board administrators also have the discretion to coordinate an arrest. But they cannot arrest everyone: gun board administrators must contend with the availability of jail space and the willingness of local jails to take in claimants. This gap between the prerogative to arrest and its feasibility means that although arrests can and do happen at gun board, administrators often rely on the *threat* of arrest as a means of compelling compliance. Using the threat of arrest as a mechanism to police would-be gun carriers, gun board administrators transpose a technique from street policing (that is, the "warning"), and, in doing so, expand the reach of the criminal justice system as they remind claimants of their precarious position between criminality and lawfulness. In this way, administrative process *expands* criminal justice by facilitating the differential flow of people into the criminal justice system and by encouraging claimants to internalize the gaze of the state and thus understand themselves as precariously subject to the law.

Not unlike the sting operations orchestrated at welfare offices, where recipients are told they have benefits waiting only to find handcuffs upon their arrival,[31] people could be and were arrested at gun boards. Over five months, I observed twenty-five instances in which claimants were arrested or directly threatened with arrest.[32] Meanwhile, broad threats—directed at no particular individual—were especially common in Wayne County. In that county, at least one gun board meeting a month included a session that addressed claimants with outstanding warrants. These claimants, usually numbering between twenty and thirty, would typically enter the auditorium en masse and be lectured on their outstanding warrants as a group. Consider one gun administrator's opening remarks to claimants with outstanding warrants, as captured in my fieldnotes:

> [The administrator] jumps to the front of the auditorium and starts pacing. . . . He calls four names off first, and tells these African American men to sit in the very front row [of the auditorium]. He [then] starts in on the lecture, "Everyone in here has an active warrant, and you are going to take care of it. You can go to jail right now. Now, I probably won't arrest you right now, but I can. So go pay your bond, get rid of the court date, get dismissal paperwork, get something that says, 'not guilty.' If you have this paperwork, we can talk to you today. If you don't, you need to go get it."

After this lecture, arrests are made; warrants for unpaid child support and violent felonies almost always resulted in arrest before cases were individually heard. In Wayne County, twelve arrests—all involving African Americans—occurred after these opening lectures.

Other kinds of warrants (e.g., for misdemeanors for unpaid parking tickets or for nonviolent felonies such as unemployment fraud) did not necessarily result in arrest. Such cases were determined by the availability of jail space, on the one hand, and the motivation of gun board members to punish certain kinds of records and particular claimants, on the other. Although a threatened arrest did not always open the valve between the gun board and the jail, such threats served as a panoptic[33] reminder to claimants that this valve could be turned. So while gun board members might quietly urge one another to "Call the jail to see if they have space," they usually presented their authority to funnel claimants into the criminal justice system in terms of their own discretion, reminding claimants of their legal vulnerability as they concealed the spatial limitations of the jail. For example, at the beginning of one gun board meeting in Wayne County, an African American woman in her thirties approached one of the gun board members as the other claimants found their seats. The gun board member insisted that the woman needed to "Go to Macomb County" to address her arrest. She argued that there was no arrest and no record. The gun board member cut her off: "You need to leave before I arrest you. You have a serious enough warrant that I could arrest you. You need to leave before I change my mind." He laughed as the woman left, saying, "She has a ten-year-old daughter waiting out there. I am becoming too nice in my old age!"

This threat of arrest was mobilized even for claimants who had no outstanding warrants, such as in cases in which gun board members "smelled marijuana" or thought an applicant "looked high" as well as in cases in which applicants acted "disorderly" by asking too many questions. One older white man was called to the gun board because he managed to obtain a medical marijuana card *and* a concealed pistol license—an illegal combination under federal law. Flummoxed by the gun board's reasoning, he asked, "Can I get that in writing?" and "Can't I ask questions?" Exasperated, one gun board member threatened arrest: "You are two seconds from being arrested for disorderly conduct." Again, such threats often did not materialize. Instead, the threat of arrest operated as a tool of discipline amid the *specter*[34] of the gun board's discretionary ability to funnel claimants into the criminal justice system.

This mobilization of the threat of arrest in the context of gun board illustrates how administrative process expands criminal justice, but not as the pipeline evoked in metaphors regarding pathways into incarceration (e.g., the school-to-prison "pipeline"). Rather, criminal and quasi-criminal records provide the wrenches with which gun board members could open the valves to criminal mechanisms, or at least threaten to open them. This link between administrative process and criminal justice is mutually beneficial. This valve-turning allows an administrative process to act as a handmaiden to criminal justice; likewise, criminal justice enhances the authority of administrators by providing a mechanism (the *threat* of arrest) to compel compliance, quell disputes, and remind claimants of their precarious position before the law.

But the administrative process also engendered its own forms of punishment—in the form of both *denying* and *revoking* gun carry licenses from people deemed statutorily or otherwise unfit to have them as well as *disciplining* and *regulating* those people to whom they are granted.

THE LICENSE TO PUNISH

Jessica James, an African American woman in her early twenties, made her way down the staircase at the gun board meeting. The first case of the day, she was accompanied by her lawyer, an African American man in his forties. Summarizing the reasoning behind the denial of the claimant's license application, a gun board member explained that she was ineligible for a gun carry license for several reasons, including two felony convictions related to illegal possession of a controlled substance. Her lawyer responded in a matter-of-fact manner:

> We were fully expecting a denial. We are working on a case with a previous judge who should have considered her under HYTA [Holmes Youthful Training Status; a mechanism for youths who committed a crime between the ages of seventeen and twenty-one[35] to remove the conviction from their records], but she was not given HYTA. She was nineteen during that case and turned twenty while the case was still under way. So we are using this as another piece of evidence to show that she's been affected by the HYTA denial.

A gun board member clarified, "So you are effectively trying to create a record?" The lawyer affirmed, "Yes, that's right. We are here to create a record." Remarkably, though "she doesn't want a [gun carry license]," the lawyer had encouraged his client to apply for and receive a near-certain denial because, he believed, it would help show that Ms. James was undergoing undue hardship as a result of her exclusion from HYTA. The lawyer's strategy was two-fold: first, to use the gun license to expose an injustice related to Ms. James's record and, second, in doing so, to create a *new* record of that harm based on the shared presumption that being denied a gun carry license constituted a kind of hardship.[36] This strategy relied on a particular presumption: that gun licenses represented a public good, and their denial represented a punishment in itself.

Legally speaking, a concealed pistol license is an administrative privilege, not a right; the U.S. Supreme Court, as of this writing, has not ruled on whether gun carry is covered under the Second Amendment. But the lawyer's strategy reflected broad-based sensibilities about the everyday politics of guns and the organization of protection and policing. Gun carry was a *social* right that hundreds of thousands of Michiganders— white and black—sought to exercise.[37] Although the denial of gun licenses is formally distinct from an arrest or detention, it carries a powerful message about civic inclusion, about who gets to be a "good guy with a gun."[38]

If carrying a gun was a right—at least, as informally understood by ordinary people—then taking that ability away could double as a punishment. In some of the cases I observed, gun boards did exactly this. Denying, revoking, or suspending a gun license served as an administrative process that provided an opportunity for punishment when criminal justice mechanisms were absent or inadequate—for example, when police may be unable to make a formal arrest but can refer a suspect to the administrative board for review. In the same way that police work is marked by an ability both to *enforce* law and also to *use* it in ways that fall short of (e.g., everyday harassment)[39] or fall outside the purview of (e.g., street justice)[40] formal justice, gun law administrators—themselves public law enforcement—could deploy punitive *administrative* techniques in the absence of formal criminal justice mechanisms.[41] Of the 936 cases I observed across two counties, roughly one in ten cases involved gun board members using denial, or threat of denial, of a gun license as a punishment (16 percent of Oakland County cases and 9 percent of Wayne County cases; see appendix A for more details). At times, I even observed cases involving police referrals that either did not involve formal charges or involved charges that had already been dismissed, especially in Oakland County. With criminal justice channels exhausted, cases ended up in gun boards for review. In such instances, gun boards could revoke, or threaten to revoke, a claimant's gun license as a punishment in itself.

Consider one case involving an African American man in his twenties who claimed that he had shot his gun in self-defense. He was charged with attempted homicide, but the case was ultimately dismissed in court. He was referred to the gun board by local police. Gun board members approached his case with suspicion as they evoked racial stereotypes; one member said the shooting "sounds like one of those basketball feud things." Gun board began by questioning the claimant about his employment status; he explained that he had two jobs at two separate group homes. Reflecting a moral, rather than legal, partition between those who are deserving and undeserving of gun carry licenses, one gun board member exclaimed, "He works at a group home—what does he need a gun for? He doesn't own a liquor store!"

The other gun board member decided to call the detective on the case and learned that the "victims never showed up, and all the witnesses moved to get out of [the city where the incident occurred]. Detective says it was a great case for felonious assault, but they were overzealous with charging him with attempted murder." Illustrating the "tough on crime" sensibility that led police to selectively embrace lawful gun access, he explained to the claimant, "I called the detective in charge. I believe in Second Amendment rights, and if I had it my way, everyone would carry a gun. But my vote is not to reinstate based on the safety of others." The claimant laughed and exclaimed, "You believe that?" The gun board member continued, "I'm dead serious. I want *everybody* to have a gun. I believe in the Second Amendment. But with rights come responsibilities." The claimant left without his license, despite having been formally convicted of no crime. In this case, the ambiguous status of gun carrying—as both a privilege requiring the licensing of the state *and* a social right as per local understandings of gun carry—created the room for administrative process to provide a stopgap for cases that "should" have been prosecuted but were not. To use the criminologist Lucia Zedner's phrasing, the board sought "to make good the failings of the criminal justice system."[42] Instead of probation or imprisonment, the offender faced indefinite revocation of his gun license.

Via license revocation, the gun board facilitates a kind of "parallel punishment" where criminal justice mechanisms are absent or inadequate. But this did not constitute the bulk of their work; gun board members weren't interested in *revoking* licenses as much as they seemed invested in *regulating* licensees. Gun board members could not just punish; they could also discipline—and not by withholding gun licenses, but by issuing them and attaching to them particular, racialized presumptions regarding public and private conduct.

DISCIPLINE AND DEGRADATION

Midway through a gun board session, one of the administrators suddenly interrupted the proceedings. Pausing a line of claimants called to the podium in the front of the large auditorium where this gun board meeting took place, he made an impromptu lecture to the roughly forty people, almost all African American, about the "responsibility" of a gun carry license:

> There is a big responsibility with a [license]. . . . It's on you. You can't get into altercations. You can't get into road rage. . . . Because as soon as someone sees you, and they see the shadow of a gun, or they see a print of a gun through your clothes, or they see you reaching for a gun, they are going to call the police. They are going to say you pulled a gun on them. . . . So you got to put your big boy pants on, put your big girl pants on, and you have to take the higher ground.

Invoking the politics of respectability, this administrator's words suggest that the gun board did more than simply process paperwork. Taking a patronizing and paternalistic tone, this gun board member saw the provision of the concealed pistol license as a vehicle of *disciplining* claimants into good behavior.

Understanding how gun boards operate as a mechanism of social control more interested in discipline than punishment requires attention to what the sociologist Megan Comfort calls "sociological ambivalence." In her book *Doing Time Together*, Comfort introduces this concept to highlight the multiple and contradictory ways in which individuals engage with penal institutions that by turns oppress and empower them. In my own observations of gun boards, the concept of sociological ambivalence was useful for bringing into focus gun board members' *own* ambivalence about gun licensing. Reflective of broader pro-gun sensibilities among law enforcement, these administrators often saw gun carry as a reasonable—and widely acceptable—response to fears about crime and disorder in Metro Detroit, and they sympathized with private civilians interested in carrying guns. At other times, however, they sought to proactively curtail access to guns to private civilians, such as those deemed dangerous to themselves or others.

This ambivalence was not merely preferential on the part of gun board administrators; it was built into the contradictory frames of legitimate violence that circulate among gun law enforcers: gun militarism and gun populism. Sometimes these frames were mutually reinforcing, but at other times, they were mutually undermining; regardless, legally armed people of color, especially men of color, were situated at their intersection. To split the difference, gun board members did not use the gun license as a vehicle of *punishment* as much as a vehicle of *discipline*. Discipline was a more much regular feature of gun board than formal sanctions, and shaming and degradation were especially common in Wayne County, where African American men most often received admonitions on responsibility.[43]

Degradation ceremonies, a concept developed by Harold Garfinkel,[44] helps to make sense of how formal administrative proceedings integrate shame, embarrassment, and accusation as a means of disciplining claimants.[45] Using Garfinkel's framework in her book *Crook County*, Nicole Gonzalez Van Cleve highlights how degradation ceremonies impart punitive "lessons" through which "racial divisions [are encoded] with symbolic meaning about violating the shared moral values of hard work, competence, and motivation."[46] When organized around controlling images (that is, stereotypes aimed at naturalizing inequality), degradation ceremonies can serve as dramatizations of racial/gender hierarchies: people positioned differently along the intersecting lines of race and gender are publicly subjected to different treatments that communicate race- and gender-specific social expectations.

Amid the specter of the high-crime, African American–majority city of Detroit and the stereotypes of black criminality that that entails,[47] African American men looking to carry guns lawfully in Metro Detroit encounter a courtesy stigma by virtue of their racial/gender identities and social locations.[48] They are held accountable to two controlling images in particular: the Thug and the Deadbeat Dad. The Thug is a version of "African American masculinity associated with criminality and poverty."[49] It has been used to justify public expenditures on policing and punishment[50] and to legitimate "attacks on African American boys' and men's bodies and minds."[51] Controlling images of African American men as criminals began to circulate in the late 1800s and early 1900s[52] but gained traction widely in the post–Civil Rights era,[53] during which "tough on crime" politics mobilized the threat of black criminality.

If the Thug stereotypes the public lives of black men, the Deadbeat Dad is tied to the private sphere. The Deadbeat Dad trope refers to "a man simply too lazy to try" and "who has simply walked away from his children and—most important—doesn't seem to care."[54] The origins of the Deadbeat Dad trope may date as far back as the 1920s,[55] but it enjoyed mass circulation under the auspices of the 1965 Moynihan Report, which declared the African American family to be in "complete breakdown" due to "out of wedlock childbearing." By 1986, Bill Moyers's *The Vanishing Family* recirculated this imagery,[56] creating a "widespread moral panic about absent fathers."[57] In my observations, gun board administrators often typecast black fathers as delinquent providers who are prone to violence within the home, and accordingly, I broaden the definition of the Deadbeat Dad to include fathers framed either as delinquently absent or abusive.

The Thug

A gun carry license is primarily a permit that regulates public behavior— that is, carrying a gun in public. Accordingly, standards for contact with police are built into the legal framework of gun licensing. Licensees who failed to disclose their status as license holders to police during stops had their licenses suspended and their files reviewed at a gun board; the gun board had the discretion to suspend licenses up to six months. Police could also suspend, revoke, or deny licenses based on "excessive police contact." I observed gun boards explicitly discuss police contact 64 times, overwhelmingly with African American men (39 times) and African American women (9 times), and most of the time in Wayne County.

Discussions of disclosure were bound up with concerns about officer safety. As one Wayne County gun board administrator noted, "Everybody—whether carrying or not—just put your hand on the wheel and say, 'I have a [gun carry license].' That puts the officer at ease." Although disclosure requirements are intended to enhance safety, such cases also served to discipline African American men according to the controlling image of the Thug. In these cases, gun board administrators enforced informal rules of conduct between African Americans and the police, particularly regarding the deference of the former to the latter.[58]

Consider one African American man called to the Wayne County gun board. Explaining his failure to disclose to an officer, the claimant asserted his awareness of appropriate conduct with police: "Over the last five years I have been stopped by as many suburban agencies as are people on this board." He used the term "suburban" to flag an awareness of the changing rules of engagement across the 8 Mile border (the street that runs between African American–majority Detroit and its whiter, wealthier suburbs). This assertion of expertise, however, backfired because it raised another set of concerns for gun board administrators: "Why [so much police contact]?" Despite documented evidence of African Americans' disproportionate contact with police due to racial profiling,[59] the gun board treated this claimant's police contact as an indicator of his individual suspiciousness.[60] Sticking to a color-blind script,[61] this claimant seemed to cede that it was ultimately *his* individual responsibility to avoid police contact. In responding to the administrator's question, he demonstrated his willingness to comply with the heightened scrutiny he warrants as a gun carry licensee: "Just because! I have a ten-year-old car. And I always have insurance. And I always disclose."

Claimants often adopted scripts that appealed to—or at least did not contradict—color-blind sensibilities. In one case, however, I did witness a claimant explicitly cite race as a factor in police stops. This African

American man's gun license was suspended because of a felony assault charge from a Detroit suburb. He explained, "I was driving, a guy flipped me off, and then flicked his cigarette into my car as I was getting in the right lane. We both called the police—and I was the one who got arrested." One administrator responded by individualizing responsibility, saying, "Road rage. You want to have a [gun carry license]? You have to be responsible. Why were you the one that got arrested?" The claimant apprehensively names race:

> CLAIMANT: Truthfully?
> ADMINISTRATOR: Yes, I want the truth.
> CLAIMANT: Because I was black, and he was white.

At these words, the panel of administrators literally threw up their hands in a show of indignation. The administrator retorted, "Watch the news: every other day people are getting killed over things that start out as nothing! You are a nice young man, you need to take the higher road!" Rather than directly address his claims, the gun board reasserted that the outcome of police encounters rests on the claimant's shoulders.[62] With this heavy-handed caution, the man's license was reinstated.

White applicants did not undergo this kind of treatment. Both Wayne and Oakland counties' gun boards tended to take a matter-of-fact approach to cases related to police contact involving white men. As a typical example, one white man who appeared to be in his sixties came to the Wayne County gun board after paying a fine for failing to disclose his status as a gun carry licensee to a police officer. An administrator informed him that his license would be suspended for six months, after which he should "come see us . . . [to] get your license back." This applicant was not questioned about the incident, he was not warned about the consequences of misbehavior, nor was he instructed on appropriate interactions with police. White men were rarely admonished, and when they were, it was often brief and even jovial. For example, one Oakland County case involved an affluent suburban police department that had entered a warning in a white man's federal record, which effectively barred the man from purchasing or possessing weapons.

Adopting a sympathetic tone, an administrator jokingly mused, "You did something to tick off [those] police!"

This joking tone was absent in cases involving African American men's police stops, although a gun board member did adopt a wise-cracking attitude toward one African American woman. This woman returned to the Wayne County gun board after a six-month suspension to claim her license. Before reissuing, an administrator reminded her how to engage with police:

> GUN BOARD MEMBER: And now you know the first thing to say is . . . ?
>
> CLAIMANT: I have my gun!
>
> GUN BOARD MEMBER [LAUGHING]: No! If you do that, they are going to start pulling their guns on you! You say, "Officer, I have a [gun carry license], and I have my weapon on me." Not, "Guess what's in my pocket!"

This kind of follow-up "quiz" was common for African Americans, but not for whites who failed to disclose. Even with the softer tone adopted by the gun board toward this woman, the gun board's warning that she should expect police to perceive her as a threat aligned with racial disparities in policing. This treatment also resonates with the growing criminalization of women of color[63] and the historically long-standing tendency for African American women to be treated as socially male by state apparatuses of social control.[64] Rather than a fleeting moment of sympathy as with the white applicant in Oakland County, this interaction both encouraged the claimant to adopt the gaze of the police officer by seeing her own legal actions as dangerous and made light of the gravity of having to do so.

At the gun board meetings I observed, African Americans, especially but not exclusively African American men, were disproportionately disciplined with regard to their interactions with police. Administrators reminded them that their guns—though legal—made them suspect to law enforcement; that they should expect guns drawn if they broke informal rules of conduct with police because their actions would be read as threatening; and that, therefore, the outcomes of police stops ultimately rested on their shoulders. Animated by the controlling image of the Thug, such encounters dramatized the subordinate position of African Americans, particularly African American men, vis-à-vis law enforcement (claimants were expected to demonstrate knowledge of, and behavioral compliance with, informal rules of conduct during police stops); vis-à-vis the gun board (administrators mobilized moralizing scripts to compel claimants to account for controlling images); and vis-à-vis other claimants (at these public gun boards, such questioning was usually reserved for African American men).

The Deadbeat Dad

Although gun carry licenses regulate behavior outside of the home, a significant portion of cases involved private matters. Of 936 gun board cases I observed, 111 involved intimate partner violence (IPV), 16 involved child support, and 3 involved child custody cases. African American men were disproportionately represented: they comprised 60 percent of IPV cases (67 African American men); 67 percent of child custody cases (2 African American men); and 100 percent of child support cases (16 African American men). The majority of cases took place in Wayne County; in Oakland County, I observed just 9 IPV cases, 2 child support, and no custody cases.

Such cases suggest that gun carry licenses were used to address a fundamental dilemma in federal gun regulation efforts related to IPV: uneven and ineffective enforcement due to poorly kept databases and inadequate interoperability across enforcement agencies.[65] My observations, especially at the Wayne County gun board, however, suggest that gun carry licenses also opened opportunities for state agents to discipline African American men according to the controlling image of the Deadbeat Dad.

To start, consider one fifty-nine-year-old African American man whose license was suspended because of a weapons charge.[66] When he admitted that he was on probation, a Wayne County administrator asked the claimant why. He explained, "Child support. I'm paying back. I'm retired now, and I owe $107,000. And I pay $100 [a month]. I've had employment issues." The administrator exasperatedly exclaimed, "That's stacks on stacks!" The claimant continued:

> CLAIMANT: I got a weapon because I was assaulted. I asked the police if I was restricted from getting a weapon, and they said no, so I sent in my paperwork.
>
> GUN BOARD ADMINISTRATOR: How much was the weapon?
>
> CLAIMANT: Between $500 and $600.
>
> GUN BOARD ADMINISTRATOR: That could have been used to pay child support!
>
> CLAIMANT: But they are grown now!
>
> GUN BOARD ADMINISTRATOR: Don't say that. Their mother paid the bill. She had to foot the bill! When they needed a fieldtrip, Pampers [diapers], someone had to pay for that! That's why you have to pay this.
>
> CLAIMANT: I take the blame, and I haven't missed a payment in three or four years.
>
> GUN BOARD ADMINISTRATOR: Your priorities are all screwed up.

Although the claimant provided a pragmatic justification for his gun license ("I was assaulted") as well as a legal one ("I asked the police if I was restricted"), this gun board administrator admonished him about his poor parenting choices, defined by his financial contributions (or lack thereof) to his family. Although the gun board appeared to be legally required to reinstate his license, they did so only after compelling the man to accept his blameworthiness ("I take the blame") and interrogating his "priorities."

In IPV cases, the gun board also compelled claimants to account for their private behaviors. This disproportionate scrutiny of African American men reflects cautionary feminist analyses[67] that IPV law enforcement promises to protect women at the cost of penetrating the privacy of marginalized groups. In IPV cases, the gun board routinely inquired about personal matters, and in cases involving African American men, I observed questioning of both the claimant *and his intimate partner.*

Consider a Wayne County case involving an African American man whose license was suspended because of a 2014 assault charge. The case opened with the administrator questioning the claimant about the details of the charge:

ADMINISTRATOR: Who [the victim] was it?
CLAIMANT: My fiancée.
ADMINISTRATOR: Is she here right now?
CLAIMANT: Yes.
ADMINISTRATOR: Ma'am, come on down!

The woman walked down from the "audience" to the podium to explain:

It was a bad argument at home, and the police came. I didn't call the police, and the police did not really speak to me. I said I did not want to press charges. It was a few days of heated argument, the kids were there, the kids were arguing too.

Listening to both the claimant and his partner account for the claimant's charge, the gun board administrator reproached both of them on responsible parenting: "That sets a bad example for kids. Both of you need to find a better way to communicate." The claimant responded, "We've been together for 14 years, three boys and three girls, we started from the bottom, and we are here now. And now after the fight we kissed and made up." The couple smiled as they talked about their kids. The gun board accepted the claimant's explanation; his license was reinstated.

For white men called to gun board because of IPV-related issues, inquiries were less inquisitive and more lighthearted. I never observed the partners of white men testify on their behalf. For example, one white man's IPV charge from Las Vegas was met with moralizing laughs before the gun board approved his license: "You know what happens in Vegas doesn't stay in Vegas!" Another white man with a misdemeanor assault charge was simply asked, "How is the relationship now?" He explained, "Wonderful. Terrible then." His license was approved, and the gun board admonished him with a threat but refrained from further questioning: "Kids don't need to see parents arguing. If there is anything else, we'll pull [the license] in a second." As these cases suggest, the gun board appeared willing to approve and reinstate the licenses of African American and white claimants alike with regard to IPV; the difference was the extensive moralizing inquiries that the former, but not the latter, experienced as a condition of their licenses.

As the public policy scholar Michael Lipsky reminds us, "The administration of public welfare has been notorious for the psychological burdens clients have to bear. These include the degradation implicit in inquiries into sexual behavior, childbearing preferences, childrearing practices, friendship patterns, and persistent assumptions of fraud and dishonesty."[68] The gun board's inquiries into the private matters of African American men complements state penetration into the private sphere of marginalized women,[69] revealing that the state's welfare interest in the private sphere extends to men as well.[70] Accordingly, the gun carry license can serve as a disciplinary mechanism for regulating private black lives: African American men were held accountable to the controlling image of the Deadbeat Dad, as they were given detailed lessons on financial responsibility and communication skills and were compelled to open up their private lives to scrutiny, accept blame for their shortcomings, and demonstrate appropriate priorities.

CONCLUSION

Much has been made of gun ownership and gun carrying as a *social* practice engaged in by millions of ordinary Americans and inflected by the politics of race, class, and gender. But it is not just a social practice; it is also a *state* practice.[71] Unlike past historical periods when gun access and use were more strictly regulated along racial lines,[72] today's gun laws are formally nondiscretionary regimes in which African American men can, and do, apply for and receive gun carry licenses. Lawfully armed African Americans are situated at the contradictory intersection of statutes that expand access to guns in line with gun populism and practices that criminalize people of color, especially men, in line with gun militarism. In seeking permission to carry a gun, such claimants push the racial/gender boundaries of legitimate violence that have been historically endorsed and enforced by state actors at local, state, and federal levels.

Michigan's gun boards—which were public at the time of my observations—provided a rare and valuable opportunity to unravel how administrators navigate gun populism versus gun militarism as they stake out the boundaries of legitimate violence. Working at the racialized crossroads of impunity and criminalization, gun board administrators improvised degradation ceremonies that place African American men in a zone of provisional citizenship. My observations show that when African Americans, particularly African American men, seek and receive gun licenses, they did not do so on the same terms as other license-seekers. Not only were African American men disproportionately called in to appear at the gun boards I observed, but they also were exposed to a different set of racialized demands in order to obtain a license. Gun board administrators—themselves largely drawn from law enforcement—nimbly and subtly deployed stereotypes and expectations as an implicit condition of the gun carry license. These stereotypes and expectations often reflected broader racialized tropes, such as the controlling images of the Thug and the Deadbeat Dad, and they were used to impart "lessons"[73] to African American men: both explicit instructions on how to conduct themselves as gun carry licensees as well as more implicit discipline regarding their position at the bottom of the racial/gender hierarchy. Incentivized by a license to carry a gun, in turn, African American men were encouraged to internalize controlling images.

By the end of 2015, Michigan gun board meetings closed their doors to the public, and gun carry licensing was reorganized within the state. Administrative gun licensing decisions are now made by the Michigan State Police, and all appeals are now directed through the county court system. The move was supported by gun rights proponents within the state, who rightly observed uneven enforcement and inconsistent protocols across Michigan counties. Gun rights advocates, however, overlooked a critical issue at play in the debate regarding Michigan's gun boards: that unequal treatment—especially along the lines of race—is not restricted to gun boards but shapes the criminal justice system from the inside out. The "solution" of centralizing decisions and routing them into county courts may well do more to strengthen, rather than unravel, the dynamics laid out here. Without recognizing the kinds of gun talk— that is, gun militarism and gun populism—that percolate through the state and society to facilitate the disparities laid out here, we merely transpose the problem. We don't solve it.

CONCLUSION

OUR GUN TALK

Police work is a mechanism for the distribution of situationally justified force in society. . . . Our expectation that policemen will use force, coupled by our refusals to state clearly what we mean by it (aside from sanctimonious homilies), smacks of more than a bit of perversity.

—Egon Bittner, *The Functions of the Police in Modern Society* (1973)

"Community policing" is often treated as standard police reform, a set of best policing practices aimed at enhancing police-community relations and, as a result, the legitimacy of public law enforcement. But history instructs otherwise. The historian Khalil Gibran Muhammad suggests that one of the earliest incantations for community policing came not from police administrators but from black residents in Philadelphia in the 1920s and 1930s.[1] In that context, the problem was slightly different from what would characterize calls for reform in the 1990s and beyond, as saturation policing in black communities was not yet administratively possible or politically imaginable. At that point in policing history, police were a simultaneously all-too-absent and all-too-aggressive force in black communities, at the ready to stop, harass, assault, and arrest community members but otherwise permissive in allowing vice institutions patronized by whites to disrupt social order. To that end, some middle-class black reformers argued that community watch groups—truly independent of the police, though not necessarily independent of the punitive spirit of the law—needed to step in to address the disorder that state-organized police not only failed to ameliorate but often aggravated.

Since the 1920s and 1930s, this impetus within African American communities would materialize in different forms, with distinctive tools, in varying relations to law enforcement, and with particular politics—including the Deacons for Defense,[2] the Black Panthers,[3] gangs such as the Divine Knights,[4] the Huey Newton Gun Club, Ceasefire's Violence Interrupters,[5] Brothers Changing the Hood,[6] and the Detroit 300,[7] to name a few. Each of these groups extends community policing beyond the comfortable arenas of graffiti, loitering, vandalism, and other examples of quality of life infractions that are often delegated to community volunteers by public law enforcement.[8] Instead, these groups engaged in the core of policing: the regulation of violence, in terms of both the regulation of criminal violence and also the exercise of legitimate violence. Regardless of whether these groups were armed (for example, peacekeeping groups like the Violence Interrupters and Brothers Changing the Hood are not armed, though they regularly insert themselves in the line of gun fire), they often focused on reducing community violence as a core aspect of their work.

Today, gun carriers also inhabit this murky space of legitimate violence, where the prerogatives of citizenship intersect with those of the state, and where community policing and policing by the community become blurred. Gun ownership and carry is overwhelmingly motivated by protection, and millions of Americans own and carry guns because they see them not just as tools to fight crime but also as a stopgap for a slow or ineffective police response. Although police reformers debate the efficacy of different initiatives and agendas, Americans are turning to guns as a measure to directly address insecurities in their lives.

Americans may well believe that the state is weak and frail, and take action—such as arming themselves—accordingly. But these individual orientations and practices do not necessarily add up to a further weakened state: as this book's analysis of gun populism suggests, the proliferation of lawful guns may embolden, rather than undermine, police prerogatives. This is why a "Molon Labe" (defiant gunspeak that dares state agents to "Come and Take it") bumper sticker next to a "Blue Lives

Matter" sticker is not at all contradictory—in today's political terrain, they can be mutually reinforcing.

But much like the police reforms that policymakers debate, the consequences of choosing to carry a gun have different consequences for different people. As one chief told me, "we don't all live life according to the same fee schedule." Though Philando Castile carried his gun for protection, the police officer who killed Castile in front of his daughter and fiancée could only see Castile's gun as indicating a violent threat. It was, of course, not just the gun that framed Castile as a violent threat rather than the generous school cafeteria supervisor that he was.[9] The social context in which his gun became dangerous was already overdetermined by practices and sensibilities—including structural racism, implicit bias, and racial profiling—that labeled Castile as a criminal.

In the aftermath of Castile's killing, as well as the killing of other boys and men of color by police, public debate has focused on police reforms that can retrain police to perceive threats differently and respond to them in ways that deescalate the potential for violent confrontation. Indeed, the past half century of U.S. policing is replete with high-minded policy reforms, data-driven law enforcement approaches, and theory-oriented policing paradigms that have aimed to reshape how police think about and carry out their everyday jobs. Community policing, hot spot policing, preventative policing, big data policing, broken windows policing, twenty-first-century policing—these initiatives promise a more effective, a less force-reliant, and a more legitimate police.

Such police reforms are often intuitively appealing because they tend to circumvent an uncomfortable impasse that the police ethnographer Egon Bittner identified decades ago. Writing about the core functions of public law enforcement, Bittner reminds us that police do two things: public law enforcement provides an institutional mechanism for the public to seek out "situationally justified use of force" (i.e., protective violence), and public law enforcement also allows the public to opt out of the core dilemma of delineating legitimate from criminal violence. Police reforms often fit well with these "perverse" (Bittner's term) public expectations: With just a little more training, a little kinder language, and a bit more data analysis, we will be able to circumvent the very issue that makes police both *inherently necessary* and *inherently problematic* in peaceful, or at least peace-wanting, democratic societies: their state-sanctioned capacity for legitimate violence.

Whether or not we can ultimately "train" our way out of this dilemma (and the effectiveness of much training remains unclear),[10] this book wagers that as long as we treat the public and private wielding of violence as separate phenomena, we are unlikely to move forward in our public debates and public policies about either. Accordingly, this book responds to Bittner's insights by unraveling the crucial points at which private and public faces of legitimate violence intertwine. In refusing to treat the politics of guns and the politics of the police as separate, this book moves beyond the obvious point that American gun culture disrupts any strict monopoly the U.S. state would have on legitimate violence. Instead, it focuses on how distinctive racial logics—gun militarism and gun populism—shape legitimate violence across state and society.

THE STATE OF GUN POLICY

According to CDC data, roughly 15,000 gun homicides and 100,000 gun injuries took place in 2017, as well as nearly 24,000 gun suicides.[11] These are overwhelming numbers—so much so that they have overwhelmed the terms of the gun debate as powerful facts that should speak for themselves.[12] These devastating facts and figures on gun violence are mobilized by both sides (but especially the gun control side) as a means to bear witness to a society-wide tragedy that exceeds words. But like the grisly war photographs[13] that were believed at one time to carry a straightforward and undeniable "truth" about the horror of war's violence, these figures hold the allure of truth, but they do not deliver. Instead, these figures are themselves distortions insofar as they require decontextualization and social leveling for their rhetorical force.

Gun violence, after all, is not an epidemic that can strike anyone, anywhere, with the same force. It is patterned, concentrated, systematic. A seven-year-old white girl in Cadillac, Michigan, sitting in her classroom faces gun terror in an era of school shootings, but she does not face the same gun terror as a thirteen-year-old African American boy in Detroit walking home from school.[14] That difference most certainly is shaped by socioeconomic inequality, differences in social cohesion between small-town and urban America, the persistent "gender gap" in violent offending and violent victimization, as well as racial differences in exposure to violent crime. But the difference is also shaped by dramatically different relationships to the state. Some children view police as heroic adults who will save them from a terrifying act of gun violence; other children, by contrast, see police as yet another potential source of terrifying gun violence rendering them vulnerable. After all, one-third of all Americans killed by strangers *are killed by police*,[15] and the roughly one thousand deaths that police perpetrate every year disproportionately leave African Americans, Native Americans, and, to a lesser extent, Latinos as fatal casualties. Whose gun terror is ameliorated by the promise of police protection versus aggravated by the threat of police violence?

It is perhaps a uniquely American frustration that gun policy in itself cannot "solve" the problem of gun violence; other countries, after all, have benefited from seemingly simple, straightforward gun policy prescriptions. But the United States is not like other countries. The United States' racial politics of policing and protection may well explain why many of these policies are all but impossible to pass in the United States, and even if they were passed, their implementation would be indelibly inflected by the politics of race that distinctively shape how legitimate violence is organized within the United States. In other words, while gun policy may often appear to center on color-blind questions about who can purchase guns, who can carry them, and what kinds of guns they can own, its foundation in racial presumptions about legitimate violence makes the promise of gun policy fundamentally different in the United States than in other places.

Accordingly, ideas—racialized ideas—about policing shape the social life of guns and the social imagination surrounding gun policy. This perhaps seems self-evident, but in most gun debates in the United States, the significance of the police—both as a practice and as an institution—has been surgically removed and sanitized. Public law enforcement emerges at the crime scene in the aftermath of a heinous act of gun violence. Police officers appear as detectives and investigators, using old-school grit to crack the coldest of cases. They are the voice boxes of doom when called on to explain to the public the latest instance of gun tragedy. In all of these instances, though, police are on the sidelines of gun violence, responding after the fact.

Police, however, are not merely on the sidelines of the gun debate. This is not only because they contribute to a sizable portion of gun deaths that disproportionately harm already vulnerable communities. It is also because they are wrapped up—professionally, ethically, and practically—in the broader politics of legitimate violence, a politics that includes the gun debate but far exceeds it. Public law enforcement is central to how gun policy is imagined and debated, and public law enforcement is central to how gun policy is executed on the ground. The gun debate rests on a whole host of presumptions about how the police will engage and enforce gun laws. At the very least, those of us invested in the politics of guns should recognize the power of these presumptions in providing the foundation for how we debate guns in society.

But, as the popularity of gun carry in the United States attests, public law enforcement does not strictly monopolize policing. This commonplace observation among law and society scholars, criminologists, and sociologists studying the police is crucial for recognizing the links between debates about public law enforcement and debates about guns. This book expands on this observation and provides a set of conceptual tools to better understand how debates about guns, on the one hand, and the police, on the other hand, are interconnected through the broader politics of race in which they are embedded. This book develops the term *gun talk* to capture the ways in which guns appear as symbolically and practically weighty objects in a variety of settings: to promote the Second Amendment; to imagine the threat of urban superpredators; to justify "tough on crime" approaches to law enforcement; to articulate newfound fears associated with active shootings; to celebrate the civilian-cum-first-responders who don guns; to condemn elites who arrogantly and ignorantly promulgate policies they do not understand; to recognize that civilians necessarily deserve the stopgap of self-defense amid the inability of police to protect *everyone*; and to decide who has crossed the threshold of deservingness in order to be able to defend oneself. Gun talk always contains assumptions about which kinds of gun use are legitimate versus criminal, about who figures as legitimate versus criminal users of guns, and about, ultimately, how guns serve as *threats* to social order versus *shields* of social order.

If gun talk communicates sensibilities about the proper place of guns in society, it necessarily looks different depending on *who* is doing the talking and *in what context*. In this book, I have focused on gun talk as related to public law enforcement, analyzing how those invested in gun politics understand and engage public law enforcement as well as how public law enforcement themselves understand and engage with gun politics and policies. Accordingly, the book focuses on key "brokers" that shape the symbolic politics of legitimate violence and the practical access to legitimate violence with respect to firearms: the National Rifle Association; police chiefs across Arizona, California, and Michigan; and gun board administrators in Michigan. The variety of these brokers illuminates that the relationship between "policing" and "guns" far exceeds public law enforcement proper. Through gun talk, organizations and actors *outside* of the state, such as the NRA, symbolically (and, in limited cases, materially) broker the legitimate violence of state agents. Likewise, through gun talk, police chiefs broker legitimate violence as they struggle to advance the goals of their respective jurisdictions, the professional agenda of the police as a profession, and the interests of the publics that they serve. And finally, gun board administrators put gun talk into action by brokering private civilian access to legitimate violence as they adjudicate the terms on which people looking to carry guns legally can do so.

These different points of brokerage reveal a pattern in how gun talk is structured—a pattern that reflects the bifurcated racialization of legitimate violence in American society. This pattern is illuminated by the two ways that gun talk tends to take shape: gun militarism and gun populism. As this book details, gun militarism captures a particular understanding of legitimate violence: namely, a state monopoly on legitimate violence aimed at an assertion of unequal relations of racial domination. Here, the emphasis is on disarming criminal gun users as *objects* of policing.

But gun militarism is not the only form of gun talk. As a counterpoint to gun militarism, gun populism draws on an embrace of "the people" and a deep suspicion of elites,[16] especially elite lawmakers who aim to regulate gun access in the United States. Gun populism centers on "law-abiding" Americans (often, though not exclusively, imagined as white, middle-class men), who are not *objects* of policing but *agents* of policing. From the perspective of gun populism, private civilian access to and enactment of legitimate violence is reflective of a broadened civic duty in a color-blind pursuit of social order. Under gun populism, armed private civilians are thus imagined as generative of social order, rather than a threat to stability (as under gun militarism). Gun militarism and gun populism are both deeply embedded in the United States' long historical legacy and ongoing politics of white supremacy and racial inequality, and they appear in contemporary discussions about gun policy as coexisting, and mutually reinforcing, forms of gun talk.

OUR GUN TALK

The NRA, police chiefs, and gun licensing officials are not the only brokers in legitimate violence. As ordinary people who can vote, choose whether to dial 911, decide on what terms and with what intentions we carry firearms, and deliberate about how we talk about guns, we are brokers, too. This means we can redraw the lines of the gun debate, rethink our own gun talk, and, in doing so, transform the terms that we have received as part of the cultural, racial, and sociolegal baggage of what it means to grow up in the contemporary United States.

Every public debate over guns provides an opportunity to reinforce gun talk as we know it—or to reinvent it. At acute moments of public despair, this may not seem possible. For example, in the aftermath of both the 2017 Las Vegas mass shooting, which left fifty-eight concertgoers and first responders dead and an unfathomable 851 injured, and the 2018 Parkland mass shooting, which left seventeen students and teachers dead and seventeen injured, headlines across the country declared that "The Gun Fight Is Over and the Gun-Rights Crowd Won" (*Detroit Free Press*),[17] "Culture Is All That's Left When Gun Policy Battles Become Pointless" (*Reason Magazine*),[18] and even "The Gun Debate That Wasn't" (CNN).[19] The vast majority of the time, Americans have fixated on the same policy elements, often spurred by high-profile and heinous, but statistically unusual, active shootings. Accordingly, the gun debate on both sides tends to recycle familiar talking points, while those already disproportionately impacted by gun violence by virtue of their racial standing within society (in intersection with class, gender, and other lines of difference) are also disproportionately silenced within the gun debate.

Noting the curious absence of voices of color in public debates about guns, gun violence experts such as Jooyoung Lee, Joseph Richardson Jr., and Desmond Patton[20] have pressed for broadening the gun debate to recognize gun violence in all its forms: active shootings, gang-related violence, negligent gun violence, and gun violence deemed justifiable by the state. But as the sociologist Nikki Jones illustrates in her ethnography of gun violence prevention efforts in a San Francisco neighborhood,[21] when swallowed up by the mantra of "tough on crime" politics, initiatives to fight gun violence stand to do much harm to communities of color. Recall Eve Ewing's insistence that gun policies may well compound the vulnerability of the very victims—boys and men of color—disproportionately likely to be victim of gun violence. As she notes, "Stricter gun laws, in this community, are not going to help address the reasons the young people were carrying the guns. They need mentors, mental health care, better schools, and jobs. Their families need support."[22]

This book suggests that there are three paths we may choose, then, as we struggle to address gun violence in society.

First, we can continue to debate gun politics and the politics of the police as separate concerns, refusing to see how the politics of race shapes *both* of these issues in ways that add up to the broader question of legitimate violence in American society. This path will not allow us to address the deeper issues driving both sets of politics, but neither will it require us to step outside of the comfortable confines of the current terms of debates about guns, on the one hand, and police, on the other. This path does not require that Americans stretch our minds (or expand our hearts) to see how the collision between gun politics and the politics of the police can lead to harm—especially for people of color.

The second path takes a reform-minded approach to the politics of the police as deeply resonant with gun politics, but ultimately it understands the current dilemmas in terms of individual-level problems requiring individual-level solutions. Eager to identify the "bad apples" in law enforcement as well as ensure that "good guys" have guns while "bad guys" do not, such a perspective will largely entail championing color-blind initiatives like community policing, implicit bias training, mandatory minimum sentencing reform, emboldened background checks, and so forth. Existing criminological scholarship suggests that the efficacy of these kinds of initiatives in addressing the problems of violence is largely shaped by the context in which they are enacted. Further, this individual-level focus will most certainly circumvent the broader issue of *legitimate violence* by focusing on reforms that largely aim to address *criminal or illegitimate violence*.

Only the third path—one that considers gun politics and the politics of the police as co-constitutive—can meaningfully advance public debates and public policy about the place of gun violence, whether legitimate or criminal, in American society. To treat these politics as co-constitutive means acknowledging the historical backdrop that intertwines them, accounting for the discursive and structural apparatuses in which they are interlocked, and reckoning with the mutual interests of those on whose behalf such politics are wagered. It means recognizing the association of blackness with criminality and whiteness with innocence as crucial for understanding the contemporary intersection of gun politics and the politics of the police. And as this book argues, this fundamentally means acknowledging *racialization* as a social process that undergirds how legitimate versus illegitimate violence is framed and, consequently, how violence is both disparately distributed and disparately impactful along the axis of race.

Together, gun populism and gun militarism form a foundation for reinforcing stark racial divisions surrounding how we live and how we die; how we disparately defend and protect lives; and whose deaths are recognized as worth grieving. There is an alternative to the reductive, unproductive debate about gun violence in the United States, and it starts by refusing to see the gun debate and police reform as isolated political projects.

METHODOLOGICAL APPROACH

What do we study when we study the police? The corpus of policing ethnographies in the twentieth and twenty-first centuries suggests that when we study the police, we study the peculiar organization of the dirty work of violence within the confines of democratic society; the unique organizational prerogatives, worldviews, and cultures attached to the state mandate of order maintenance and social control; the practical mechanisms by which one "becomes" a police officer; how police officers manage themselves vis-à-vis the public; and, finally, how policing does, or does not, reflect and reproduce broader identities and inequalities with respect to race, class, gender, sexuality, and other lines of difference. This scholarship reveals that ethnography is not merely a method of data *collection*; it is also an approach to data analysis that emphasizes the meaning-making mechanisms by which social worlds come to be reproduced and, at times, resisted. (Accordingly, I consider a range of methods—including observation and interviews—to be ethnographic by virtue of data analysis.)

Ethnography also implies a particular understanding of the self as researcher; the policing scholar Peter Kraska,[1] for example, notes that his own engagement in paramilitary policing forced him to edge up to the limits of his own comfort with his masculine sense of self. He writes frankly about the raw enjoyment he vicariously experienced by virtue of participating in a particular police culture. Other ethnographers vary to the extent that they trouble, versus trade on, the context of policing as a risky endeavor for an academic to engage and immerse oneself in. The untroubled version of this presentation of the ethnographic self in the context of policing studies resonates with what Victor Rios calls "cowboy ethnography": the tendency for ethnographers to treat their field sites as exotic spaces in which to excavate subtle and salacious "truths" that are hard won by virtue of the ethnographer's unique grit and perspicacity.[2] This framing of ethnography as a feat in which the highly trained and educated researcher enters an unfamiliar realm draws parallels between the ethnographic endeavor and the colonial impulse, whereby the heroism of ethnography is really the entitlement to exploitation. Indeed, as Rios and others note, the ethnographer often structurally occupies a privileged position vis-à-vis those whom the ethnographer studies; the ethnographer (and the ethnographer's career) is also the one most likely to benefit, while study participants may even be harmed by the ethnographer's "findings," or subsequent appropriations thereof. Policing ethnographers hint of cowboy ethnography in the heroic, uncanny, risky, and even dangerous "tales from the field" they tell, but with a twist: the power differential between police and the people who study police is never clear, but it is most certainly not reducible to the prototypical cowboy ethnography involving the white, middle-class, educated suburbanite going "native" in a poor community of color.

As that white, middle-class, educated suburbanite, I found that my own encounters with police could not be pigeonholed into the schematics that sociologists typically use to outline researcher positionality vis-à-vis research subjects. In some cases, I found myself indeed facing interviewees who wielded profound power, especially as they did exactly what I asked them to do: speak frankly about the intersection of guns and policing. I recall one chief in particular who, during an interview, explicitly and cruelly disparaged people killed by the police and their families; it was unusually brash and disrespectful compared to every other chief I had interviewed. In a split second, I had to decide whether to push and probe, and how far, or to simply let the comments hang in the air, juggling the need to maintain rapport, maintain the data-collection process, and—most immediately—preserve my own composure, especially of my often overly expressive face. Other times, though, it was not me but my interviewee who had to fight the urge to squirm. If many police chiefs wielded the social and structural power to say what they wanted and how they wanted to say it and had practice doing so as the public face of their departments, a handful of chiefs seemed uneasy, not so much with the subject content but with the prospect of speaking about their life's work. These were generally chiefs in smaller, more remote, and more insular towns, far removed from the concerns of the so-called big-city chiefs. They had less practice in interacting with the public; they often became a chief not because they had long aspired to be one but because the vacancy was open and they could competently fill it; they disliked the politics of policing. Other chiefs, nevertheless, clearly relished talking to me *because of* the politics; through their responses to my questions, these chiefs explicitly and implicitly recruited me to the project of expanding gun rights, of restricting gun access, or—especially in California—of identifying the hypocrisy of lawmakers. And finally, for a handful of chiefs, I was neither a threat nor an opportunity—I was simply an irritation; I recall one chief in particular who buried his head in paperwork as I asked him questions, signing documents as he blurted out pithy responses. Rather than a researcher or a writer, I was just another member of the public, spreading police resources thin by posing yet another request for service.

The broader conversations in sociology about researcher positionality tend to underplay these more nuanced power dynamics that unravel in the context of data collection—as do human ethics review boards through which this project was vetted at the University of Toronto, the University of California, Irvine, and the University of Arizona. In the case of human ethics review boards, the project's approval required that I neither record police nor take signatures nor collect any identifiable data that could link data to individual chiefs. In addition to anonymizing biographical details that chiefs provided, I reminded them as part of the informed consent process that they could and should be guarded with any details that could identify them. I write "reminded" here instead of "informed" (as in "informed consent") because police are almost always aware that they speak to the public at their own discretion, as are they aware of the stakes of speaking to the public, especially during the time period (2014–2017) in which these interviews were conducted. Indeed, in stark contrast to the research subject imagined by human ethics boards as deeply unaware of the risks (and, at times, rewards) of research participation, chiefs generally well understood what they were getting into. Interestingly, it was in the state where police had the *most* political power[3]—California—that police were most inquisitive with regard to me, my motivations, and my research project. One chief, I recall, participated only after I assured him that the research was not funded by George Soros or his ilk. Other California chiefs opened the interview by remarking on the vulnerability that they were exposing themselves to by virtue of talking to me—a seemingly absent concern in Arizona and Michigan. To the extent that California is popularly understood as a highly politicized "lawsuit capital of the country" (as one chief noted) and that chiefs I interviewed largely spoke out against the liberal consensus in the state, they were absolutely justified in their concerns. Power, risk, vulnerability—these are not axes that can be anticipated before research starts (as human ethics boards assume), nor could they be homogenized into a binary relationship between the researcher and her subjects (as even critics of cowboy ethnography often assume).

• • •

Although police ethnographers have provided a wealth of insight, especially on the racial dynamics of urban policing, they tend to focus on large, urban police departments that are not representative of the vast majority of police departments, which are located in small or medium-sized rural and suburban areas. My choice to engage in a variety of methods conducive to ethnographic analysis—in-depth reading of newspaper accounts and other media related to the National Rifle Association's engagement with law enforcement; in-depth interviews with police chiefs in Arizona, California, and Michigan; and observations of gun boards in Michigan—reflects my attention to how meanings about gun violence, gun politics, gun policy, and gun law enforcement are forged in tandem, as well as a choice to capture the rich variations within and across different policing contexts within the United States.

Regarding my observations of gun licensing procedures, I was limited in terms of data availability; gun records are generally sealed from Freedom of Information Act requests, and most gun licensing decisions happen behind closed doors, beyond the purview of the public. Michigan's gun board system—though now defunct—provided a crucial opportunity while it existed to understand not just what police *thought* but also what they *did* with respect to staking out the boundaries of legitimate violence in the form of lawfully carried guns. To collect data, I attended meetings of two county-level gun boards in Metro Detroit for five months in 2014. During my research, Wayne County met twice a month for morning and afternoon sessions; Oakland County met once a month for a morning session. As notetaking was not disruptive, I wrote detailed synopses of each case, including the demographics of the prospective licensee (race, gender, age); the initial sanction (denial, suspension, or revocation); the reason the claimant was called to the gun board (e.g., a disqualifying arrest, conviction, or referral); the conversation between gun board members and the claimant; and the outcome (approval, denial, suspension, revocation, or pending/reschedule). I compiled a database of 936 cases (106 from Oakland, 830 from Wayne) through my observations, treating each individual called before a gun board as a separate case. Most cases were resolved within minutes, depending on the presentation of proper paperwork and the eagerness of administrators to accelerate decisions, but some cases lasted as long as thirty minutes. I categorized the sanctions attached to these cases according to the emergent analytical themes: procedural pains; denials/threat of denial; and arrest/threat of arrest. See table 1.

The two county-level gun boards I studied served different populations: an urban, economically depressed area, which includes Detroit, that is disproportionately poor and African American (Wayne County) and a wealthier, whiter suburb (Oakland County). Nevertheless, gun carrying is common in both Wayne County and Oakland County. In these two counties, African Americans are issued concealed pistol licenses at rates slightly higher than their population rates, based on 2013 CPL data obtained from the Michigan State Police. However, even accounting for this slight increase in rates, African Americans still com-

TABLE 1. Gun Board Cases by Analytical Theme

	Total Cases	Procedural Pains (% of Cases)	Denial / Threat of Denial (% of Cases)	Arrest / Threat of Arrest (% of Cases)
Wayne County	830	340 (41%)	75 (9%)	24 (3%)
Oakland County	106	40 (38%)	17 (16%)	1 (1%)

TABLE 2. African American Representation at Gun Board Cases

	Wayne County	Oakland County
African American % of Population	40	14.4
African American % of Issued Gun Licenses (2013 MSP data)	43	21
African American % of Those Called to Gun Board (2014 observational data)	72	58

prised a disproportionate number of claimants called to gun board. See table 2. Note that though the population of Wayne County was about 1.5 times that of Oakland County, about *eight times* the number of cases were processed at the Wayne County gun board meetings. Because people are called to gun board because of contact with the criminal justice system, this suggests Wayne County residents' greater exposure to the criminal justice system.

If gun board observations zeroed in on one specific context (Metro Detroit), interviews with police chiefs allowed me insight into a diversity of jurisdictions across three states. Although most studies of policing tend to focus on one, or a handful, of jurisdictions, this research engages chiefs across more than six dozen jurisdictions, peeling away at the social reality that most police departments do not look like the kinds of departments featured in most ethnographic studies of policing. To do so, however, I would not be able to engage in the preferred method for qualitatively studying police (that is, embedded ethnography) but, instead, would have to rely on a different method: in-depth interviews. In some ways, my choice in research methods no doubt reflected the *practical exigencies* of my own research objectives.

That said, interviews were not chosen simply for their practical convenience. Interviews, as the sociologist Allison Pugh has argued,[4] allow researchers to tap into emotional valences, social anxieties, and wrought expectations in ways that neither participant observation nor survey methods facilitate. Because interviews permit researchers to understand not just *how* research subjects feel but also "how it feels to feel that way,"[5] interviews give researchers a glimpse into the "emotional landscape" (to use Pugh's term) in which a given culture is emboldened, bent, and sometimes broken by those for whom culture does work. It matters not just to recognize *that* police cope with conflicting cultural demands with respect their objectives and prerogatives as police—including "dueling"[6] racial frames that animate those demands, objectives, and prerogatives. It also matters *how* they coped—for example, that police conjure up emotions of domination, thrill, and adventure in some contexts (i.e., urban gun violence) but emotions of shame, devastation, and inadequacy in others (i.e., active shooters). Interviews allowed me a window—always framed and thus always partial—into how police feel as they navigate these imaginaries and how these imaginaries, in turn, are mobilized to reproduce (and at times resist) the conditions that fuel the conflicts police face.

Public law enforcement agencies are complex organizations. I chose to interview those at the top of these organizations: police chiefs. These are people within law enforcement who typically have decades of policing experience as well as unique insight into policy implementation as both managers and frontline workers. Their years of experience allowed me to examine how dramatic changes in gun policy over the past several decades have affected police. Furthermore, chiefs must interact with the public, especially on issues such as the use of force, and thus are illuminating interview subjects with regard to the popular justificatory narratives regarding gun policy, gun politics, and gun violence.

The interviews with police chiefs took place from 2014 to 2017 in Arizona (2017), California (2015–2016), and Michigan (2014–2015), a

TABLE 3. Geographic Breakdown of Interviewee Jurisdictions in Michigan (N = 23)

Greater Detroit Area	35%
Greater Lansing Area	22%
Western Michigan	30%
Northwestern Michigan	13%

TABLE 4. Geographic Breakdown of Interviewee Jurisdictions in California (N = 36)

Bay Area	19%
Greater Los Angeles Area	33%
Inland Empire	14%
Central Valley	33%

TABLE 5. Geographic Breakdown of Interviewee Jurisdictions in Arizona (N = 20)

Greater Tucson Area	15%
Greater Phoenix Area	15%
Greater Prescott Area	20%
Northern Arizona	25%
Southern Arizona	25%

period when issues of police use of lethal force became increasingly salient as a public issue. See tables 3, 4, and 5 for the geographic breakdown of sampled jurisdictions. Across all three states, the modal police chief was an older white man who had decades of police experience (see table 6). Note also that one in four police chiefs nationwide are members of the NRA,[7] whereas in my data, roughly one in six California and Michigan chiefs and one in three Arizona chiefs are members. These figures undercount support for the NRA, however; many more chiefs expressed support for the NRA (e.g., "I'm not a member of the NRA, but I think they do a lot in terms of education of kids about gun safety, education about hunting"). At the same time, NRA members also

TABLE 6. Chief Demographics by State

State	% Male	% White	Average Age
Arizona	95	95	52
California	97	86	53
Michigan	96	91	55

cited grievances and/or lukewarm feelings about the organization ("I'm a member of the NRA. . . . And I don't support everything they do, obviously, but I join them because I'm against the slippery slope" or "I'm not a big NRA guy, but I had to join to teach their courses").

In California, there are more than three hundred jurisdictions; I focused on jurisdictions from San Diego County in the south to Sacramento County in the north. In Arizona and Michigan (Lower Peninsula), because there are fewer jurisdictions, I contacted every public law enforcement agency with publicly available contact information. This resulted in a total sample of 20 Arizona chiefs (of 66 Arizona agencies contacted; 30 percent response rate); 23 Michigan chiefs (of 104 Michigan agencies contacted; 22 percent response rate); and 36 California chiefs (of 208 jurisdictions contacted; 17 percent response rate). I rarely received an explicit decline from police chiefs who did not participate in the study; therefore, I have no way of knowing whether chiefs received information about the study and decided against participating or whether my initial contact was screened and/or deleted (in many jurisdictions, the contact method was a generic police contact email or online form). Although the chiefs I interviewed hailed from diverse jurisdictions, my sample likely skewed toward jurisdictions that had a greater emphasis on community policing because such jurisdictions are more likely to have an online presence, provide a variety of ways of contacting police, actively monitor community input and contact, and be responsive to community communication. (For that matter, the high response rate in Arizona may very well reflect a broader, state-level cultural emphasis on police-community relationships as compared to the more professionalized police forces in states like California.) Interviewees' jurisdictions were also probably more likely to be, if not resource-rich, at least not resource-strapped; while I interviewed chiefs in many smaller and less resourced jurisdictions, at the very least, police chiefs needed the resource of time to meet with me. Lastly, my interviews likely skewed away from jurisdictions experiencing scandal or public relations crisis; while I did not contact chiefs who were currently under investigation, I had no way of knowing the internal politics of jurisdictions.[8]

As compared to survey methods and observation, interviews allowed police chiefs to frame their own politics of guns—whether private or public guns. Interviews were semi-structured to cover a consistent range of topics, allow for probing, and enable interviewees to direct the interview as warranted. Topics focused on policing background, experiences with violence (as victims and perpetrators), attitudes on and experiences with enforcing gun regulation, and opinions on gun policy measures (see appendix C for the interview guide). I gave each chief the choice of interview location; all but two chose to meet at their respective headquarters. Interviews lasted between thirty minutes and two hours.

As with all data, interview data are shaped by the context in which they are gathered. My presence and positionality, as well as the research setting, shaped how police chiefs talked about guns to me. At times, police chiefs imputed identification with me and my aims by alluding to my middle-class identity and my presumed affiliations with either side of the gun debate. Occasionally, police skirted on the edge of flirting, conveniently conjuring up examples that would put me in the role of girlfriend. Likely, my gender reduced any perceived threat I might pose to these men, but my race and class status aligned with the power structure—indeed, as a white woman in her early and mid-30s, I was the ideal victim on whose behalf projects of police protection are often enabled. Sitting at this particular juncture likely enhanced my ability to talk to largely "law-and-order" conservative men. But I was also aided by another set of factors: my previous research on guns gave me broad knowledge not just about policing and gun law enforcement but also about firearms and gun culture, and the conservative sensibilities that the latter entails. Somewhat unexpectedly—as I had not anticipated the deep overlap in sensibilities between police chiefs and concealed gun carriers—I pivoted my previous expertise on gun carriers to this new interview setting. Given that I am not a member of the law enforcement community, I relied on my knowledge about firearms, firearms law, and gun politics to establish rapport with interviewees. At times, this meant engaging in small talk regarding gun mechanics and self-defense techniques to demonstrate that I wasn't an outsider to the world of firearms; at other times, it meant referencing examples from my previous research on gun carriers to show that I understood the subtleties of gun law. Needless to say, I had much to learn from the police chiefs I interviewed, and thus I also built up my ability to probe over the course of my research, reviewing and recoding interviews throughout the process to identify and pursue emergent patterns.

It is tempting to present my interview skills as uniquely capable of collecting the kind of data I was able to obtain for this project. In some cases, I know that interviewees talked to and encouraged one another to talk to me—a feather in my cap that I was effectively interviewing them. At the same time, most of my interviews came from contacting prospective interviewees through publicly available contact information; though many surely searched the Internet for my online footprint, few had any reason to talk to me other than interest in the project. For that reason, I believe that the primary skill I brought as an interviewer wasn't my deftness in posing questions about guns, gun policy, and gun politics to police—it was that I had even bothered to ask these questions in the first place. Furthermore, despite an abiding liberal presumption—at least as I've seen among sociologists—that Americans don't or won't talk bluntly about "sensitive" topics such as race, police (and, in my experience, Americans more generally) are rather open about their attitudes on a wide variety of topics.[9]

· · ·

My positionality shaped not only how I served as a collector of data; it also shaped my analysis process. I take a perhaps uniquely ambivalent view on the American project of guns, gun culture, and gun politics. On the one hand, I am disgusted by the heinous distribution of gun violence in the United States: the nearly 40,000 gun deaths that occur annually, and the attempts of some gun advocates to discount nearly 24,000 (according to the CDC data for 2017) of these as suicide (read: not gun crime) and to discount the nearly fifteen-fold greater risk[10] of gun homicide victimization for black men as compared to white men as "black-on-black crime" (read: not "our" problem); the prevalence (if dramatically reduced over the past hundred years) of accidental or negligent shootings alongside some prosecutors' disparate readiness to criminally charge children of color and their parents for these acts; and the legalization, institutionalization, and normalization of justifiable homicide, especially in the form of Stand Your Ground laws that have been shown to increase the likelihood that alleged defensive shootings involving black victims will be deemed justifiable as compared to those involving white victims.[11] On the other hand, I am well aware that people must navigate social contexts not of their choosing. Unlike those tenured professors in academia who have one of the few remaining stable and secure jobs in an economy now defined by flexibility (if you are an apologist) and precariousness (if you are a realist), most Americans do not live in the proverbial gated community—or their gates are getting very, very rusty. Attempting to navigate their own personal realities of vulnerability, whether that be based in criminological, social, political, economic, or other kinds of insecurities, many Americans have made a calculated decision to include guns in their lives as a stopgap for the failure of other security apparatuses such as police. They recognize that having a gun entails certain risks—but so does not having a gun. And for many Americans, the political valence of guns—their association, for example, with white supremacy, police violence, and so forth—is crowded out by the personal valence of security they provide and the alternative meanings that are *also* associated with guns. If we look over the course of American history, they are not wrong: while guns have emboldened white supremacists and empowered projects of racial cleansing, guns have also provided a modicum of security, political power, and civic dignity to the most disenfranchised Americans in the form of the negro militias, the Deacons for Defense, the Black Panthers, and other groups. As Maj Toure, an African American and self-proclaimed "black guns matter" activist, notes of the ambivalence of the Second Amendment: "I don't give a f*** who they meant it for. It's mine now."[12]

Accordingly, I am aware (and readers should be aware, too) that as with any analysis, my personal background, my academic training, and my social standing have shaped my ability—sometimes as binoculars, sometimes as blinders—to cull contradictions, identify patterns, and suss out linkages across the micro-, meso-, and macro-level social dynamics shaping the intersection of the politics of the police and the politics of guns. During my data analysis for this book, I took an abductive approach that iteratively moved me through, and back to, multiple literatures that ranged from directly to obliquely related to my central research questions. This happened both while I was "in the field" (whether that meant sitting in a police chief's office or observing gun licensing proceedings) and long after it. Likewise, I turned to trusted colleagues—particularly colleagues I knew would bring a different background, both intellectual and personal, to bear on this project— to identify blind spots, encourage me to refine an analysis further, or to abandon a line of inquiry altogether. As such, my research approach embraced a "sociological double-consciousness approach." As the sociologists Victor Rios, Nikita Carney, and Jasmine Kelekay note, "The sociological double-consciousness approach urges researchers to acknowledge and operationalize our power-blindness and our implicit and explicit biases, and to embrace messy, kaleidoscopic data and experiences."[13]

I began the data analysis process as many qualitative researchers do—with the assistance of qualitative data analysis software, in this case Atlas.ti. I deductively developed codes in tandem with the major themes of the interview guide for interview data (e.g., "gun carry"; "gun bans"; and so forth) and with respect to major existing theories related to gun ownership, policing, and race for both interview and gun board observation data. Nevertheless, I largely developed my codebook based on coding and recoding of my data, adding codes to reflect empirically derived themes. Furthermore, my analysis approach reflected the different kinds of qualitative data I used in this study; for the nearly one thousand gun board cases I analyzed, it was easier to develop clear-cut categorizations of different kinds of cases based on violation, demographics of the claimants, and outcomes. For this reason, I relied more on quantitative descriptors when presenting these data as compared to the interview data. Alternatively, the seventy-nine chiefs I interviewed across three states provided an empirically robust window into the politics of guns from the perspective of police, but this was a theoretically motivated, rather than empirically representative, sample of police chiefs. Accordingly, I relied more heavily on qualitative descriptors as compared to my discussion of gun board data to emphasize the processes and patterns in meaning-making that characterized the multiple ways that police chiefs wrestled with the intersection of guns and policing.

While I produced a neat if elaborate coding scheme that helped me to arrange data points into a coherent, book-length argument, I became increasingly aware of the reality that any particular sociological point of mine was almost always eclipsed by the singularity of any particular data point—especially with regard to the interview data. After all, each of us contains multitudes—even, perhaps especially, the police chiefs who spend much of their time distilling the complexities of policing for both their agencies and the outside world.

As I grappled with what this meant for data analysis, I decided to attend a creative writing workshop, largely with the intent of enhancing my writing techniques. But as that workshop delved deeper into questions of narrative, tone, and mood, I grew increasingly aware of the God Trick—to use the feminist theorist Donna Haraway's term[14]— often embedded in ethnographic writing, or what the policing ethnographer John Van Maanen labels the realist tone.[15] I came to appreciate that rather than merely allowing the reader into an unfamiliar world, ethnographic writing just as much serves to construct the author as intellectual—such that the narrative objective is often not just about providing a particular experience for the reader; it is also about advancing the career goals of the author by consolidating her "voice" as an intellectual (hence the professional tragedy that academics may feel compelled to make decisions about their first books based on tenure expectations rather than intellectual ingenuity).

This creative writing workshop also provided the tools to escape this conundrum. It gave me a different approach to thinking about the analytical process, one in which I could pause to prioritize the narrative voice of respondents before leveling up that voice into my own analysis. I integrated a new stage into my data analysis process; after coding and writing analytical memos about major themes and trends within the coded data, I opted to write composite memos that illustrated—based on key data, but in narrativized, composite form—the core dynamics I was uncovering in my analysis. Doing so allowed me an opportunity to play with different narrative voices and to inhabit the worldviews of interviewees in a different way. It allowed me to differently imagine myself as author; in embracing this move, my goal was not simply to "give voice" to my research participants but also to force myself to keep coming back to the social world they inhabited. These memos helped ensure that my analysis would not pull the data "off the rails" of the social realities I intended to capture.

To illustrate, then, I close this methodological appendix with three of these memos: one on gun militarism, one on gun populism, and one on police reform. If abductive analysis places emphasis on theoretically resolving contradictions and ambiguities within data as a means of generating sociological insight, then I found that these narrative memos provided a practical means of wrestling with these contradictions and ambiguities, forcing me to sit with them rather than "jump the gun" to analytical resolution. To be clear: I wrote these memos as evocative, messy, deeply ambivalent—with the goal not of "resolving" them through a neat sociological analysis but by providing space to sit with the discomfort that these data necessarily pose. They are composites of multiple chiefs, rather than reflecting a single research subject or interviewee. As such, these memos harness the power of fiction in the service of data analysis. As envisioned by the sociologists Josh Page and Phil Goodman, "Fiction is suffused with disruptive potential; it can force us to question assumptions that affect how we elicit and interpret research subjects' stories."[16] Sociologists, by virtue of the work they do, tend to cut up social lives and social worlds into discrete data points, but narrativizing, and renarrativizing, these data points provide a crucial means to reckon with the inherent discomfort of the sociological enterprise in the hopes of forging a more genuine sociology.

On Gun Militarism: Discarded Lives

Chief Richardson grew up in a house of strict discipline. He knew never to touch his father's gun, let alone play with it. He rode dirt bikes. He played in the woods. He watched good old spaghetti Westerns and the early cop shows, like *Adam-12*. He still liked the drama of good and evil, but he hated the gratuitous violence. He doesn't like to watch a whole lot of television anymore.

After all, he had spent enough years working in the high-crime, high-minority town, and he had spent many years teaching in the police academy. He found the change palpable, especially over the last few years. So much killing. Is it violent video games? Social media? These days, people don't understand that guns kill. They think guns are cool, that you pick one up, shoot off a few rounds, and it's like a movie. They don't realize that this is permanent. This isn't a video game, where you can kill an alien 100 times, and then you regenerate.

He felt older than the passing years, and had a harder and harder time understanding the people he ran into on the job, the suspects, the parents, the kids. He could even see it in the younger police recruits who are used to video-game violence: the kids watch the media that glorifies guns, they play the video games, and they all want to have toy guns, BB guns, air softs. And sometimes even real guns, too. That's why he wanted to bring back the most severe punishments, across the board, for anything involving a gun *to teach these damn kids a lesson.*

But because he knew he was dealing with kids who didn't know any better, sometimes he managed to offer some fatherly—stern fatherly—compassion. After all, he had responded recently to a weapons call. Someone saw a weapon—a brandished weapon. The caller didn't realize that it was just thirteen-year-olds, three African American kids, playing. He arrived on the scene, and two of the boys ran off, leaving one of the boys frozen in step, clutching the gun in his hands. Deer in the Headlights. The boy tried to turn toward the chief, tried to mouth words, tried to get something to come out that was audible, but the boy was just too stunned. And the chief sensed this. So he tried to jolt him back to life in the best way he knew: "One more step, and I'm going to drop you." The chief liked to remind himself that he could have, and he told himself he would have been in the right, to shoot. But he didn't have to; the boy let go of the gun.

His dilemma came down to this: how do we get the kid who sees guns as so glamorous, and fun, and cool to not grow up to be a piece of crap who is threatening people's lives?

His very first time in court was for an arraignment for a kid who had been charged with murder in the second degree. For the *second time.* It took a few minutes for the judge to understand that this was his second trial for second-degree murder in less than a year because the kid got probation. The shock of that moment in court still stunned him. Over time, he only became surer of it: *those people need to go away. They need to be gone. If we are not going to incapacitate those people, what is the point of our prison system?* As far as he could tell, there was only one answer: zero tolerance for a gun that crosses the line, and truth in sentencing.

He felt like his whole career was learning a lesson over, and over, and over that he still couldn't totally accept: the capacity of so many people to have such a total disregard for the value of life, and the incapacity of the criminal justice system to do much at all about it.

On Gun Populism: Shame on Us

Though the sting had dulled over the years, the snap of Chief Clarkson's gun in his holster still pricked him with failure.

He wasn't directly involved. As luck would have it, the tragedy had just barely missed him: he was working in Colorado at the time, and had friends who were there, but his agency hadn't been part of the response that day. He hadn't personally secured the exterior of the suddenly infamous high school. He hadn't waited for a specialized unit, one that everyone was sure had specifically trained for these kinds of events (though he hated calling them "events"), one that would certainly minimize the foul scene playing out in the mind of every parent who waited at the caution tape staked out in the muddy April soil. He hadn't had to explain to these parents that the police knew how to handle what was going on, that they were trained to negotiate in these kinds of circumstances, and that the experts would do their jobs. He hadn't had to stand there, he hadn't had to hear the kids screaming, and he hadn't had to wonder at that visceral moment whether police really knew what they were doing.

Back then, he was Officer Clarkson, not Chief Clarkson. At that early point in his career, he hadn't trained other officers, he hadn't been on SWAT, and he certainly hadn't had a hand in directing his agency's policy on responses to shooting massacres. That would all come later.

Looking back on that April day, though, Clarkson can't help but kick himself. He knew the protocol wasn't right. They all knew it wasn't right. And they all felt the same sense of failure, of having failed society, because they let all those kids down.

Twenty years later, he still couldn't shake the feeling of stinging *failure*.

That sting had followed him, and probably made him more apprehensive than he otherwise would be about "following the rules" when he got tested in the field. He hadn't had the chance to make a whole lot of life-or-death decisions while on the force—his entire career had been spent in affluent suburban areas and sleepy rural towns, the kinds of places where everyone knows there just isn't a whole lot of violence. Normal places with normal people. Well, maybe not so normal. He'd never look at a place as normal again, not after Columbine, then Virginia Tech, then Aurora, then Sandy Hook, then Orlando, then San Bernardino.

Despite the appearance of complacency that he had developed over his years of policing sleepy suburbs and small towns, he had reckoned with the fact that there *is* a time, a place, and a reason to shoot first: and that time was April 20, 1999; that place was Columbine High School; and that reason was the unshakable weight of having contributed to the screaming, the bleeding, the dying, all because you were waiting for someone else to arrive. That's no time to sit around and "secure the area." He was done with passing responsibility on to someone else. He felt, they all felt, like failures—and that's because they *were* failures.

So he found it offensive, intolerable, that some people thought they could fix this just with gun control. *They* let society down. *They* were the ones who failed. Background checks were not useless, not at all, and it's true that the teachers, the counselors, and even the parents, too, could have done something to prevent all of this. But if it wasn't guns, it would have been bombs. Or cars. Or something else. Look at France! And whatever that was, the police—not the parents, not the teachers, not the counselors, not even the gun carriers, although he was happy to have their help if he needed it—were really the only ones *absolutely obligated to do something.* Because when it came right down to it, he knew that police are the only first responders, the only ones responsible for those casualties counts. That's not to say police can save everyone. But if police abdicate their responsibility to those kids, those screaming, bleeding, dying kids in Columbine, in Sandy Hook, or in who-knows-where-next?

A police officer can't change the world, but he can carry his gun. And that's why he never left home without it.

On Reform: At the Pinnacle of Privilege

Chief Williams started at the beginning. His beginning.

As he told it, his dad was a bit of a crook—he had to move around because his dad had cheated the wrong people. They were poor. They shared flats with other families, attending schools where there was a lot of poverty. His parents, poor and white, quite frankly did not have the luxury of thinking themselves to be superior to anyone.

But then they all moved to Northern California, and suddenly he went from a school in a poor black neighborhood to a bubble. He was one of the poorest kids there, and as soon as he could, he got a job so that he could buy a sweater, a shirt, and pants to look like the other kids. And as soon as he could do it again, he did. That's when he started realizing: *it isn't about your color. It's about what happened to you because of your color.*

When he came of age in the late 1960s, he didn't have much to set himself up for life—a driver's license and a high school diploma. He turned to public law enforcement because it was the best pay and best benefits he could find. But even so, he realized a profound truth: he was at the pinnacle of privilege. *I was a twenty-one-year-old white male. What a lucky deal! So what about the kid whose parents took him across the border and he's "illegal" here? What about the black kid?*

That's why he's not so interested in changing the law. Changing the law is just changing the rules. He thinks we need to do something different: we need to change the game, and change who gets to play. He doesn't care about drugs; he thinks that all of that just echoes the Puritans. He's sure that we should be rehabilitating people. But not just that. We need to start *understanding* people. *We should be asking them who they are, where they come from, what they are about. And we should be doing this even for violent offenders.* He's especially worried about the young people—the people, as he sees it, who are simply not yet in control of their destiny, but who have bad influences that bring them into crime.

He ponders: *If I was king and I wanted to affect crime, I would stop thinking about prisons. I would go to Oakland, and spend a gazillion dollars. For at least two generations. I'd get those kids a nutritious breakfast. Then I'd buy them lunch. Then I'd have them do after-school programs. Then I'd get them dinner. Then I'd take them safely home. I'd show them the way out. You and I cannot imagine what it is like to be a nine- or ten-year-old, scared to go to school because there might be drive-bys. I would give them scholarships. I would do whatever I could to give them the stability that they need.*

It's do-able, he insists, but you'd have to do it for a few generations. He's aware, though, that people don't follow through. We have no will. People just don't get it. And the cops don't get it, either. He thinks about the Oakland Police Department: *I strongly believe that part of the training in Oakland—or anywhere else, for that matter—should be immersion with black families. These new recruits should eat*

*dinner with them. Get immersed. And if you can't do that—
fine. You just won't be hired.*

*Or how about this: you tell your new recruits to walk to a
certain address, say, the No Tell Motel. And there you'll find a
panel of black people, just everyday people, who talk to you,
who feel you out, who figure out what kind of officer you might
become. And sure, you could do it with panels of Asians, His-
panics. Even white people—but they'd have to be at the Mar-
riott! Or how about you have a big ball, and you invite your
average residents. Including the homeless guy hanging out in
front of the hotel. You get everyone in a room, and you parade
the new officers on the stage, and everyone can vote, and that's
how the hiring decision can happen! I'm riffing here, but if you
want to change anything, you have to change hiring. Gun laws
are nothing compared to that.*

He couldn't care less about gun laws as compared to getting officers to just listen to people. Talk to them. Go door
to door—and, sure, it might freak out people to have police
officers at their door asking questions. But he's not doing it
for those people. He's doing it for the officers, so they can
see that not everyone who lives in a particular area or looks
a certain way is a criminal.

We don't all live life according to the same fee schedule.

It was his warning for anyone willing to listen.

APPENDIX B
PROCEDURES FOR PROTECTING RESEARCH SUBJECTS

As per my human ethics approvals from the University of Toronto, the University of California, Irvine, and the University of Arizona, all interviews were conducted at a location of the interviewee's choice. At the start of each interview, I gave each research subject an information sheet about the research and their rights as research subjects; to protect research subjects, I did not take signatures for consent but instead asked for consent verbally. Likewise, I did not record interviews; I took handwritten notes during interviews, which were later (usually within less than twenty-four hours) transcribed into narratives. All data were deidentified, and at times I changed details in order to further protect research subject confidentiality. Likewise, I follow the policing scholar Peter Moskos[1] and refer only to pertinent characteristics of a chief (such as state of residency) when introducing an excerpt. When I do use names, they are pseudonyms. Nevertheless, the reader should know that while at times I introduce pseudonyms for ease of readability, I have honored the request of those chiefs who did not even want to be identified by pseudonym; this was a concern that a handful of chiefs voiced, particularly in California. Overall, I use pseudonyms sparingly in order to avoid readers triangulating data to identify a particular chief.

APPENDIX C
INTERVIEW GUIDE

1. How long have you worked in your current jurisdiction? Can you provide a rough sketch of your background as a police officer?

2. Can you recall the earliest moment you knew that you would go into police work? What attracted you to this line of work?

3. Is gun crime common in your jurisdiction?
   a. Is gun violence a top concern for your agency?
   b. Have you personally been the victim of gun violence?
   c. Have you ever used (whether display or discharge) your firearm in the line of duty?

4. Do you carry a gun while off-duty, and if so, why?
   a. As a member of this community, does your status as a police officer make you feel *more* at risk of gun crime?

5. How do you feel about citizens being able to own/carry guns?
   a. Do you feel more safe, less safe, or about the same knowing that civilians can and do own guns *legally*? What about carry?
   b. Do you think that current mechanisms (background checks, training requirements, required disclosure to police) are adequate? What would you change, if anything?
   c. Have you encountered cases where people were given the ability to own or carry but should not have been—either in your opinion or legally?
   d. Have you encountered cases where people have been denied the ability to own or carry but should have been given the ability— either in your opinion or legally?

6. What do you feel about Stand Your Ground laws?
   a. What is your department's procedure for handling justifiable homicide laws? Has there been any specialized training in this regard?
   b. Can you think of a case that should have been deemed self-defense but wasn't?
   c. Can you think of a case that should not have been deemed self-defense but was?

7. What are your feelings about personal protection orders and gun bans? Is this effective?

8. What are your procedures for seizing guns?
   a. In what cases does your department typically seize guns? What typically triggers a gun seizure? Domestic violence? Mental health issues?

9. Do you believe certain classes of guns (e.g., assault weapons) should be banned or heavily regulated?
   a. What would such a ban look like on the ground? Do you feel you have the resources to execute it? How would this differ from current strategies to get illegal guns off the street?

10. Mandatory minimum drug laws have recently come under attack—and some people are raising similar questions about mandatory minimum gun laws. What is your opinion on mandatory minimum gun laws?
    a. Are cases typically pursued on mandatory minimum gun charges?
    b. Do mandatory minimum gun laws reduce crime?

11. Would you personally prefer laws surrounding civilian gun ownership and carry to be changed in any way? Should they be more restrictive, more lenient, or just about the same?

12. Are you a member of the NRA or the Brady Campaign, or politically active regarding guns? Have you ever felt compelled to be politically involved?

13. The International Association of Police Chiefs has often spoken out in favor of gun control. However, other organizations that represent law

enforcement—as well as individual police chiefs—have spoken out in favor of expanded gun rights.

a. Which perspective better characterizes public law enforcement?

b. To what extent do you believe that police should be involved in gun politics at all?

Notes

INTRODUCTION: AN ARMED SOCIETY IS A POLICED SOCIETY

1. Schuppe (2016).
2. Winsor (2016).
3. Butler (2017).
4. Fisher (2016).
5. Neidig (2016).
6. French (2017).
7. See the Movement for Black Lives (2016) and Black Lives Matter (2019) on the movement's broad program.
8. Graham (2016).
9. Boddie (2017).
10. Felony stops involve police contact with individuals believed to have committed or be planning to commit a violent offense. These multiple-officer stops involve the threat or use of force by police; officers, for example, may unholster their guns as they order suspects to exit a vehicle or demonstrate that their waistbands are not concealing a firearm.
11. Butler (2017); Jones (2018); Maynard-Moody and Musheno (2003); Stoughton (2014; 2016); Stuart (2016); Zimring (2017).
12. Morin et al. (2017).
13. Butler (2017).
14. There is a useful debate regarding the circumscription of violence, and whether it "necessarily includes physicality in either the action or its effect" (Walby 2013: 101; see also Bourdieu 1991; Butler 2011; Ray 2011). For the purposes of this book, I focus on threat or enactment of physical violence involving guns.
15. Weber (1946).
16. Burnett (2016); Crime Prevention Research Center (2020); Gallup (2019); Parker et al. (2017).
17. Carlson (2015); Stroud (2012); Mencken and Froese (2019).
18. Carlson (2015; 2018).
19. Miller (2010).
20. Rose (2013).
21. Kendi (2017); Seamster and Ray (2018).
22. Kraska (2007); see also Balko (2013).

23. Stoughton (2014: 226).
24. Smith and Williams (2016).
25. Armstrong and Carlson (2019); Dow (2016); Rios (2011).
26. This is vitally underscored by the #SayHerName campaign (Crenshaw et al. 2015); see also Madriz (1997). Furthermore, the consequences of police harassment and violence against boys and men of color is not confined to them; it reverberates in a variety of forms of violence against girls and women. See Butler (2017); Comfort (2008); Jones (2018).
27. E.g., Butler (2017); Forman (2017); Muhammad (2011); Rios (2011).
28. According to Feagin (2013: xi), racial frames represent "a broad and persisting set of *racial stereotypes, ideologies, interlinked interpretations and narratives, . . . visual images, . . . racialized emotions, and racialized reactions to language accents*" (emphasis in the original). This definition reflects a broad body of scholarship on race and crime control starting with W.E.B. Du Bois, across sociology (e.g., Bonilla-Silva 2006; Feagin 2013), history (e.g., Kendi 2017; Muhammad 2011), psychology (e.g., Gutsell and Inzlicht 2012; Payne 2006), and law (e.g., Harris 1993; Gonzalez Van Cleve and Mayes 2015).
29. Carlson (2015).
30. Carlson (2015).
31. See Jones (2018) on masculinity, gun violence, and the politics of respectability.
32. Sociological and political analyses of the state also provide a foundation for understanding gun populism, unraveling Weber's (1946) argument that the "right" to use violence—both the capacity to deploy violence and the ability to do so "legitimately"—is dynamically and intimately connected to the "politics" over which "states" and "groups within a state" struggle. Recall, for example, Black's (1983) contention that much crime is justice by another name. In contexts where access to legitimate, state-centric channels of redress is limited, individuals take justice into their own hands. Claims by historical criminologists (e.g., Roth 2012) that homicide rates are inversely related to trust in government institutions are likewise suggestive. Underscoring legitimate violence as a sociological phenomenon, Elias (1939) reminds us that violence becomes monopolized by the state through a contingent "civilizing" process of social-psychic and structural processes. Furthermore, Weber's (1946) designation of the state as a "human community," especially when paired with an understanding of the state as interpenetrating civil society (Foucault 1977; Mann 1986), anticipates subsequent scholarship that proclaims that the state has no clear a priori boundaries (Mitchell 1991).
33. Spierenburg (2006: 113).
34. Obert (2018) shows, across these contexts, that communities struggled to reinvent order maintenance as social order (whether due to industrialization, emancipation, or frontier expansion) transformed around them. His book traces how these struggles produced new forms of organized violence: public law enforcement, private security firms, and white supremacist militias.

35. Dunbar-Ortiz (2014; 2018); Madley (2016).
36. Drawing on an ethnography of local security arrangements in Colombia, Gordon (2019: 3, 17) analyzes the social psychological mechanisms among residents *and* police by which "extrajudicial violence *and* legal authority can be viewed as legitimate simultaneously" such that "extrajudicial violence [can be] viewed as a legitimate complement to, rather than a replacement for, legal authority." Likewise, in her ethnography of immigration-restrictionist and pro-immigrant activists on the Arizona border, Elcioglu (2015; 2017) emphasizes how appraisals of state efficacy embolden nonstate actors to engage in policing and patrol activities that buttress state legitimacy while simultaneously undermining the state's strict monopoly on legitimate violence. Explicitly extending Elias's (1939) theory of the civilizing process to a "no rules" weapons fighting group, Gong (2015) analyzes how participants interactionally draw lines between legitimate violence (i.e., "civilized" violence) and illegitimate violence (i.e., impulsive and undisciplined violence). Although rule of law matters in shaping the limits of legitimate violence for participants, Gong (2015: 611, 613) also found that some members of the group were military and law enforcement who participated to cultivate dispositions that they believed regular police training did not. Such findings disrupt the insularity of police subcultures of violence, suggesting that norms surrounding private violence co-constitute public actors' sensibilities surrounding legitimate violence.
37. Bonikowski (2016); Brubaker (2017); Müller (2017).
38. Carlson (2014; 2015); McDowall and Loftin (1983); Simon (2003); Steidley (2019).
39. Bonilla-Silva (2006); Feagin (2013); Gonzalez Van Cleve and Mayes (2015).
40. Harris (1993).
41. When whiteness is considered in studies of policing, it often serves as a justificatory backdrop for the policing of "out of place" black and brown bodies (e.g., Meehan and Ponder 1992) or used to signal a *lack* of police attention that whites experience as compared to people of color. Whites experience less harassment in the context of investigatory stops than African Americans (Epp, Maynard-Moody, and Haider-Markel 2014), while analyses of white suburban drug dealers found that respondents had little interaction with police (Jacques 2017; Jacques and Wright 2015). The treatment of whiteness as a "racial lack" reflects the invisibility of whiteness and its conflation, as Dyer (2008: 12) notes, with "the human condition." As the criminologists Smith and Linnemann (2015: 101) describe with respect to whiteness and policing, "it is the normalized 'invisible weight' of whiteness that provides meaning for the difference and crafted inferiority of the other."
42. Maghbouleh (2017).
43. Lipsitz (2008: 76); see also Oliver and Shapiro (2013); Rothstein (2017). Harris (1993: 1725) argues that whiteness affords both a negative freedom (e.g., a lack of police attention) and also a positive liberty (e.g., entitlement to different treatment) insofar as whiteness itself is a form of property.

44. As Butler (2017: 12) points out, in addition to the psychosocial benefits of safety and security offered by police, there are material ways that whites benefit from the criminal justice system: "the American criminal justice enhances the property value of whiteness. . . . [A] vote for a conservative is an investment in the property value of one's whiteness. The criminal process makes white privilege more than just a status symbol, and more than just a partial shield from the criminal process. . . . [B]y reducing competition for jobs, and by generating employment in law enforcement and corrections, especially in the mainly white rural areas where prisons are often located, the Chokehold delivers cash money to many working-class white people."
45. See Collins (2002) on "controlling images."
46. Note that although Fanon's *Wretched of the Earth* (2007) focuses on the Algerian context, his analysis of a bifurcated system of racial governance—consent for whites, coercion for people of color—resonates with these frames of gun populism and gun militarism in the U.S. context.
47. Du Bois (1995); Morris (2015); Muhammad (2011).
48. Stuart (2016).
49. Greenberg (2005); Hadden (2001).
50. Greenberg (2005).
51. Reviewing centuries of racial ideas in North America, Kendi (2017) concludes that U.S. history cannot be distilled into a racial teleology moving from regress to progress but rather represents a "three-way argument" animated by multiple projects of racial inequality, alongside pushes for antiracism. See also Seamster and Ray (2018).
52. Fernandez and Gould (1994).
53. Fernandez and Gould (1994).
54. Fernandez and Gould (1994).
55. Garland (2001); Hinton (2016); Muhammad (2011); Murakawa (2014); Simon (2007); Tonry (1995; 2011); Wacquant (2001).
56. Ackerman and Furman (2013); Aguirre (2012); Armenta (2017); Beckett and Herbert (2009); Beckett and Murakawa (2012); Garland (2001); Hinton (2016); Murakawa (2014); Simon (2007); Tonry (1995; 2011); Wacquant (2001).
57. Giffords Law Center to Prevent Gun Violence (2017).
58. Wood (2017).
59. A recent analysis conducted by 24/7 Wall St. and featured in *USA Today* ranked Arizona sixteenth in the United States for gun violence (Frohlich and Harrington 2018).
60. McCombie (2011).
61. Arizona's state constitution frames the right to keep and bear arms as follows: "The right of the individual citizen to bear arms in defense of himself or the State shall not be impaired, but nothing in this section shall be construed as authorizing individuals or corporations to organize, maintain, or employ an armed body of men." The final clause has a strange ring to it, given that the

Second Amendment to the U.S. Constitution opens with the prefatory clause, "A well-regulated Militia, being necessary to the security of a free State." The historical preeminence of the mining industry as a site of private policing, however, helps explain the curiosity of this Arizona provision.

62. United States Fish and Wildlife Service (2017).

63. Hopper Usher (2019).

64. Mack (2018).

65. Frohlich and Harrington (2018).

66. Giffords Law Center to Prevent Gun Violence (2017).

67. Wood (2017).

68. See Judicial Council of California (2019).

69. E.g., Moen (2018).

70. E.g., Albanesius (2014).

71. Note that there is no statewide system in California for issuing concealed pistol licenses on a nondiscretionary basis.

72. Frohlich and Harrington (2018).

73. Giffords Law Center to Prevent Gun Violence (2017).

74. Wood (2017).

75. See Forman (2017); Kraska (2007); Stoughton (2014; 2016).

76. See Jones (2018) on the politics of respectability.

CHAPTER 1: GUN POLITICS IN BLUE

1. See Morin et al. (2017) for police opinion data on the assault weapons ban, gun rights versus gun control, and other measures. See Avery (2013) for police opinion data on the assault weapons ban, concealed carry, and other measures.

2. McClellan (2010).

3. Kahr (1916).

4. The NRA offers grants to police departments as part of its NRA Foundation Grant program and its range development program. See NRA Foundation (2019) and NRA Range Services (2019).

5. Note that the NRA established its Law Enforcement Division in 1960. As of July 2019, the Division boasted of more than thirteen thousand active instructors who specialize in police training. The Division also organizes police shooting competitions as well as provides insurance and other benefits to public law enforcement. See NRA Law Enforcement, Military and Security (2019).

6. Recall that this is what the sociologists Fernandez and Gould (1994) analyze as an "itinerant broker."

7. Bayley and Shearing (1996); Zedner (2005).

8. Marx and Archer (1971); Simon (2007).

9. Greenberg (2005: 26, 27).

10. Greenberg (2005: 34).
11. In the decade after the Civil War, freed slaves exercised their newfound rights—including the right to keep and bear arms and organize into a militia. When the North encouraged state militias as a means of establishing order in the Reconstruction South, freed slaves joined to provide protection to fellow freedmen and Republicans—and thus they became known as "negro militias." As the historian Otis Singletary (1971) notes, these militias were widely praised in the North and among black Southerners as vehicles of security, dignity, and citizenship. But among white Southerners, these forces inspired brutal backlash. As Singletary (1971: 152) writes, "It is ironic that the organization of this protective force, because of its racial implications, actually aided in the destruction of the very thing it was created to protect." Amid economic upheaval, the negro militias—and the broader project of black political emancipation they represented—riled white vigilantes who would terrorize and torture freed slaves, and their descendants, for decades. Note that the last Ku Klux Klan–orchestrated lynching, of Michael Donald, took place as recently as 1981.
12. Hadden (2001: 218).
13. Hadden (2001: 218–219).
14. Hadden (2001: 218).
15. Garland (2005).
16. Greenberg (2005: 3).
17. Harring (1983).
18. Vitale (2017: 37)
19. Foucault (1977); Harring (1983).
20. Woodward (1955).
21. See Muhammad (2011). Furthermore, the "scientific" charities of the nineteenth century (Stuart 2016), which were facilitated by fledgling public law enforcement at the time, typically excluded African Americans from the social support they offered. As a result, so-called ethnic whites—Italians, Polish, Germans, and other Eastern and Southern Europeans—would assimilate economically and politically, while African Americans would remain isolated as workers and as citizens.
22. Prassel (1972: 129).
23. Greenberg (2005: 68).
24. Brown (1991); Prassel (1972).
25. Kopel (2014).
26. Greenberg (2005).
27. See Carrigan and Webb (2013). Thousands of Mexican Americans (known at the time as Tejanos) were lynched from the late nineteenth to the early twentieth centuries. In addition, the Texas Rangers waged a brutal campaign on the border of Texas and Mexico, executing nearly three hundred Tejanos in 1915 alone and facilitating the transfer of almost two hundred thousand

acres of land from Tejano to Anglo hands. The Texas Rangers are widely considered the precursor to the U.S. Border Patrol, which was founded in 1924.

28. As another example, in 1917 in Southern Arizona, Sheriff Henry C. Wheeler deputized hundreds of citizens to participate in the "Bisbee Deportation" of thirteen hundred mine strikers, including many innocent Mexican Americans working in the mines; within a few years, the U.S. government took it upon itself to expel up to two million Mexicans and Mexican Americans living in the United States. Finally, brutal forms of repression—often targeting Chinese and Mexican laborers—were employed by private policing agencies at the behest of railroad and mining companies. Recall that concerns about the brutality of these organized private policing groups lie behind the wording of Arizona's right to keep and bear arms provision.

29. Arguably, U.S. policing took Sir Robert Peel's notion of democratic policing-by-consent and, while perhaps not inverting it, flipped it sideways. Sir Robert Peel is often considered the founder of modern policing, articulating in 1829 the British Metropolitan Police Act to found the London Police as we know it. He proclaimed police as a highly trained, professional, and incorruptible force that represented the will of the people, who for their part have consented to be policed. In the Peelian tradition, public law enforcement is the exemplar social contract: I, the citizen, consent to your, the police officer's, capacity to use the full force of the state against me, in exchange for protecting me from fellow citizens and thus enhancing the broader social order. Policing-by-consent necessarily emphasized law enforcement as community members, whereby "the police are the public and the public are the police, the police being only members of the public who are paid to give full-time attention to duties which are incumbent on every citizen in the interests of community welfare and existence" (Kopel 2019: 17–18).

30. Hadden (2001); Vitale (2017).

31. Muhammad (2011).

32. Hernández (2017); Muhammad (2011).

33. As LeFave (1970: 104) writes in his dissertation on the National Rifle Association, "Evidence was abundant and much publicized by police and other officials that the number of shootings in the United States was extremely high. Many attributed the difficulty to the easy availability of mail-order pistols and revolvers accessible to anyone for six or eight dollars. In 1920, 71.8 per cent of all murders were committed with a gun. Against a backdrop of rising complaints and demands for gun controls, Congress passed two laws during the decade of the twenties. One in 1924 was a simple tax measure levying an excise on the sale of arms and ammunition. More pertinent to the problem, the shipment of concealable weapons through the mails was outlawed in 1927." Leddy (1985: 216), referring to a quotation from the *American Rifleman* in 1927, notes: "In the twenties a new type of crime began. Robberies of banks and the use of guns by criminals became much more common. A spectacular

crime wave replaced the calm period of the late nineteenth and early twentieth century. In those good old days a policeman's gun was merely a symbol of office, never fired, and sometimes even nonfunctional: 'The gun was part of the uniform—a symbol of authority—just that and nothing more. Most police departments [were] ruled by men who cherished the traditions of the two fisted cop who ruled Bedlam with his hands and night stick.'"

34. This was especially so as African Americans fled the South and headed North in what would become known as the "Great Migration."
35. McGirr (2015).
36. Adler (2015: 43).
37. Adler (2015: 43).
38. McGirr (2015: 84).
39. McGirr (2015: 86).
40. McGirr (2015: 93).
41. McGirr (2015: 71).
42. Kahr (1916: 169).
43. Morrison (1995).
44. Bright and Maccar (2017).
45. Morrison and Vila (1998: 514).
46. Kahr (1916: 169).
47. Morrison (1995: 350).
48. Morrison (1995: 339).
49. Cited in Morrison (1995: 338).
50. Morrison and Vila (1998: 516).
51. LeFave (1970: 101–102).
52. New York Times Staff (1927).
53. New York Times Staff (1927).
54. New York Times Staff (1927). It is interesting that this chief made these statements in 1927, just two years after an African American doctor named Ossian Sweet defended himself and his family with firearms against a white mob (under the auspices of a homeowners' association) that terrorized his residence after he moved into an all-white block. Detroit's police department responded to white-on-black crime with apathy; had the police intervened, Sweet might not have had to fire shots in self-defense.
55. Morrison (1995: 481).
56. In the next decades, police would apparently favor firearms controls: "In response to a questionnaire circulated at the 1950 meeting of the Attorney General's Conference on Organized Crime, 255 members of the International Association of Chiefs of Police favored restriction while only twenty-three opposed controls" (LeFave 1970: 152–153).
57. Simon (2007).
58. Note that these terms refer to racial tropes—or what Collins (2002) calls "controlling images." For the origins of the term *superpredator,* see DiIulio (1995).

59. Sergel (1962: 2C).
60. Griffith (2010).
61. Whitten (1963: A27).
62. For example, Louisville's *Courier-Journal* (1965) notes, "All efforts to pass regulatory legislation has been stymied largely by the lobbying efforts of the National Rifle Association." Likewise, Senator Thomas J. Dodd, who reintroduced a defeated bill to regulate mail-order guns, noted in 1965 that "the gunrunners are more powerful than the American people who I believe want this law." The *Arizona Republic* reprint of the *Congressional Quarterly* (1965) article explained, "He [Dodd] blamed the failure to report the bill on the 'almost hysterical efforts' by a 'small but loud and well-organized hard-core minority.' . . . The private organization most actively involved in firearms legislation is the National Rifle Association, which in 1963 had more than 600,000 members and 400,000 affiliates and a total income of just under $4 million. . . . [T]he NRA does not register under the Federal Regulation of Lobbying Act because its stated purpose is not to influence Congress but merely to 'inform' or 'educate' its members and the public."
63. Berg (1967: 6A).
64. Avery (1965: 28).
65. Anderson (1965: 20).
66. Carper (1965: B1).
67. Moley (1965: 9A).
68. Friedman (1975: 5A).
69. Lane (1967).
70. Police buying own carbines (1967).
71. Riots and guns (1968: A22). The NRA, it should be noted, was inconsistent in its support for armed African American groups up through the 1960s. On the one hand, it provided charters for rifle clubs that pursued civil rights, including the group organized by the civil rights activist Robert Williams in Monroe, North Carolina, that desegregated the public library and the swimming pool (Williams 1998). At the same time, when given the opportunity to weigh in on the Mulford Act of 1967, the California law that outlawed open carry after the emergence of the armed Black Panthers, the NRA supported what many gun rights proponents, antiracist activists, and at least one former FBI agent (Leonardatos 1999) would decades later see as a clear-cut example of racially motivated firearms restrictions. Schmitz (1967), a California lawmaker, noted after the passage of the Mulford Act that "members of the National Rifle Association in California should know that their organization, despite its record of opposing gun control bills in the past, favored this bill and that without NRA support it almost certainly would have been defeated."
72. See Carlson (2015).
73. Buchwald (1967: 36).
74. Washington Post Staff (1975).

75. Washington Post Staff (1975).
76. Marx and Archer (1971: 58, 59).
77. Marx and Archer (1971: 58).
78. Marx and Archer (1971: 58).
79. Congressional Quarterly (1965).
80. L. L. (1968).
81. Though police militarization was visible in the war on alcohol and in the police response to riots throughout the twentieth century, policing historians often credit the 1980s and 1990s as the era of police militarization.
82. Turner and Fox (2017).
83. These terms represent commonplace tropes and metaphors emerging from the war on crime. As Kraska (1996: 420) notes, the "'war' metaphor . . . filter[s] solutions to the complex social problems of crime and substance abuse." This filtering is reinforced by racial tropes such as *gangbangers* or *superpredators*—what Collins (2002) calls "controlling images"—that justify inequality, legitimate discrimination, and render tolerable the overt coercion of marginalized groups.
84. See, e.g., Forman (2017).
85. For a detailed look at the racial politics of this case, see *The Central Park Five*, a 2012 documentary by Ken Burns, Sarah Burns, and David McMahon.
86. Eschholz et al. (2002).
87. Hurwitz and Peffley (1997: 375).
88. DiIulio (1995).
89. See Collins (2002). I will return to the concept of controlling images, particularly the controlling image of the thug, in chapter 5.
90. Recall the definition of police militarization from the introduction to this book: "the process whereby civilian *police* increasingly draw from, and pattern themselves around, the tenets of militarism and the military model" (Kraska 2007; see also Balko 2013).
91. Murch (2015: 165–166).
92. Romero (2014).
93. Margasak (1986: 03A).
94. McNamara (1988: 10A).
95. See, e.g., Kopel (2004).
96. United Press International (1983: 7B).
97. Nelson (1984: 9A).
98. New York Times Editorial Board (1983: A18).
99. According to Mezzacappa (1984: A11), "Legislation that would have banned armor-piercing 'cop-killer' bullets was pulled from the House calendar at the last minute yesterday, killing any chance for a vote on the issue this year. The measure was apparently a victim of its own controversial nature. House members did not want to record a vote on the legislation—which pitted the National Rifle Association (NRA) against most of the nation's law enforcement organizations—so close to an election."

100. Herbers (1985: 1).
101. Philadelphia Inquirer (1986: A12).
102. Gates (1989).
103. Freed (1989: 1).
104. Lamar (2001).
105. Keenan and Walker (2004).
106. Parker (2012).
107. Although the Stockton school shooting helped spark political engagement more broadly, police involvement was largely galvanized around the problem of urban crime.
108. Balko (2013).
109. See https://www.nraila.org/articles/20140820/anti-gun-lobbying-organizations
110. Annin (1992).
111. Houston (1989: 21A).
112. Annin (1992).
113. Annin (1992).
114. For example, Police Chief Howells of Allentown, PA, would ascend to the NRA's board of directors (Fegely 1987) as other cops distanced themselves from the organization in the 1980s; in the 1990s, the Los Angeles and San Jose officers turned to the NRA for assistance, including legal assistance (e.g., Freed 1989).
115. Pyle (2001). Note that although this essay originally appeared on http://www.2ampd.net/Articles/Pyle/LeroyPyle-Biography.htm, it has since been archived by the Wayback Machine, according to which it was last live on March 2, 2017.
116. De Parle (1990: A1).
117. Baye (2015).
118. Pyle (2001).
119. Lee (1991).
120. Annin (1992).
121. Baye (2015).
122. Fraternal Order of Police (2019).
123. Freedman (2013).
124. Fields (2000: B1).
125. Bedard (2015).
126. Eilperin and Rosenwald (2016).
127. NRA-ILA (2017a).
128. Hamburger and Horwitz (2013); Roberts (2004).
129. Baye (2015).
130. Law Enforcement Officers Safety Act (2003: 4).
131. Ammoland (2017).
132. NRA-ILA (2017b).
133. See https://www.nracarsforfreedom.com/
134. See https://www.youtube.com/watch?v=tOfLjGg5gP0

135. Note that two-thirds of FOP's national delegates must agree on a candidate for a presidential endorsement to move forward; the organization did not endorse a candidate in 2012. See Jackman (2016).

CHAPTER 2: THE WAR ON GUNS

1. Note that whereas the term *police militarization* (Kraska 1996; 2007; Stoughton 2014) refers to a social *process* of increased interpenetration of military mindset, tactics, strategies, and personnel with public law enforcement, I use *gun militarism* to specifically highlight sensibilities, policies, and practices that idealize a particular distribution of legitimate violence within American society.
2. See https://www.snopes.com/fact-check/gun-deaths-wars/
3. Gramlich (2019); Pilkington (2018).
4. Follman et al. (2015).
5. Gardner (2006).
6. NRA-ILA (2000).
7. Gaston (2019); Gaston and Brunson (2018).
8. Balko (2014).
9. Schenwar (2014).
10. Denvir (2016).
11. United States Sentencing Commission (2016).
12. Shannon et al. (2017).
13. Du Bois (1995); see also Muhammad (2011).
14. See https://twitter.com/eveewing/status/978647407201280002
15. Alexander (2012); Comfort (2008); Forman (2017); Lerman and Weaver (2014); Pager (2008); Western (2018).
16. Forman (2017: 51).
17. Balko (2014).
18. See Alexander (2012) on the war on drugs; Hinton (2016) on the war on poverty; McGirr (2015) on the war on alcohol.
19. Fernandez and Gould (1994).
20. Consider, too, that both illegal and legal gun use is often wrapped up in attempts to cope with adverse social circumstances (Barragan et al. 2016; Carlson 2015; Harcourt 2010), and the lines between legitimate and illegitimate coping are themselves blurry (Broidy and Santoro 2018).
21. See Spitzer (2015: 40–41) for an overview of gun laws by type from 1607 to 1934.
22. Cottrol and Diamond (1991); Johnson (2014).
23. Winkler (2011: 239).
24. Austin (2008); Bloom and Martin (2013); Nelson (2011).
25. Winkler (2011: 244); see in particular chapter 8, "By Any Means Necessary," for a more detailed discussion of the impact of the Black Power movement on the introduction and passage of the 1967 Mulford Act.

26. Leonardatos (1999).
27. Hofer et al. (2000).
28. Forman (2017: 65).
29. As Forman (2017: 75) notes, "Young's view—that private citizens should be able to keep guns in their homes while criminals who use them should face harsh sentences—was in line with the beliefs of many black citizens."
30. Lowenthal (1993: 79).
31. Claiborne (1998).
32. According to a Pew study of police attitudes (Morin et al. 2017), "about two-thirds of police (68%) . . . believe the country's marijuana laws should be re-laxed"; one-third of police "support legalizing marijuana for both private and medical use."
33. Zimring (1972).
34. For a review of the relationship between gun availability and gun violence, see Cook and Goss (2014).
35. Inordinately measured by their capacity to prevent crime, police chiefs rightly feel "set up" to fail at this mandate—not least because the relationship be-tween what police do and how crime rates fluctuate is often tenuous at best. See Meares and Neyroud (2015); Stoughton (2016).
36. Scholars of police subculture show that these attitudes are prevalent among the public law enforcement community more broadly. See, e.g., Herbert (1998; 2001); Hunt (1984; 1985; 1990); Manning (1977); Micucci and Gomme (2005); Reiner (2010); Sierra-Arévalo (2016); Skolnick (2011); Skolnick and Fyfe (1993); Terrill, Paoline, and Manning (2003); Van Maanen (1973; 1978); Wad-dington (1999); Westley (1953); see also Morin et al. (2017).
37. See Martinson (1974) on rehabilitative justice—and its discontents.
38. Simon (2014).
39. Reiter and Pifer (2015).
40. See https://www.cdcr.ca.gov/News/prop47.html
41. Uggen and McElrath (2013).
42. A large literature has documented the sheer breadth of these costs and the myriad forms they take. As a starting point, see Alexander (2012); Comfort (2008); Forman (2017); Lerman and Weaver (2014); Pager (2008); Western (2018). On the conservative "Right on Crime" movement, see Dagan and Teles (2016).
43. E.g., Herbert (1998; 2001); Hunt (1984; 1985; 1990); Manning (1977); Mi-cucci and Gomme (2005); Reiner (2010); Sierra-Arévalo (2016); Skolnick (2011); Skolnick and Fyfe (1993); Terrill, Paoline, and Manning (2003); Van Maanen (1973; 1978); Waddington (1999); Westley (1953); see also Morin et al. (2017).
44. Waddington (1999).
45. Herbert (1998); Campeau (2015); Maynard-Moody and Musheno (2003); see also Swidler (1986).

46. Manning (1977).
47. Alpert, MacDonald, and Dunham (2005); Beckett, Nyrop, and Pfingst (2006); Welch (2007).
48. Carroll and Gonzalez (2014); Novak and Chamlin (2012); Smith and Alpert (2007).
49. Stoughton (2014: 225).
50. Stoughton (2016: 632).
51. Stoughton (2014: 226).
52. Stoughton (2016: 635).
53. Stoughton (2016: 637).
54. Stoughton (2016: 639).
55. Forman (2017: 156).
56. Anderson (2012); Bobo and Charles (2009); Muhammad (2011); Russell-Brown (1999).
57. Forman (2017: 156); see also Murch (2015).
58. Ramey and Steidley (2018: 839) "find that the relative size of minority populations is consistently and nonlinearly associated with 1033 Program participation." As further evidence of this association between police militarization and racial domination, they note that this relationship applies only to military equipment—not to nonmilitary supplies also transferred via the 1033 Program, such as tools and medical supplies.
59. Balko (2013); Kraska (1996; 2007).
60. See, e.g., Epp, Maynard-Moody, and Haider-Markel (2014) on the social foundations of racial profiling.
61. Kraska (2007: 507).
62. Stoughton (2014: 228).
63. Hunt (1984: 287, 288); see also Hunt (1990).
64. Herbert (2001: 56, 58, 59).
65. Cooper (2008).
66. Herbert (2001); Hunt (1984; 1990).
67. Herbert (2001).
68. Herbert (2001); Hunt (1984; 1990).
69. Slotkin (1973 [2000]).
70. Herbert (2001); Hunt (1984; 1985; 1990).
71. Williams (2015).
72. Anderson (2012); Bobo and Charles (2009); Collins (2002); Forman (2017); Muhammad (2011); Gonzalez Van Cleve and Mayes (2015).
73. Omi and Winant (2014).
74. Bonilla-Silva (2006); Harris (2012); Gonzalez Van Cleve and Mayes (2015).
75. Note that chiefs have become increasingly concerned about terrorism in the aftermath of 9/11, after which local police departments became increasingly involved in antiterrorist activities; see Huq and Muller (2008). Although this chief connects "gangsters" to the threat of terrorism, terrorism

was most commonly raised in the context of active shootings, which I analyze in chapter 3.

76. Jones (2018).
77. Braga (2003); Papachristos and Wildeman (2014); Papachristos, Wildeman, and Roberto (2015); Wintemute (2015).
78. Braga (2003); Kennedy (2011). Note, however, that these initiatives have often turned on creating divides *within* communities—between upstanding and disreputable residents—under the banner of crime fighting. See Jones (2018).
79. After my interviews with police chiefs, California lawmakers somewhat limited the breadth of the state's felony murder rule. Police have spoken in opposition to this law, which went into effect in 2019 following court challenges. See Smith (2018).
80. Russell-Brown (2009).
81. E.g., Alexander (2012); Butler (2017); Epp, Maynard-Moody, and Haider-Markel (2014); Forman (2017); Gonzalez Van Cleve (2016); Jones (2018); Lerman and Weaver (2014); Pager (2008); Tonry (1995); Wacquant (2001); Western (2018).
82. Du Bois (2015: 4).
83. Dow (2016).
84. Epp, Maynard-Moody, and Haider-Markel (2014).
85. Voigt et al. (2017).
86. See findings from the Stanford Open Policing Project at https://openpolicing .stanford.edu/findings/
87. Mitchell and Caudy (2015).
88. For example, the Stanford Open Policing Project finds that police conduct more than fifty thousand traffic stops every day. See https://openpolicing.stanford .edu/findings/
89. Ross (2015). Note, however, that although police brutality against African Americans has gained the most attention in popular media and debates, Native Americans are the racial group that experiences disproportionately the greatest number of police homicides, according to *The Guardian* data posted at https://www.theguardian.com/us-news/ng-interactive/2015/jun/01/the -counted-police-killings-us-database. This disparity, combined with the public silence on it, helped galvanize the Native Lives Matter initiative of the Lakota People's Law Project. See https://www.lakotalaw.org/resources/native -lives-matter. As they note, "We aim to influence a public discourse that routinely ignores the fact that Native Americans suffer the most adverse effects of a structurally unjust criminal justice system. Proportionally, Native Americans are the most likely racial group to be killed by the police. Native American men are admitted to prison at four times the rate of white men, and Native women at six-fold the rate of white women."
90. Weber (1946).

CHAPTER 3: NEVER OFF DUTY

1. Cullen (2009: 66–67).
2. Muschert (2007: 355).
3. Willis-Chun (2011: 50). And as the sociologists William Mingus and Bradley Zopf (2010: 67, 68) note, "white privilege involves more than the ability to ignore race. It also controls the focus of official attention in crimes that involve white victims. . . . [T]he shooting of whites by someone else who is also white is considered so out of the ordinary that it receives massive media and governmental attention while more mundane violence, an everyday occurrence in poor urban areas, is ignored and attributed to a culture of poverty (often read as Black or Latino culture)."
4. Snow (1997).
5. The emergence of SWAT was itself spawned by a deep sense that traditional methods of policing had failed to stand up to the demands of the 1960s and 1970s. Riots, political uprisings, assassinations, generalized disorder, and at least one mass shooting—the 1966 Bell Tower massacre at the University of Texas, Austin—revealed a threat of chaos that seemingly lay just beneath the uneasy patina of American democracy. As SWAT units appeared in large and small jurisdictions alike and were used for routine policing activities—usually related to drug raids but, at least in some jurisdictions, also as part of regular patrol activities—SWAT teams became an increasing presence across the United States. Their use, however, was starkly racially disparate, as they were disproportionately deployed to police racial minorities. As such, these paramilitary units became quintessential components of the urban war on drugs, one that not only reinforced a *culture* that encouraged aggressive policing tactics but also gave police broad *legal* powers to stop, detain, arrest, and use force. The sociologist Christian Parenti (2000: 112) describes SWAT units as an "urban counterinsurgency bulwark," quoting one SWAT officer who explained, "Those people out there—the radicals, the revolutionaries, and the cop haters—are damned good at using shotguns, bombs, or setting ambushes, so we've got to be better at what we do."
6. Muschert (2007: 359).
7. Blair et al. (2013: 12).
8. Associated Press (2009).
9. Hybrid masculinity involves both "selective incorporation of performances and identity elements associated with marginalized and subordinated masculinities and femininities" and selective disavowal of hypermasculine attributes such that "the willingness to temper one's masculinity is viewed as a sign of confidence" (Young 2017: 1364; see also Pascoe and Hollander [2016: 72, 68] on antirape slogans and masculinity). Recent scholarship reveals that race- and class-privileged men (Bridges and Pascoe 2014) in the contexts of conservative politics (Heath 2003; Messner 2007; Stein 2005), sport (Anderson 2010),

and even violence (Carlson 2018; Stroud 2012; Young 2003) are reframing masculinity to selectively integrate care and compassion to navigate and justify their engagement in these areas.

10. Messner (2007: 467).

11. Berkowitz, Lu, and Alcantara (2018).

12. McGinty et al. (2014). Consider the roughly fifteen thousand gun homicides, more than one thousand police-perpetrated gun homicides, as well as roughly twenty-four thousand gun suicides that have occurred annually in recent years (Gramlich 2019; Pilkington 2018); whereas, for comparison, recall the *Washington Post* data showing that 1,135 people have been killed in active shootings since 1966 (Berkowitz, Lu, and Alcantara 2018).

13. Florida and Boone (2018).

14. Turk (2004: 271).

15. Altheide (2009: 1366).

16. See Phillips (2016) on active shootings, police myths, and the adoption of patrol rifles.

17. Note, however, that this contrasts with law enforcement's broad-brush refusal of new responsibilities with regard to immigration enforcement (e.g., Harris 2006) and, as discussed later in this chapter, mental health.

18. Huq and Muller (2008).

19. Follman, Aronson, and Pan (2018); Fox and Levin (1998); Madfis (2014).

20. Kellner (2015); Larkin (2011); Madfis (2014); Newman and Fox (2009); Tonso (2009).

21. Fox and Levin (1998).

22. Follman, Aronson, and Pan (2018).

23. Duxbury, Frizzell, and Lindsay (2018).

24. Metzl and MacLeish (2015).

25. Mingus and Zopf (2010: 73).

26. Metzl (2010).

27. Heitzeg (2015). Though not directly related to gun crime, consider, for example, the case of Sandra Bland, who allegedly committed suicide in a jail cell in Waller County, Texas, after being arrested for assaulting a police officer during a traffic stop. The initial public outcry centered on two opposing frames: either Bland was an unstable aggressor toward police, or she was a victim of police aggression. This binary was aided by the tendency to associate mental illness with whiteness, a tendency challenged by commentators, activists, and Bland's friends and family. By 2017, Texas passed a law called the Sandra Bland Act, which "mandates county jails divert people with mental health and substance abuse issues toward treatment, makes it easier for defendants to receive a personal bond if they have a mental illness or intellectual disability, and requires that independent law enforcement agencies investigate jail deaths." See https://www.texastribune.org/2017/06/15/texas-gov-greg-abbott-signs-sandra-bland-act-law/

28. Regarding more broadly the frustrations of frontline workers at the intersection of mental health and law enforcement, see Chiarello (2015). See also the literature on "transinstitutionalization," whereby criminal justice institutions are increasingly charged with addressing mental illness (e.g., Primeau et al. 2013; Reiter and Blair 2015).
29. Ford (2015).
30. Bonilla-Silva (2006).
31. This was especially the case under President Obama's Twenty-first-Century Policing Initiative.
32. Rahr and Rice (2015: 3).
33. Stoughton (2016: 632).
34. Messner (2007: 467).
35. Young (2003).
36. See Messner (2007) on the "Kindergarten Commando" and Young (2003) on masculinist protection.
37. Police off-duty carry has been a largely understudied phenomenon, however. See Fyfe (1980).
38. Carlson (2015).
39. The *New York Times* wagered that the ruling means that "police officers in some cases [could] avoid jury trials in controversial shootings in which officers believed they were acting in self-defense but might have had other options." See Robles (2018).
40. Before, policy stated that police "may" intervene. See Rosenblatt (2018).
41. The commission was charged with investigating the Parkland school shooting and its lessons for future prevention and response.
42. Burch and Blinder (2019).
43. Bittner (1973).
44. Swidler (1986).
45. Morin et al. (2017).

CHAPTER 4: WHEN THE GOVERNMENT DOESN'T COME KNOCKING

1. White (2017).
2. Ruelas (2017).
3. Ruelas (2017).
4. Carlson (2015).
5. Ruelas (2017).
6. The *Phoenix New Times*, in this regard, had an atypical headline: "Armed civilian praised for shooting undocumented suspect who attacked trooper"; see Stern (2017).
7. Arizona law enforcement described him as "a known drug user but has no criminal history that we can find"; he was also an officer for the Mexican federal police. He had crossed the border and was turned away at least once, and

police claimed he was in the United States without authorization. See Holland (2017).

8. Kravarik and Elam (2017).
9. ABC15.com Staff (2017).
10. Bonikowski (2016); Brubaker (2017); Müller (2017).
11. In *Cop Knowledge*, Christopher Wilson (2000: 16) uses the term *police populism* to describe a police trope that emerged in the 1960s to describe "the labor of a dedicated, hard-bitten knight of the city, an everyday man-in-shirtsleeves servant of the mostly white working class, solving crimes not through eccentric genius but by shoe leather, hard work, and pragmatic adherence to often-tedious procedure. And as such they exhibit not simple authoritarianism or paramilitary values, but a long-recognized double-edged potential in populist ideology, applications that are progressive and reactionary, liberal and authoritarian all at once. . . . [A] classic pitfall of critical analysis is to mistake the cultural or media entanglement with policing for complicity with a generalized, monolithic (or hegemonic) political authority, rather than with this historically contingent and more particular political sub-culture." In this excerpt, Wilson is interested in understanding broad-based cultural representations of police; his is the only use of the term *populism* with respect to policing of which I am aware. My development of gun populism is somewhat different; I use this concept to clarify how (1) police understand themselves by (2) blurring the lines between state and nonstate actors with respect to the deployment of legitimate violence.
12. Greenberg (2005: 34).
13. Greenberg (2005); Hadden (2001).
14. Garland (2005).
15. Dunbar-Ortiz (2018); Greenberg (2005); Hadden (2001); Obert (2018); Vitale (2017).
16. Verma (2015); see also Page (2011).
17. Though perhaps motivated by the politics of their position as chiefs, this assessment is not an inaccurate take on California laws passed since the 1990s; see Zimring, Hawkins, and Kamin (2001) on California sentencing laws.
18. Page (2011); Reiter (2016); Zimring, Hawkins, and Kamin (2001).
19. Simon (2014).
20. Petersilia (2013).
21. Kail (2016).
22. Aviram (2015); Simon (2014).
23. Gusfield (1986); see also Page (2011).
24. McGreevy (2016).
25. Carlson (2015).
26. See also Black (1983); McDowall and Loftin (1983); Smith and Uchida (1988). But see Wilcox (2002).
27. Lipsky (2010).

28. Bell (2000).
29. Note that this inverts Brayne's (2014) concept of "system avoidance."
30. John Lott (2013) is the progenitor of the "more guns, less crime" study that found that increasing lawful gun carry was correlated with lowered crime rates. Some scholars have reproduced the results (Plassmann and Whitney 2003); many have criticized Lott's findings as an artifact of the study's statistical approach (e.g., Ayres and Donohue 2002) and quality of data (e.g., Duggan 2001).
31. Müller (2017).
32. Pager (2008).
33. Shannon et al. (2017). Note that these records not only bar someone from obtaining a concealed pistol license but may also shape voting, employment, welfare eligibility, and other informal and formal collateral consequences. See Allard (2002); Chin (2002); Manza and Uggen (2008); Pager (2008).
34. Carlson (2015; 2018); Shapira, Jensen, and Lin (2018). Racial disparities in licensing rates reflect both racial differences in demand *and* systematic differences in how licenses are processed for African Americans versus whites (Shapira, Jensen, and Lin 2018). States releasing public gun licensing data show that African Americans are armed at rates equal to (e.g., Michigan, suggesting that demand overwhelms disproportionate disqualification) or less than (e.g., Texas, suggesting disparate demand and/or disparate disqualification) their white counterparts.
35. A review of historical accounts of guns and self-defense reveals that the trope of the armed citizen is historically rooted in a republican ideal of citizenship reflecting the prerogatives of hegemonic white masculinity. Dunbar-Ortiz (2018); Filindra and Kaplan (2016); Light (2017).
36. Omi and Winant (2014); see also Harris (2012).
37. As of February 1, 2018, 621,327 residents were licensed to carry a firearm concealed, comprising 8 percent of the adult population (Mack 2018).
38. Note that under Arizona state law, an eighteen-year-old may lawfully possess a handgun, provided it is not purchased from a federally licensed firearms dealer, and openly carry it; an individual must be twenty-one years old to carry it concealed.
39. Although chiefs in Arizona more consistently embraced this stance than chiefs in California and Michigan, these brands of populism were not mutually exclusive across states. For example, though he was in the minority in the context of California, one California chief illustrated a sentiment that aligned with co-policing (as per Arizona) and system exposure (as per Michigan) when he explained, "Yes, I am comfortable with concealed carry. You know, the only concealed carry that is a problem are parolees with firearms in their belts—not someone who studied for carrying. I don't know who is armed around me, but my feeling is—if there's an off-duty cop next to me in the store when I need back up, I'm going to want that back up. And I don't see what's the difference

between that off-duty cop and the responsible citizen. There is zero difference."

40. Zimring (2017).
41. Zimring (2011).
42. Kurtzleben (2017).
43. According to Gerney, Parsons, and Posner (2013), the state ranks fourth for gun violence and eleventh for gun homicides. As noted earlier, a more recent analysis ranked Arizona sixteenth in the United States for gun violence (Frohlich and Harrington 2018). 2017 CDC data also rank Arizona eighteenth for its rate of gun deaths. For CDC data, see https://www.cdc.gov/nchs/pressroom/sosmap/firearm_mortality/firearm.htm
44. Kahan and Braman (2003).
45. Omi and Winant (2014).
46. Note that when Zamudio encountered the shooter, another bystander had already disarmed him; Zamudio nearly shot the bystander, thinking he was armed. Realizing his mistake by noting the locked slide, he quickly assisted the bystander and helped to restrain the shooter. See Ruelas (2018).
47. Dagan and Teles (2016).
48. See Omi and Winant's (2014) analysis of racial code words.
49. Foley (1998); Pierce (2018).
50. Maynard-Moody and Musheno (2003).
51. In Michigan, these orders are called "personal protection orders." I used the more general language of "restraining orders" here for reasons of accessibility.
52. Note, however, that historically police have been reluctant to see domestic violence as a public crime as opposed to a personal conflict. Indeed, the introduction of restraining orders and other mechanisms to address domestic violence represents a top-down protocol change in which police dramatically shifted their practices surrounding domestic violence. Scholars of gender and policing have documented historical tendencies among law enforcement to, on the one hand, deprioritize domestic violence as a legitimate policing problem and, on the other hand, identify with the perpetrators as opposed to female victims of domestic violence; see, for example, the sociologists Anastasia Prokos and Irene Padavic's provocatively titled article, "There oughtta be a law against bitches" (2002). See also Bumiller (2009); Desmond and Valdez (2013).
53. See Collins (2002) on "controlling images."
54. The Lautenberg Amendment, in particular, has been the subject of debate because it prohibits gun possession for a person convicted of a domestic violence misdemeanor, even if the act occurred prior to the passing of the Amendment. Although some critics argue that this violates the Ex Post Facto Clause of the U.S. Constitution, which prohibits ex post facto laws, at least two challenges to the law on this basis have been rejected by U.S. courts in *United States v. Brady* (1994) and *United States v. Waters* (1994).

55. Sometimes they saw open carry in an advantageous light; one California chief noted, "I actually wish we still had open carry. Because I can see the threat! Like with the Hell's Angels, I want them to wear their stuff, I want to see it!" Others offered apathy, like the Arizona chief who told me, "We have people in this town—several who open carry in this town. That's just—that's how this town is." And still others were ambivalent, like the Michigan chief who told me that "open carry: it's a right, but I don't know. Your nice guy: he's going to have it in a holster on the side. But your criminal won't have it in a holster; he'll just wear it in front. But come on. It's legal, but it's like wearing a KKK hood at the Nation of Islam." And finally, some vehemently opposed it; one Michigan chief admitted, "This is emotionally driven. I don't have the data. But I would outlaw open carry. There is no reason for it, this isn't the Wild West. . . . The only reason to do this in Michigan—I have not seen it in other states, but in Michigan—is to stick it to the man. And I think something's wrong with people who do that." Several police chiefs, especially in Michigan, saw open carriers as unstable or antisocial. One chief noted, "I'm okay if someone has a CPL. I am bothered, really bothered by open carry. Based on my life experience as a law enforcement officer, people who push open carry have issues of some sort. They are antisocial." Another Michigan chief noted, "I think it's a macho thing. [At one gathering] one of them came up to me and said the whole 'It's my right to carry' thing. Well, I said, 'I think you are just an asshole.'" In the interview, I verified that he actually said that. He went on: "Yes! Because it just scares people—and it's like, why are you even there? This is not the forum for that. I'm not opposed to it on principle, but just get your CPL, and hide it. . . . [T]hey give gun rights a bad name."
56. Siegel (2018).
57. Guzman (2018).
58. This pattern echoes the moral improvisation and identity work observed to shape frontline work more generally; see Maynard-Moody and Musheno (2003).
59. Carlson (2015).

CHAPTER 5: LEGALLY ARMED BUT PRESUMED DANGEROUS

1. As with police chiefs, all names of gun board claimants and administrators are pseudonyms.
2. Herbert (2009); Thacher (2019); Vargas (2016).
3. Fernandez and Gould (1994).
4. For a breakdown of firearms laws regarding concealed carry, see the NRA-ILA's "Right to Carry Laws" at https://www.nraila.org/gun-laws/. As of August 2019, only nine states issue concealed pistol licenses under a "may-issue" system, and only Vermont does not issue licenses to carry at all, as it allows concealed carry without a license for legal gun owners. All other states issue

licenses on a shall-issue basis, although many also allow concealed carry without a license (in such states, licenses are still issued for the purposes of specialized concealed carry or concealed carry out-of-state). Note that, historically, gun carry has been heavily regulated by law (Spitzer 2015) and strictly circumscribed by custom (Churchill 2007), with "early state governments routinely exercis[ing] their police powers to restrict the time, place and manner in which Americans used their guns" (Churchill 2007: 162). Treated as a "civic right" that "belonged to citizens who exercised it when they acted collectively for public defense" (Cornell 2006: 572), several Southern states banned concealed carry from the 1810s to the 1830s in an effort to suppress dueling (Cramer 1999). In the aftermath of the Civil War, however, Southern states began introducing licensing systems to buttress a white monopoly on lawful access to publicly carried guns, especially under the Jim Crow system that prevailed from the late nineteenth to the mid-twentieth centuries (Cottrol and Diamond 1991; Johnson 2014). In order to obtain a license, an individual had to appear before licensing officials, who were charged with making decisions involving the issuance of concealed carry licenses to eligible Americans. Note that this decision-making authority could reside in one individual (such as a sheriff) or a board of individuals (i.e., a "gun board"). Under this gun licensing apparatus, *any* person who wanted a gun license had to petition officials to demonstrate need for a firearm. Because licenses were issued at the discretion of state administrators, this system became known as "may-issue" licensing.

5. A note about generalizability should be made up front: although a handful of states maintain similar systems (Rose 2013), most states have no public board dedicated to this purpose; instead, claimants must file a court appeal (as is now the case in Michigan) or submit a written administrative appeal.

6. "Controlling images," as Patricia Hill Collins (2002: 69) notes, "are designed to make racism, sexism and poverty appear to be natural, normal and a part of everyday life."

7. Note that statistics about the number of guns, the number of gun owners, and the number of concealed carriers are frustrating at best. As there is no national registry of firearms or firearms owners, we do not know exactly how many guns circulate within the United States and in how many hands. Background checks and manufacturing data suggest that there are "more guns than people" (Ingraham 2018) in the United States, while survey data suggest that the percentage of gun owners has been erratic (Gallup 2019) or has declined (General Social Survey 2019) over the past several decades. In contrast, gun carrying appears by all measures to be increasing; although it is not possible to measure the number of gun carriers in states that allow permitless gun carry, the issuance of gun carry licenses has steadily increased since John Lott's Crime Prevention Research Center began compiling the data in 2014; their report issued in 2019 tallies 18.66 million licensed gun carriers. See Crime Prevention Research Center (2020).

8. Myrick (2013).
9. Monahan (2010); see also Gilliom (2001).
10. Butler (2017); Epp, Maynard-Moody, and Haider-Markel (2014); Jones (2018); Rios (2011). As the legal scholar and former prosecutor Paul Butler (2017: 61, 65) explains, "It turns out arrests, which *precede* incarceration, are an even bigger deal. That's because for most kinds of arrests—for low-level crimes called misdemeanors—police and prosecutors don't care really whether you are guilty. That's not the point of the arrest. African American men are arrested mainly so that they can be officially placed under government surveillance. . . . [A]rrests enable a set of surveillance practices."
11. This is similar to what Kohler-Hausmann (2013) calls "misdemeanor justice"; see also Feeley (1979).
12. Similar to Kohler-Hausmann's (2013) analysis of "procedural harassment," I developed this term as an extension of what Sykes (1958) calls the "pains of imprisonment" to administrative settings. Sykes describes a variety of deprivations that are built into the experience of imprisonment; I use *procedural pains* to designate the frustrating hurdles built into administrative procedures so that they double as a punitive process evocative of Feeley's (1979) thesis that the "process is the punishment."
13. Myrick (2013); see also Gurusami (2018); Jacobs (2015); Lageson (2017).
14. Lipsky (2010: 90).
15. Shannon et al. (2017); Soss and Weaver (2017).
16. For Detroit, see Apel (2015) and Sugrue (2014); see also Sampson (2008) and Vargas (2016) on Chicago.
17. Lipsky (2010: 83).
18. Lipsky (2010: 132).
19. E.g., "with the law"; see Ewick and Silbey (1998) on legal consciousness. See also Maynard-Moody and Musheno (2003) on moral improvisation.
20. Jacobs (2015).
21. Stivers (2007: 48).
22. Jacobs (2015).
23. Van Maanen (1978); Waddington (1999).
24. Maynard-Moody and Musheno (2003).
25. Ewald (2016: 30, 29, 30, 29).
26. Recall, also, the discussion in chapter 4 on "system exposure."
27. Note that whereas Pager (2008) addresses felony convictions, subsequent research has suggested how this extends to misdemeanor and administrative contexts. See, e.g., Kohler-Hausmann (2013).
28. This sentiment is especially felt among California law enforcement; see Page (2011).
29. Simon (2003).
30. For a revelatory analysis of the entanglement between child support and criminal justice systems, see Haney (2018).
31. Gustafson (2011).

32. The reliance on arrests and threats of arrest in Wayne County as compared to Oakland County resonates with Gonzalez Van Cleve's (2016) findings in Cook County courts and with scholarship on the "racial empathy gap" more broadly: poor African American populations tend to be dealt with more harshly and more punitively. Another factor may be that, in wealthier Oakland County, outstanding warrants that might have elicited arrest "downstream" in the context of the gun board had already been addressed further upstream by other law enforcement mechanisms. These factors further suggest the utility of the valve-turning metaphor (as opposed to a "pipeline") insofar as administrators may decide to deploy different kinds of tactics, ranging from symbolic to carceral, depending on their own sociolegal sensibilities as well as the sociolegal and material resources at their disposal.

33. Foucault (1977).

34. Page (2011).

35. In 2015, the upper age limit was increased to twenty-four.

36. Ewald (2016).

37. Carlson (2015).

38. Lerman and Weaver (2014); Mettler and Soss (2004).

39. Rios (2011); Stuart (2016).

40. Van Maanen (1978).

41. Considering the repercussions for driving under the influence (DUI), Jennifer Earl (2008: 765) explains, "In some cases, administrative legal settings serve as an initial stop in a larger judicial process, while at other times they parallel criminal or civil systems. . . . It is interesting to consider the extent to which these administrative hearings are used to augment the punishment meted out on the criminal side or to ensure that some formal punishment occurs, since these administrative hearings involve different burdens of proof and thus may well lead to the removal of licenses from individuals who are able to avoid conviction on the criminal charge of DUI."

42. Zedner (2016: 9); see also Beckett and Murakawa (2012).

43. This is also evident in scholarship on courts (Gonzalez Van Cleve 2016) and the welfare system (Soss, Fording, and Schram 2011).

44. Garfinkel (1956).

45. Garfinkel (1956: 422–423) establishes criteria for "successful" ceremonies that "effect the ritual destruction of the person denounced" (421) by framing the denounced "as a representative of a 'type' of person . . . that poses an affront to common values" such that "the denouncement can serve not just as a personal punishment but as a broader warning about, and affirmation of, community values."

46. Gonzalez Van Cleve (2016: 68).

47. Detroit is, e.g., colloquially disparaged as a "murder capital" by Greater Metro area residents; see Carlson (2015).

48. Harris, Evans, and Beckett (2011).

49. Dow (2016: 175).

50. Jackson and Carroll (1981); Tonry (2011); Wacquant (2001).
51. Dow (2016: 182).
52. Du Bois (1995); Muhammad (2011).
53. Collins (2004: 159).
54. Edin and Nelson (2013: 165, 188).
55. Marks and Palkovitz (2004).
56. Edin and Nelson (2013: 165).
57. Freeman (2003: 33).
58. Cooper (2008).
59. E.g., Butler (2017); Epp, Maynard-Moody, and Haiden-Markel (2014); Forman (2017); Rios (2011).
60. As another example, in a case involving an assault charge rather than a police interaction, an African American man in Oakland County said that he exposed his firearm after being called a racial slur by a customer; instead of acknowledging the slur, an administrator commented: "I think he just got upset, and wanted to just say, 'Oh, here's my gun!'"
61. Bonilla-Silva (2006).
62. Had this claimant "watched the news" leading up to this meeting, he would have viewed public outrage over the police killings of Eric Garner and Michael Brown in addition to other acts of public and private violence; it is not clear to which of these incidents the administrator refers, but it is worth noting that this formed the broader context in which the administrator urged the claimant to "watch the news."
63. Chesney-Lind (2006).
64. Haley (2013).
65. Vigdor and Mercy (2006).
66. Because gun records are sealed, my ability to ascertain the details of the case is limited to public proceedings. A "weapons charge" likely refers to carrying in an authorized manner, for example, concealed carrying into a designated "pistol-free" zone such as the secured area of an airport or a public school.
67. Bumiller (2009).
68. Lipsky (2010: 93).
69. Bumiller (2009); Roberts (2009).
70. See, e.g., Randles (2013).
71. See, e.g., Dubber (2000); Ewald (2016).
72. Cottrol and Diamond (1991); Johnson (2014).
73. Gonzalez Van Cleve (2016).

CONCLUSION: OUR GUN TALK

1. Muhammad (2011).
2. Hill (2004); Strain (1997).
3. Austin (2008); Bloom and Martin (2013); Nelson (2011).

4. This is a fictionalized name that the anthropologist Laurence Ralph (2014) uses in his study of a Chicago-area gang.
5. Butts et al. (2015); Slutkin, Ransford, and Decker (2015).
6. This is the pseudonym that the sociologist Nikki Jones (2018) uses for the peacekeeping group she studied in San Francisco.
7. Briggs (2004).
8. See, e.g., Carr (2005).
9. An NPR story notes that "Philando Castile frequently paid for the lunches of students who owed money or couldn't afford them" (Van Sant 2019); carrying on this legacy, the Philando Castile Relief Foundation works to alleviate children's lunch debts.
10. For example, on implicit bias training and policing, see James (2017); on de-escalation training and policing, see Engel, McManus, and Herold (2020).
11. For 2017 figures, see Gramlich (2019) and Pilkington (2018). On surviving, and living with, gunshot wounds, see Lee (2012).
12. Kahan and Braman (2003).
13. Sontag (2003).
14. Armstrong and Carlson (2019).
15. Ball (2016).
16. Bonikowski (2016); Brubaker (2017); Müller (2017).
17. Kaffer (2017).
18. Tuccille (2018).
19. Fox (2018).
20. Lee, Richardson, and Patton (2018).
21. Jones (2018).
22. See https://twitter.com/eveewing/status/978647407201280002

APPENDIX A: METHODOLOGICAL APPROACH

1. Kraska (1996).
2. For feminist critique and practical navigation of the "ethnographic fixations" of solitary research, intimacy and danger, see Hanson and Richards (2019).
3. On criminal justice unions in California, see Page (2011).
4. Pugh (2013).
5. Pugh (2013: 49).
6. Kendi (2017); see also Seamster and Ray (2018).
7. Thompson et al. (2006).
8. That said, I know that at least one interview was cancelled because the chief had been removed between agreeing to the interview and our interview date; I only knew because his emails were forwarded to an assistant chief, who politely declined the interview.
9. This cannot be chalked up to a "Trump effect"; most of my interviews took place before Trump was elected, and many took place long before he became a viable contender for the Republican nomination

10. Riddell et al. (2018).
11. Roman (2013).
12. Philly Voice Staff (2017).
13. Rios, Carney, and Kelekay (2017: 508).
14. Haraway (2003).
15. Van Maanen (2011).
16. Page and Goodman (2018: 15).

APPENDIX B: PROCEDURES FOR PROTECTING RESEARCH SUBJECTS

1. Moskos (2008).

Bibliography

ABC15.com Staff. (2017). Arizona trooper ambushed: Good Samaritan says God put him there to help save trooper. *ABC15.com*. December 17. https://www .abc15.com/news/region-phoenix-metro/west-phoenix/dps-to-give-update-on -trooper-ambushed-on-i-10-in-tonopah

Ackerman, A. R., and R. Furman. (2013). The criminalization of immigration and the privatization of the immigration detention: Implications for justice. *Contemporary Justice Review* 16 (2): 251–263.

Adler, J. S. (2015). Less crime, more punishment: Violence, race, and criminal justice in early twentieth-century America. *Journal of American History* 102 (1): 34–46.

Aguirre, A. (2012). Arizona's SB1070, Latino immigrants and the framing of anti-immigrant policies. *Latino Studies* 10 (3): 385–394.

Albanesius, C. (2014). Smith & Wesson to sell fewer guns in Calif. over microstamping law. *PC Mag*. January 24. Accessed January 22, 2019. https://www.pcmag .com/article2/0,2817,2429893,00.asp

Alexander, M. (2012). *The New Jim Crow: Mass Incarceration in the Age of Colorblindness*. New York: New Press.

Allard, P. (2002). *Life Sentences: Denying Welfare Benefits to Women Convicted of Drug Offenses*. Washington, DC: Sentencing Project.

Alpert, G., J. MacDonald, and R. Dunham. (2005). Police suspicion and discretionary decision-making during citizen stops. *Criminology* 43:407–434.

Altheide, D. (2009). The Columbine shootings and the discourse of fear. *American Behavioral Scientist* 52:1354–1370.

Ammoland. (2017). White House petition for national concealed carry reciprocity HR 38. *Ammoland*. August 1. Accessed July 18, 2019. https://www.ammoland .com/2017/08/white-house-petition-for-national-concealed-carry-reciprocity -h-r-38/#axzz5u3ua2pKM

Anderson, A. W. (1965). Self-protection. *Chicago Tribune*. March 11. Accessed November 4, 2018, from ProQuest.

Anderson, E. (2010). *Inclusive Masculinity: The Changing Nature of Masculinities*. New York: Routledge.

Anderson, E. (2012). The iconic ghetto. *Annals of the American Academy of Political and Social Science* 642:8–24.

Annin, P. (1992). The NRA woos the cops. *Newsweek*. January 13. Accessed November 4, 2018, from ProQuest.

Anonymous. (1985). Ban sales of "cop-killer" bullets. *Sun Sentinel*. December 26. Accessed January 23, 2019, from ProQuest.

Apel, D. (2015). *Beautiful Terrible Ruins: Detroit and the Anxiety of Decline*. New Brunswick, NJ: Rutgers University Press.

Armenta, A. (2017). *Protect, Serve, and Deport: The Rise of Policing as Immigration Enforcement*. Oakland: University of California Press.

Armstrong, M., and J. Carlson. (2019). Speaking of trauma: The race talk, the gun violence talk, and the racialization of gun trauma. *Palgrave Communications* 5 (1): 1–11.

Associated Press. (2009). Shoot first: Columbine High School transformed US police tactics. *Fox News*. April 18. Accessed November 18, 2018. https://www .foxnews.com/story/shoot-first-columbine-high-school-massacre-transformed -u-s-police-tactics

Austin, C. J. (2008). *Up against the Wall: Violence in the Making and Unmaking of the Black Panther Party*. Fayetteville: University of Arkansas Press.

Avery, B. (1965). NRA stands firm on '65 arms control. *Arizona Republic*. April 5. Accessed January 23, 2019, from ProQuest.

Avery, R. (2013). Police gun control survey: Are legally-armed citizens the best solution to gun violence? *Police One*. April 8. Accessed July 17, 2019. https:// www.policeone.com/gun-legislation-law-enforcement/articles/6186552-Police -Gun-Control-Survey-Are-legally-armed-citizens-the-best-solution-to-gun -violence/

Aviram, H. (2015). *Cheap on Crime: Recession-Era Politics and the Transformation of American Punishment*. Oakland: University of California Press.

Ayres, I., and J. Donohue III. (2002). Shooting down the more guns, less crime hypothesis. NBER Working Paper no. 9336. National Bureau of Economic Research.

Balko, R. (2013). *Rise of the Warrior Cop: The Militarization of America's Police Forces*. New York: PublicAffairs.

Balko, R. (2014). Shaneen Allen, race and gun control. *Washington Post*. July 22. Accessed November 8, 2018. https://www.washingtonpost.com/news/the-watch /wp/2014/07/22/shaneen-allen-race-and-gun-control/?utm_term= .3a153f378b38

Ball, Patrick. (2016). Violence in blue. *Granta 134: No Man's Land*. March 4. Accessed January 6, 2019. https://granta.com/violence-in-blue/

Barragan, M., N. Sherman, K. Reiter, and G. E. Tita. (2016). "Damned if you do, damned if you don't": Perceptions of guns, safety, and legitimacy among detained gun offenders. *Criminal Justice and Behavior* 43 (1): 140–155.

Baye, R. (2015). Police advocacy group leaves few fingerprints. March 25. *Time*. https://time.com/3756739/law-enforcement-alliance-campaign-finance/

Bayley, D. H., and C. D. Shearing. (1996). The future of policing. *Law and Society Review* 30 (3): 585–606.

Beckett, K., and S. Herbert. (2009). *Banished: The New Social Control in Urban America*. Oxford: Oxford University Press.

Beckett, K., and N. Murakawa. (2012). Mapping the shadow carceral state: Toward an institutionally capacious approach to punishment. *Theoretical Criminology* 16 (2): 221–244.

Beckett, K., K. Nyrop, and L. Pfingst. (2006). Race, drugs, and policing. *Criminology* 44:105–137.

Bedard, P. (2015). Police say Obama bullet ban isn't needed, AR-15 round isn't a threat. *Washington Examiner*. March 3. Accessed November 4, 2018. https://www.washingtonexaminer.com/police-say-obama-bullet-ban-isnt-needed-ar-15-round-isnt-a-threat

Bell, D. (2000). CCW bill targeted for more battles. *Detroit Free Press*. December 19.

Berg, W. (1967). Riflemen hit anti-NRA editorial. *Detroit Free Press*. November 9. Accessed November 4, 2018, from ProQuest.

Berkowitz, B., D. Lu, and C. Alcantara. (2018). The terrible numbers that grow with each mass shooting. *Washington Post*. March 14. Accessed November 18, 2018. https://www.washingtonpost.com/graphics/2018/national/mass-shootings-in-america/?utm_term=.eab750cd9f46

Bittner, E. (1973). *The Functions of the Police in Modern Society*. Chevy Chase, MD: National Institute of Mental Health, Center for Studies of Crime and Delinquency.

Black, D. (1983). Crime as social control. *American Sociological Review* 48 (1): 34–45.

Black Lives Matter. (2019). What we believe. Accessed January 22, 2019. https://blacklivesmatter.com/about/what-we-believe/

Blair, J., T. Nichols, D. Burns, and J. Curnutt. (2013). *Active Shooter Events and Response*. Boca Raton, FL: CRC Press.

Bloom, J., and W. E. Martin. (2013). *Black against Empire: The History and Politics of the Black Panther Party*. Berkeley: University of California Press.

Bobo, L., and C. Charles. (2009). Race in the American mind. *Annals of the American Academy of Political and Social Science* 621:243–259.

Boddie, E. C. (2017). Philando Castile and the terror of an ordinary day. *New York Times*. June 20. Accessed January 6, 2019. https://www.nytimes.com/2017/06/20/opinion/philando-castile-and-the-terror-of-an-ordinary-day.html

Bonikowski, B. (2016). Three lessons of contemporary populism in Europe and the United States. *Brown Journal of World Affairs* 23 (1): 9–24.

Bonilla-Silva, E. (2006). *Racism without Racists: Color-Blind Racism and the Persistence of Racial Inequality in America*. Lanham, MD: Rowman & Littlefield.

Bourdieu, P. (1991). *Language and Symbolic Power*. Cambridge, MA: Harvard University Press.

Braga, A. (2003). Serious youth gun offenders and the epidemic of youth violence in Boston. *Journal of Quantitative Criminology* 19:33–54.

Brayne, S. (2014). Surveillance and system avoidance: Criminal justice contact and institutional attachment. *American Sociological Review* 79 (3):367–391.

Bridges, T., and C. J. Pascoe. (2014). Hybrid masculinities: New directions in the sociology of men and masculinities. *Sociology Compass* 8 (3): 246–258.

Briggs, B. (2014). On the streets with the Detroit 300 community police force's A-team. *The Guardian.* June 27. https://www.theguardian.com/cities/2014/jun/26/city-streets-detroit-300-community-police-forces-armed

Bright, S., and D. Maccar. (2017). History of NYPD sidearms. *Range365.* December 14. Accessed November 4, 2018. https://www.range365.com/history-nypd-sidearms

Broidy, L., and W. A. Santoro. (2018). General strain theory and racial insurgency: Assessing the role of legitimate coping. *Justice Quarterly* 35 (1): 162–189.

Brown, R. M. (1991). *No Duty to Retreat: Violence and Values in American History and Society.* Oxford: Oxford University Press.

Brubaker, R. (2017). Why populism? *Theory and Society* 46 (5): 357–385.

Buchwald, Art. (1967). Everyman's escalation. *Newsday.* May 27. Accessed November 4, 2018, from ProQuest.

Bumiller, K. (2009). *In an Abusive State: How Neoliberalism Appropriated the Feminist Movement against Sexual Violence.* Durham, NC: Duke University Press.

Burch, A., and A. Blinder. (2019). Parkland officer who stayed outside during shooting faces criminal charges. *New York Times.* June 4. https://www.nytimes.com/2019/06/04/us/parkland-scot-peterson.html

Butler, J. (2011). *Bodies That Matter.* London: Taylor & Francis.

Butler, P. (2017). *Chokehold: Policing Black Men.* New York: New Press.

Butts, J. A., C. G. Roman, L. Bostwick, and J. R. Porter. (2015). Cure violence. *Annual Review of Public Health* 36:39–53.

Campeau, H. (2015). "Police culture" at work: Making sense of police oversight. *British Journal of Criminology* 55 (4): 669–687.

Carlson, J. (2014). States, subjects and sovereign power: Lessons from global gun cultures. *Theoretical Criminology* 18 (3): 335–353.

Carlson, J. (2015). *Citizen-Protectors: The Everyday Politics of Guns in an Age of Decline.* Oxford: Oxford University Press.

Carlson, J. (2018). Legally armed but presumed dangerous: An intersectional analysis of gun carry licensing as a racial/gender degradation ceremony. *Gender and Society* 32 (2): 204–227.

Carper, E. (1965). Officials return gun lobby fire. *Washington Post.* May 13. Accessed November 4, 2018, from ProQuest.

Carr, P. J. (2005). *Clean Streets: Controlling Crime, Maintaining Order, and Building Community Activism.* New York: New York University Press.

Carrigan, W. D., and C. Webb. (2013). *Forgotten Dead: Mob Violence against Mexicans in the United States, 1848–1928.* Oxford: Oxford University Press.

Carroll, L., and M. L. Gonzalez. (2014). Out of place. *Journal of Research in Crime and Delinquency* 51:559–584.

Chesney-Lind, M. (2006). Patriarchy, crime, and justice: Feminist criminology in an era of backlash. *Feminist Criminology* 1 (1): 6–26.

Chiarello, E. (2015). The war on drugs comes to the pharmacy counter: Frontline work in the shadow of discrepant institutional logics. *Law and Social Inquiry* 40 (1): 86–122.

Chin, G. J. (2002). Race, the war on drugs, and the collateral consequences of criminal conviction. *Journal of Gender, Race and Justice* 6:253.

Churchill, R. H. (2007). Gun regulation, the police power, and the right to keep arms in early America. *Law and History Review* 25 (1): 139–176.

Claiborne, W. (1998). Starting today, California packs toughest gun-sentencing law. *Washington Post*. January 1. Accessed November 8, 2018. https://www .washingtonpost.com/archive/politics/1998/01/01/starting-today-california -packs-toughest-gun-sentencing-law/cef57ead-f714–4546-b938–89c86aea26ac /?utm_term=.409ecc90c5d1

Collins, P. H. (2002). *Black Feminist Thought: Knowledge, Consciousness, and the Politics of Empowerment*. New York: Routledge.

Collins, P. H. (2004). *Black Sexual Politics: African Americans, Gender, and the New Racism*. New York: Routledge.

Comfort, M. (2008). *Doing Time Together: Love and Family in the Shadow of the Prison*. Chicago: University of Chicago Press.

Congressional Quarterly. (1965). Battle on firearms control resumes. *Arizona Republic*. February 10. Accessed July 17, 2019, from ProQuest.

Cook, P. J., and K. A. Goss. (2014). *The Gun Debate: What Everyone Needs to Know*. Oxford: Oxford University Press.

Cooper, F. R. (2008). "Who's the man?": Masculinities studies, terry stops, and police training. *Columbia Journal of Gender and Law* 18:671.

Cornell, S. (2006). Early American origins of the modern gun control debate. *Stanford Law and Policy Review* 17:571–596.

Cottrol, R. J., and R. T. Diamond. (1991). The Second Amendment: Toward an Afro-Americanist reconsideration. *Georgetown Law Journal* 80:309.

Courier-Journal Staff. (1965). Some check on our traffic in firearms is imperative. *Courier-Journal*. February 9. Accessed July 17, 2019, from ProQuest.

Cramer, C. E. (1999). *Concealed Weapon Laws of the Early Republic*. Westport, CT: Greenwood.

Crenshaw, K., A. J. Ritchie, R. Anspach, R. Gilmer, and L. Harris. (2015). Say her name: Resisting police brutality against black women. African American Policy Forum, Center for Intersectionality and Social Policy Studies, Columbia Law School.

Crime Prevention Research Center. (2020). Annual reports on the number of concealed handgun permits. Crime Prevention Research Center. Accessed February 11, 2020. https://crimeresearch.org/tag/annual-report-on-number -of-concealed-handgun-permits/

Cullen, D. (2009). *Columbine*. New York: Twelve.

Dagan, D., and S. M. Teles. (2016). *Prison Break: Why Conservatives Turned against Mass Incarceration*. Oxford: Oxford University Press.

De Parle, J. (1990). Police chief vs. officer: Symbolic rift on guns. *New York Times*. June 21. Accessed November 4, 2018, from ProQuest.

Denvir, D. (2016). A better gun control. *Jacobin*. September 1. Accessed November 8, 2018. https://www.jacobinmag.com/2016/09/gun-control-mass-incarceration -drug-war-nra-shooters

Desmond, M., and N. Valdez. (2013). Unpolicing the urban poor: Consequences of third-party policing for inner-city women. *American Sociological Review* 78 (1): 117–141.

DiIulio, J. J. (1995). The coming of superpredators. *Weekly Standard*. November 27.

Dow, D. M. (2016). The deadly challenges of raising African American boys: Navigating the controlling image of the "thug." *Gender and Society* 30 (2): 161–188.

Du Bois, W.E.B. (1995). *The Philadelphia Negro*. Philadelphia: University of Pennsylvania Press.

Du Bois, W.E.B. (2015). *Souls of Black Folk*. New Haven, CT: Yale University Press.

Dubber, M. D. (2000). Policing possession: The war on crime and the end of criminal law. *Journal of Criminal Law and Criminology* 91:829.

Duggan M. (2001). More guns, more crime. *Journal of Political Economy* 109 (5): 1086–1114.

Dunbar-Ortiz, R. (2014). *An Indigenous Peoples' History of the United States*, vol. 3. Boston: Beacon Press.

Dunbar-Ortiz, R. (2018). *Loaded: A Disarming History of the Second Amendment*. San Francisco: City Lights Books.

Duxbury, S., L. Frizzell, and S. Lindsay. (2018). Mental illness, the media and the moral politics of mass violence. *Journal of Research in Crime and Delinquency* 55:766–797.

Dyer, R. (2008). The matter of whiteness. Pp. 9–14 in *White Privilege*, ed. P. Rothenberg. New York: Worth.

Earl, J. (2008). The process is the punishment: Thirty years later. *Law and Social Inquiry* 33 (3): 735–778.

Edin, K., and T. J. Nelson. (2013). *Doing the Best I Can*. Berkeley: University of California Press.

Eilperin, J., and M. Rosenwald. (2016). White House wants to make it easier for law enforcement to use "smart guns." *Washington Post*. April 29. Accessed November 4, 2018. https://www.washingtonpost.com/politics/white-house-wants-to -make-it-easier-for-law-enforcement-to-use-smart-guns/2016/04/29/88a7183a -0e1e-11e6–8ab8–9ad050f76d7d_story.html?utm_term=.3bfb3106c317

Elcioglu, E. F. (2015). Popular sovereignty on the border: Nativist activism among two border watch groups in southern Arizona. *Ethnography* 16 (4): 438–462.

Elcioglu, E. F. (2017). The state effect: Theorizing immigration politics in Arizona. *Social Problems* 64 (2): 239–255.

Elias, N. (1939). *The Civilizing Process*. New York: Pantheon Books.

Engel, R. S., H. D. McManus, and T. D. Herold. (2020). Does de-escalation training work? A systematic review and call for evidence in police use-of-force reform. Early View: *Criminology and Public Policy*. https://doi.org/10.1111/1745-9133.12467

Epp, C. R., S. Maynard-Moody, and D. P. Haider-Markel. (2014). *Pulled Over: How Police Stops Define Race and Citizenship*. Chicago: University of Chicago Press.

Eschholz, S., B. S. Blackwell, M. Gertz, and T. Chiricos. (2002). Race and attitudes toward the police: Assessing the effects of watching "reality" police programs. *Journal of Criminal Justice* 30 (4): 327–341.

Ewald, A. C. (2016). Rights restoration and the entanglement of US criminal and civil law: A study of New York's "Certificates of Relief." *Law and Social Inquiry* 41 (1): 5–36.

Ewick, P., and S. S. Silbey. (1998). *The Common Place of Law: Stories from Everyday Life*. Chicago: University of Chicago Press.

Fanon, F. (2007). *The Wretched of the Earth*. New York: Grove/Atlantic.

Feagin, J. R. (2013). *The White Racial Frame*. New York: Routledge.

Feeley, M. (1979). *The Process Is the Punishment*. New York: Russell Sage Foundation.

Fegely, T. (1987). Howells nominated for NRA board of directors. *Morning Call*. January 6. Accessed November 4, 2018, from ProQuest.

Fernandez, R. M., and R. V. Gould. (1994). A dilemma of state power: Brokerage and influence in the national health policy domain. *American Journal of Sociology* 99 (6): 1455–1491.

Fields, G. (2000). Gun conundrum: More on streets, fewer incidents. *Wall Street Journal*. December 11. Accessed November 4, 2018, from ProQuest.

Filindra, A., and N. J. Kaplan. (2016). Racial resentment and whites' gun policy preferences in contemporary America. *Political Behavior* 38 (2): 255–275.

Fisher, A. (2016). "Bulletproof warrior" police training canceled in Santa Clara. *Reason Magazine*. August 2. Accessed October 14, 2018. https://reason.com/2016/08/02/bulletproof-police-philado-castile/

Florida, R., and A. Boone. (2018). Where do mass shootings take place? *CityLab*. Accessed October 4, 2018. https://www.citylab.com/life/2018/03/where-do-mass-shootings-take-place/554555/

Foley, N. (1998). *The White Scourge: Mexicans, Blacks, and Poor Whites in Texas Cotton Culture*, vol. 2. Berkeley: University of California Press.

Follman, M., G. Aronson, and D. Pan. (2018). A guide to mass shootings in America. *Mother Jones*. July. Accessed November 18, 2018. https://www.motherjones.com/politics/2012/07/mass-shootings-map/

Follman, M., J. Lurie, J. Lee, and J. West. (2015). The true cost of gun violence. *Mother Jones*. April. Accessed November 8, 2018. https://www.motherjones.com/politics/2015/04/true-cost-of-gun-violence-in-america/

Ford, M. (2015). America's largest mental hospital is jail. *The Atlantic*. June. Accessed November 11, 2018. https://www.theatlantic.com/politics/archive/2015/06/americas-largest-mental-hospital-is-a-jail/395012/

Forman, J., Jr. (2017). *Locking Up Our Own: Crime and Punishment in Black America*. New York: Farrar, Straus and Giroux.

Foucault, M. (1977). *Discipline and Punish: The Birth of the Prison*. New York: Vintage.

Fox, J. A., and J. Levin. (1998). Multiple homicide: Patterns of serial and mass murder. *Crime and Justice* 23:407–455.

Fox, L. (2018). The gun debate that wasn't. *CNN*. March 1. Accessed January 6, 2019. https://www.cnn.com/2018/03/01/politics/gun-debate-this-week-congress/index.html

Fraternal Order of Police. (2019). A history of the Fraternal Order of Police. Fraternal Order of Police. Accessed July 18, 2019. https://www.fop.net/CmsPage.aspx?id=13

Freed, D. (1989). 2 LAPD officers join NRA-backed lawsuit against gun ordinance. *Los Angeles Times*, Valley Edition. February 22. Accessed November 4, 2018, from ProQuest.

Freedman, D. (2013). NRA, gun politics keep ATF in crossfire. *Houston Chronicle*. November 29. Accessed November 4, 2018. https://www.houstonchronicle.com/news/nation-world/nation/article/NRA-gun-politics-keep-ATF-in-crossfire-5022561.php

Freeman, T. (2003). Loving fathers or deadbeat dads. Pp. 33–49 in *Gender, Identity and Reproduction*, ed. S. Earle and G. Letherby. London: Palgrave Macmillan.

French, D. (2017). The Philando Castile verdict was a miscarriage of justice. *National Review*. June 17. Accessed February 12, 2020. https://www.nationalreview.com/corner/philando-castile-verdict-was-miscarriage-justice/

Friedman, S. (1975). Chances for handgun control legislation improving. *Detroit Free Press*. March 16. Accessed January 23, 2019, from ProQuest.

Frohlich, T. C., and J. Harrington. (2018). States with the most (and least) gun violence: See where your state stacks up. *USA Today*. February 21. Accessed December 12, 2018. https://www.usatoday.com/story/news/nation/2018/02/21/states-most-and-least-gun-violence-see-where-your-state-stacks-up/359395002/

Fyfe, J. J. (1980). Always prepared: Police off-duty guns. *Annals of the American Academy of Political and Social Science* 452 (1): 72–81.

Gallup. (2019). Guns. *Gallup Historical Trends*. Accessed August 28, 2019. https://news.gallup.com/poll/1645/guns.aspx

Gardner, B. R. (2006). Separate and unequal: Federal tough-on-guns program targets minority communities for selective enforcement. *Michigan Journal of Race and Law* 12 (2): 305–349.

Garfinkel, H. (1956). Conditions of successful degradation ceremonies. *American Journal of Sociology* 61 (5): 420–424.

Garland, D. (2001). *The Culture of Control*. Oxford: Oxford University Press.

Garland, D. (2005). Penal excess and surplus meaning: Public torture lynchings in twentieth-century America. *Law and Society Review* 39 (4): 793–834.

Gaston, S. (2019). Producing race disparities: A study of drug arrests across place and race. *Criminology* 57 (3): 424–451. https://doi.org/10.1111/1745–9125 .12207

Gaston, S., and R. K. Brunson. (2018). Reasonable suspicion in the eye of the beholder: Routine policing in racially different disadvantaged neighborhoods. *Urban Affairs Review.* https://doi.org/10.1177/1078087418774641

Gates, D. (1989). Ban assault rifles: Yes. *Christian Science Monitor.* February 27. Accessed November 4, 2018. https://www.csmonitor.com/1989/0227/d2weap .html

General Social Survey. (2019). Trends in gun ownership in the United States, 1972– 2018. *NORC at the University of Chicago.* Accessed August 28, 2019. https://www .norc.org/PDFs/GSS%20Reports/GSS_Trends%20in%20Gun%20Ownership _US_1972–2014.pdf

Gerney, K., C. Parsons, and C. Posner. (2013). *America under the Gun.* Washington, DC: Center for American Progress.

Giffords Law Center to Prevent Gun Violence. (2017). Gun law score card. Accessed January 22, 2019. https://lawcenter.giffords.org/scorecard/

Gilliom, J. (2001). *Overseers of the Poor: Surveillance, Resistance, and the Limits of Privacy.* Chicago: University of Chicago Press.

Gong, N. (2015). How to fight without rules: On civilized violence in "de-civilized" spaces. *Social Problems* 62 (4): 605–622.

Gonzalez Van Cleve, N. (2016). *Crook County: Racism and Injustice in America's Largest Criminal Court.* Stanford, CA: Stanford University Press.

Gonzalez Van Cleve, N., and L. Mayes. (2015). Criminal justice through "colorblind" lenses: A call to examine the mutual constitution of race and criminal justice. *Law and Social Inquiry* 40 (2): 406–432.

Gordon, J. (2019). The legitimation of extrajudicial violence in an urban community. *Social Forces.* https://doi.org/10.1093/sf/soz015

Graham, D. (2016). The Second Amendment's second-class citizens. *The Atlantic.* July. Accessed January 6, 2019. https://www.theatlantic.com/politics/archive /2016/07/alton-sterling-philando-castile-2nd-amendment-guns/490301/

Gramlich, J. (2019). What the data say about gun deaths in the U.S. Pew Research Center. August 16. Accessed February 12, 2020. https://www.pewresearch.org /fact-tank/2019/08/16/what-the-data-says-about-gun-deaths-in-the-u-s/

Greenberg, M. A. (2005). *Citizens Defending America: From Colonial Times to the Age of Terrorism.* Pittsburgh: University of Pittsburgh Press.

Griffith, D. (2010). National Rifle Association and law enforcement: Celebrating 50 years of teamwork. *Police Magazine.* September 13. Accessed January 23, 2019. https://www.policemag.com/340387/national-rifle-association-and-law -enforcement-celebrating-50-years-of-teamwork?page=2

Gurusami, S. (2018). The carceral web we weave: Carceral citizens' experiences of digital punishment and solidarity. *Punishment and Society* 21 (4): 435–453.

Gusfield, J. R. (1986). *Symbolic Crusade.* Urbana: University of Illinois Press.

Gustafson, K. S. (2011). *Cheating Welfare: Public Assistance and the Criminalization of Poverty.* New York: NYU Press.

Gutsell, J. N., and M. Inzlicht. (2012). Intergroup differences in the sharing of emotive states. *Social Cognitive and Affective Neuroscience* 7 (5): 596–603.

Guzman, D. (2018). Video shows woman calling police over BBQ at Lake Merritt. SFGate. May 10. Accessed December 12, 2018. https://www.sfgate.com/g00/bayarea/article/Oakland-barbecue-Lake-Merritt-Sunday-confrontation-12902520.php?i10c.encReferrer=aHR0cHM6Ly93d3cuZ29vZ2xlLmNvbS8%3d&i10c.ua=1&i10c.dv=6

Hadden, S. E. (2001). *Slave Patrols: Law and Violence in Virginia and the Carolinas.* Cambridge, MA: Harvard University Press.

Haley, S. (2013). "Like I was a man": Chain gangs, gender, and the domestic carceral sphere in Jim Crow Georgia. *Signs: Journal of Women in Culture and Society* 39 (1): 53–77.

Hamburger, T., and S. Horwitz. (2013). Gun advocates divided over background checks. *Washington Post.* March 5. Accessed November 4, 2018. https://www.washingtonpost.com/world/national-security/gun-advocates-divided-over-background-checks/2013/03/05/2eee5136-84f2-11e2-9d71-f0feafdd1394_story.html?utm_term=.17338c693fa9

Haney, L. (2018). Incarcerated fatherhood: The entanglements of child support debt and mass imprisonment. *American Journal of Sociology* 124 (1): 1–48.

Hanson, R., and P. Richards. (2019). *Harassed: Gender, Bodies, and Ethnographic Research.* Berkeley: University of California Press.

Haraway, D. (2003). Situated knowledges: The science question in feminism and the privilege of partial perspective. Pp. 21–46 in *Turning Points in Qualitative Research: Tying Knots in a Handkerchief,* ed. Y. S. Lincoln and N. K. Denzin. Walnut Creek, CA: AltaMira Press.

Harcourt, B. E. (2010). *Language of the Gun: Youth, Crime, and Public Policy.* Chicago: University of Chicago Press.

Harring, S. L. (1983). *Policing a Class Society: The Experience of American Cities, 1865–1915.* New Brunswick, NJ: Rutgers University Press.

Harris, A., H. Evans, and K. Beckett. (2011). Courtesy stigma and monetary sanctions: Toward a socio-cultural theory of punishment. *American Sociological Review* 76 (2): 234–264.

Harris, C. (1993). Whiteness as property. *Harvard Law Review* 106:1707–1791.

Harris, D. (2006). The war on terror, local police, and immigration enforcement. *Rutgers Law Journal* 38:1.

Harris, F. (2012). *The Price of the Ticket: Barack Obama and the Rise and Decline of Black Politics.* Oxford: Oxford University Press.

Heath, M. (2003). Soft-boiled masculinity: Renegotiating gender and racial ideologies in the Promise Keepers movement. *Gender and Society* 17 (3): 423–444.

Heitzeg, N. A. (2015). "Whiteness," criminality, and the double standards of deviance / social control. *Contemporary Justice Review* 18 (2): 197–214.

Herbers, J. (1985). Police groups reverse stand and back controls on pistols. *New York Times*. October 27. Accessed November 4, 2018, from ProQuest.

Herbert, S. (1998). Police subculture reconsidered. *Criminology* 36 (2): 343–370.

Herbert, S. (2001). "Hard charger" or "station queen"? Policing and the masculinist state. *Gender, Place and Culture: A Journal of Feminist Geography* 8 (1): 55–71.

Herbert, S. (2009). *Citizens, Cops, and Power: Recognizing the Limits of Community*. Chicago: University of Chicago Press.

Hernández, K. L. (2017). *City of Inmates: Conquest, Rebellion, and the Rise of Human Caging in Los Angeles, 1771–1965*. Chapel Hill: University of North Carolina Press.

Hill, L. E. (2004). *The Deacons for Defense: Armed Resistance and the Civil Rights Movement*. Chapel Hill: University of North Carolina Press.

Hinton, E. (2016). *From the War on Poverty to the War on Crime*. Cambridge, MA: Harvard University Press.

Hofer, P., K. Blackwell, K. Burchfield, J. Gabriel, and D. Stevens-Panzer. (2000). Report of the Firearms Policy Team. U.S. Sentencing Commission. January 6. Accessed November 8, 2018. https://www.ussc.gov/sites/default/files/pdf/research-and-publications/working-group-reports/firearms/20000106-use-firearms-during-crime/firearms.pdf

Holland, C. (2017). DPS identifies man who shot, wounded trooper near Tonopah. *Cleveland 19 News*. January 16. Accessed December 17, 2018. https://www.cleveland19.com/story/34271139/dps-identifies-man-who-shot-wounded-trooper-near-tonopah/

Hopper Usher, K. (2019). Report: Hunting and fishing bring billions to Michigan. *Cadillac News*. January 15. Accessed January 22, 2019. https://www.cadillacnews.com/news/report-hunting-and-fishing-bring-billions-to-michigan/article_7a03fd86-59fd-5d13-b20f-97e5324b00c2.html

Houston, P. (1989). NRA mailings put members on red alert. *Star Tribune*. July 30. Accessed November 4, 2018, from ProQuest.

Hunt, J. (1984). The development of rapport through the negotiation of gender in field work among police. *Human Organization* 43:283–296.

Hunt, J. (1985). Police accounts of normal force. *Urban Life* 13 (4): 315–341.

Hunt, J. (1990). The logic of sexism among police. *Women and Criminal Justice* 1:3–30.

Huq, A., and C. Muller. (2008). The war on crime as precursor to the war on terror. *International Journal of Law, Crime and Justice* 36:215–229.

Hurwitz, J., and M. Peffley. (1997). Public perceptions of race and crime: The role of racial stereotypes. *American Journal of Political Science* 41 (2): 375–401.

Ingraham, C. (2018). There are more guns than people in the United States, according to a new study of global firearm ownership. *Washington Post*. June 19. Accessed August 28, 2019. https://www.washingtonpost.com/news/wonk/wp/2018/06/19/there-are-more-guns-than-people-in-the-united-states-according-to-a-new-study-of-global-firearm-ownership/

Jackman, T. (2016). Fraternal Order of Police union endorses Trump. *Washington Post.* September 16. Accessed November 4, 2018. https://www.washingtonpost .com/news/true-crime/wp/2016/09/16/fraternal-order-of-police-union -endorses-trump/?utm_term=.537a84367aaf

Jackson, P. I., and L. Carroll. (1981). Race and the war on crime: The sociopolitical determinants of municipal police expenditures in 90 non-southern US cities. *American Sociological Review* 46 (3): 290–305.

Jacobs, J. B. (2015). *The Eternal Criminal Record.* Cambridge, MA: Harvard University Press.

Jacques, S. (2017). "A run-in with the cops is really few and far between": Negative evidence and ethnographic understanding of racial discrimination by police. *Sociological Focus* 50 (1): 7–17.

Jacques, S., and R. Wright. (2015). *Code of the Suburb: Inside the World of Young Middle-Class Drug Dealers.* Chicago: University of Chicago Press.

James, T. (2017). Can cops unlearn their unconscious biases? *The Atlantic.* December 23. Accessed February 12, 2020. https://www.theatlantic.com/politics /archive/2017/12/implicit-bias-training-salt-lake/548996/

Johnson, N. (2014). *Negroes and the Gun.* Amherst, NY: Prometheus Books.

Jones, N. (2018). *The Chosen Ones: Black Men and the Politics of Redemption.* Oakland: University of California Press.

Judicial Council of California. (2019). Gun violence restraining orders. *California Courts: The Judicial Branch of California.* Accessed August 28, 2019. https://www .courts.ca.gov/33961.htm

Kaffer, Nancy. (2017). Las Vegas shooting: The gun debate is over and the gun-rights crowd won. *Detroit Free Press.* October 2. Accessed January 6, 2019. https://www.freep.com/story/opinion/2017/10/02/las-vegas-proves-gun -debate-is-over-gun-rights-crowd-won-nancy-kaffer-column/724724001/

Kahan, D. M., and D. Braman. (2003). More statistics, less persuasion: A cultural theory of gun-risk perceptions. *University of Pennsylvania Law Review* 151 (4): 1291–1327.

Kahr, F. J. (1916). Intensive training necessary in teaching the policeman to shoot. *American Rifleman* 61:169.

Kail, S. (2016). The unintended consequences of California Proposition 47. *Pepperdine Law Review* 44:1039.

Keenan, K. M., and S. Walker. (2004). An impediment to police accountability: An analysis of statutory law enforcement officers' bills of rights. *Boston University Public Interest Law Journal* 14:185.

Kellner, D. (2015). *Guys and Guns Amok: Domestic Terrorism and School Shootings from the Oklahoma City Bombing to the Virginia Tech Massacre.* New York: Routledge.

Kendi, I. (2017). *Stamped from the Beginning: The Definitive History of Racist Ideas in America.* New York: Random House.

Kennedy, D. M. (2011). *Don't Shoot: One Man, a Street Fellowship, and the End of Violence in Inner-City America.* New York: Bloomsbury USA.

Kohler-Hausmann, I. (2013). Misdemeanor justice: Control without conviction. *American Journal of Sociology* 119 (2): 351–393.

Kopel, D. (2004). The return of a legislative legend. *National Review Online*. March 1. Accessed October 2, 2019. http://davekopel.org/NRO/Return-of-a-Legislative -Legend.htm

Kopel, D. (2014). The posse comitatus and the office of sheriff: Armed citizens summoned to the aid of law enforcement. *Journal of Criminal Law and Criminology* 104:761.

Kopel, D. (2019). Brief for amici curiae in the case of *Rocky Mountain Gun Owners v. State of Colorado*. Accessed October 2, 2019. http://davekopel.org/Briefs/Colorado /Amicus%20Brief%20CLEFIA%20and%20Sheriffs-June10-corrected.pdf

Kraska, P. (1996). Enjoying militarism. *Justice Quarterly* 13:405–429.

Kraska, P. (2007). Militarization and policing. *Policing* 1:501–513.

Kravarik, J., and S. Elam. (2017). Armed stranger with a gun saves wounded cop. *CNN*. March 17. Accessed December 17, 2018. https://www.cnn.com/2017/03 /17/us/beyond-the-call-of-duty-arizona/

Kurtzleben, D. (2017). Fact check: Is Chicago proof that gun laws don't work? *National Public Radio*. October 5. Accessed November 30, 2019. https://www.npr .org/2017/10/05/555580598/fact-check-is-chicago-proof-that-gun-laws-don-t -work

Lageson, S. E. (2017). Crime data, the internet, and free speech: An evolving legal consciousness. *Law and Society Review* 51 (1): 8–41.

Lamar, J. V. (2001). Gaming for assault rifles. *Time*. June 24. Accessed November 4, 2018. http://content.time.com/time/magazine/article/0,9171,151492,00 .html

Lane, B. (1967). Police test anti-riot arsenal. *Los Angeles Sentinel*. November 30. Accessed November 4, 2018, from ProQuest.

Larkin, R. W. (2011). Masculinity, school shooters, and the control of violence. Pp. 315–344 in *Control of Violence*, ed. W. Heitmayer, H.-G. Haupt, A. Kirschner, and S. Malthaner. New York: Springer.

Law Enforcement Officers Safety Act. (2003). Report from the Committee on the Judiciary. House of Representatives, 108th Congress, 2nd session. Washington, DC: U.S. Government Printing Office.

Leddy, E. (1985). The National Rifle Association: The evolution of a social movement. PhD dissertation. Fordham University.

Lee, G. (1991). Taking the fight against gun control to the police. *Washington Post*. August 15. Accessed November 4, 2018. https://www.washingtonpost.com /archive/politics/1991/08/15/taking-the-fight-against-gun-control-to-the -police/c1de803d-9213–4bad-9892-c9055836508f/?noredirect=on&utm_term =.73ee496e7f20

Lee, J. (2012). Wounded: Life after the shooting. *Annals of the American Academy of Political and Social Science* 642 (1): 244–257.

Lee, J., J. Richardson Jr., and D. Patton. (2018). Three gun violence scholars on what is missing from America's gun control debate. *Vice*. May 24. Accessed

January 6, 2019. https://www.vice.com/en_ca/article/7xmxky/three-gun-violence-scholars-on-what-is-missing-from-americas-gun-control-debate

LeFave, D. G. (1970). The will to arm: The National Rifle Association in American society, 1871–1970. PhD dissertation. University of Colorado.

Leonardatos, C. D. (1999). California's attempts to disarm the Black Panthers. *San Diego Law Review* 36:947.

Lerman, A. E., and V. M. Weaver. (2014). *Arresting Citizenship: The Democratic Consequences of American Crime Control*. Chicago: University of Chicago Press.

Light, C. E. (2017). *Stand Your Ground: A History of America's Love Affair with Lethal Self-Defense*. Boston: Beacon Press.

Lipsitz, G. (2008). The possessive investment in whiteness. Pp. 67–90 in *White Privilege*, ed. P. Rothenberg. New York: Worth.

Lipsky, M. (2010). *Street-level bureaucracy: Dilemmas of the individual in public service*. 30th anniversary edition. New York: Russell Sage Foundation.

L. L. (1968). Letter to the editor: Sees National Rifle Association being made a "whipping boy." *Indianapolis Star*. July 21. Accessed November 4, 2018 from ProQuest.

Lott, J. R. (2013). *More Guns, Less Crime*. Chicago: University of Chicago Press.

Lowenthal, G. T. (1993). Mandatory sentencing laws: Undermining the effectiveness of determinate sentencing reform. *California Law Review* 81: 61–124.

Mack, J. (2018). Michigan gun numbers by county. *MLive.com*. February. Accessed January 22, 2019. https://www.mlive.com/news/index.ssf/2018/02/michigan_gun_ownership_by_the_1.html

Madfis, E. (2014). Triple entitlement and homicidal anger. *Men and Masculinities* 17:67–86.

Madley, B. (2016). *An American Genocide: The United States and the California Indian Catastrophe, 1846–1873*. New Haven, CT: Yale University Press.

Madriz, E. I. (1997). Images of criminals and victims: A study on women's fear and social control. *Gender and Society* 11 (3): 342–356.

Maghbouleh, N. (2017). *The Limits of Whiteness: Iranian Americans and the Everyday Politics of Race*. Stanford, CA: Stanford University Press.

Mann, M. (1986). The autonomous power of the state. Pp. 109–136 in *States in History*, ed. J. A. Hall. Oxford: Oxford University Press.

Manning, P. K. (1977). *Police Work: The Social Organization of Policing*. Cambridge, MA: MIT Press.

Manza, J., and C. Uggen. (2008). *Locked Out: Felon Disenfranchisement and American Democracy*. Oxford: Oxford University Press.

Margasak, L. (1986). Police shoot for tougher gun control. *Minneapolis Star and Tribune*. January 10. Accessed November 4, 2018, from ProQuest.

Marks, L., and R. Palkovitz. (2004). American fatherhood types. *Fathering* 2 (2): 113–130.

Martinson, R. (1974). What works? Questions and answers about prison reform. *Public Interest* 35:22.

Marx, G. T., and D. Archer. (1971). Citizen involvement in the law enforcement process: The case of community police patrols. *American Behavioral Scientist* 15 (1): 52–72.

Maynard-Moody, S. W., and M. C. Musheno. (2003). *Cops, Teachers, Counselors: Stories from the Front Lines of Public Service.* Ann Arbor: University of Michigan Press.

McClellan, A. (2010). A half-century of service. *The American Rifleman.* April 13. Accessed November 4, 2018. https://www.americanrifleman.org/articles/2010/4/13/a-half-century-of-service/

McCombie, B. (2011). Arizona, a mecca for gun makers. *Gun Digest.* July 20. Accessed January 22, 2019. https://gundigest.com/article/arizona-a-mecca-for-gun-makers

McDowall, D., and C. Loftin. (1983). Collective security and the demand for legal handguns. *American Journal of Sociology* 88 (6): 1146–1161.

McGinty, E., D. Webster, M. Jarlenski, and C. Barry. (2014). News media framing of serious mental illness and gun violence in the United States, 1997–2012. *American Journal of Public Health* 104:406–413.

McGirr, L. (2015). *The War on Alcohol: Prohibition and the Rise of the American State.* New York: W. W. Norton.

McNamara, J. (1988). For police, an arms race. *USA Today.* August 9. Accessed November 4, 2018, from ProQuest.

Meares, T. L., and P. Neyroud. (2015). *Rightful Policing.* U.S. Department of Justice, Office of Justice Programs, National Institute of Justice.

Meehan, A., and M. Ponder. (2002). Race and place. *Justice Quarterly* 19: 399–430.

Mencken, F. C., and P. Froese. (2019). Gun culture in action. *Social Problems* 66 (1): 3–27.

Messner, M. A. (2007). The masculinity of the governator: Muscle and compassion in American politics. *Gender and Society* 21 (4): 461–480.

Mettler, S., and J. Soss. (2004). The consequences of public policy for democratic citizenship: Bridging policy studies and mass politics. *Perspectives on Politics* 2 (1): 55–73.

Metzl, J. M. (2010). *The Protest Psychosis: How Schizophrenia Became a Black Disease.* Boston: Beacon Press.

Metzl, J., and K. T. MacLeish. (2015). Mental illness, mass shootings, and the politics of American firearms. *American Journal of Public Health* 105:240–249.

Mezzacappa, D. (1984). "Cop-killer" bullet bill withdrawn. *Philadelphia Inquirer.* September 27. Accessed November 4, 2018 from ProQuest.

Micucci, A. J., and I. M. Gomme. (2005). American police and subcultural support for the use of excessive force. *Journal of Criminal Justice* 33 (5): 487–500.

Miller, L. L. (2010). The invisible black victim. *Law and Society Review* 44 (3–4): 805–842.

Mingus, W., and B. Zopf. (2010). White means never having to say you're sorry: The racial project in explaining mass shootings. *Social Thought and Research* 31:57–77.

Mitchell, O., and M. S. Caudy. (2015). Examining racial disparities in drug arrests. *Justice Quarterly* 32 (2): 288–313.

Mitchell, T. (1991). The limits of the state. *American Political Science Review* 85 (1): 77–96.

Moen, B. (2018). California firearms manufacturer moving to Wyoming. *US News and World Report.* January 23. Accessed January 22, 2019. https://www.usnews .com/news/best-states/wyoming/articles/2018-01-23/california-firearms -manufacturer-moving-to-wyoming

Moley, R. (1965). FBI report shows need for gun bill. *Detroit Free Press.* July 31. Accessed November 4, 2018, from ProQuest.

Monahan, T. (2010). *Surveillance in the Time of Insecurity.* New Brunswick, NJ: Rutgers University Press.

Morin, R., K. Parker, R. Stepler, and A. Mercer. (2017). Behind the badge. Pew Research Center. January 11. Accessed November 7, 2018. http://www .pewsocialtrends.org/2017/01/11/behind-the-badge/

Morris, A. D. (2015). *The Scholar Denied: W.E.B. Du Bois and the Birth of Modern Sociology.* Oakland: University of California Press.

Morrison, G. B. (1995). A critical history and evaluation of American police firearms training to 1945. PhD dissertation. University of California, Irvine.

Morrison, G. B., and B. J. Vila. (1998). Police handgun qualification: Practical measure or aimless activity? *Policing: An International Journal of Police Strategies and Management* 21 (3): 510–533.

Moskos, P. (2008). *Cop in the Hood: My Year Policing Baltimore's Eastern District.* Princeton, NJ: Princeton University Press.

The Movement for Black Lives. (2016). A vision for black lives: Police demands for black power, freedom and justice. Accessed January 22, 2019. https://policy .m4bl.org/.

Muhammad, K. G. (2011). *The Condemnation of Blackness.* Cambridge, MA: Harvard University Press.

Müller, J. W. (2017). *What Is Populism?* Harmondsworth, UK: Penguin.

Murakawa, N. (2014). *The First Civil Right: How Liberals Built Prison America.* Oxford: Oxford University Press.

Murch, D. (2015). Crack in Los Angeles: Crisis, militarization, and black response to the late twentieth-century war on drugs. *Journal of American History* 102 (1): 162–173.

Muschert, G. W. (2007). The Columbine victims and the myth of the juvenile superpredator. *Youth Violence and Juvenile Justice* 5 (4): 351–366.

Myrick, A. (2013). Facing your criminal record: Expungement and the collateral problem of wrongfully represented self. *Law and Society Review* 47 (1): 73–104.

Neidig, H. (2016). NRA: "The reports from Minnesota are troubling." *The Hill.* July 8. Accessed February 12, 2020. https://thehill.com/blogs/blog-briefing -room/news/287062-nra-the-reports-from-minnesota-are-troubling

Nelson, A. (2011). *Body and Soul: The Black Panther Party and the Fight against Medical Discrimination.* Minneapolis: University of Minnesota Press.

Nelson, L. (1984). The NRA is protecting a vicious cop-killer. *Detroit Free Press*. October 22. Accessed November 4, 1984, from ProQuest.

New York Times Editorial Board. (1983). Kill the "cop-killer" bullet. *New York Times*. August 29. Accessed November 4, 2018, from ProQuest.

New York Times Staff. (1927). Plan to bar arms to all criminals. *New York Times*. January 29. Accessed July 19, 2019. https://www.nytimes.com/1927/01/29 /archives/plan-to-bar-arms-to-all-criminals-baker-lowden-and-mills-speak .html

Newman, K., and C. Fox. (2009). Repeat tragedy: Rampage shootings in American high school and college settings, 2002–2008. *American Behavioral Scientist* 52 (9): 1286–1308.

Novak, K, and M. Chamlin. (2012). Racial threat, suspicion, and police behavior. *Crime and Delinquency* 58:275–300.

Novak, W. J. (2008). The myth of the "weak" American state. *American Historical Review* 113 (3): 752–772.

NRA Foundation. (2019). Grants. *NRAFoundation.org*. Accessed July 17, 2019. https://www.nrafoundation.org/grants/

NRA Law Enforcement, Military and Security. (2019). Law enforcement, military, and security. *LE.NRA.org*. Accessed July 17, 2019. https://le.nra.org/

NRA Range Services. (2019). Range services. *RangeServices.NRA.org*. Accessed July 17, 2019. https://rangeservices.nra.org/

NRA-ILA. (2017a). In case you missed it: Head of FOP debunks gun control lobby's main argument against the Hearing Protection Act. *NRAILA.org*. Accessed November 4, 2018. https://www.nraila.org/articles/20170928/in-case-you-missed -it-head-of-fop-debunks-gun-control-lobby-s-main-argument-against-the hearing-protection-act

NRA-ILA. (2017b). Disaffected gun control activist exposes Bloomberg's "top-down bureaucracy." *NRAILA.org*. Accessed November 4, 2018. https://www .nraila.org/articles/20170901/disaffected-gun-control-activist-exposes -bloomberg-s-top-down-bureaucracy

NRA-ILA. (2000). NRA praises U.S. House for national "Project Exile" passage. *NRAILA.org*. Accessed November 8, 2018. https://www.nraila.org/articles /20000411/nra-praises-us-house-for-national-pr

Obert, J. (2018). *The Six-Shooter State: Public and Private Violence in American Politics*. Cambridge: Cambridge University Press.

Oliver, M., and T. Shapiro. (2013). *Black Wealth / White Wealth*. New York: Routledge.

Omi, M., and H. Winant. (2014). *Racial Formation in the United States*. New York: Routledge.

Page, J. (2011). *The Toughest Beat: Politics, Punishment, and the Prison Officers Union in California*. Oxford: Oxford University Press.

Page, J., and P. Goodman. (2018). Creative disruption: Edward Bunker, carceral habitus, and the criminological value of fiction. *Theoretical Criminology*. https:// doi.org/10.1177/1362480618769866

Pager, D. (2008). *Marked: Race, Crime, and Finding Work in an Era of Mass Incarceration*. Chicago: University of Chicago Press.

Papachristos, A., and C. Wildeman. (2014). Network exposure and homicide victimization in an African American community. *American Journal of Public Health* 104:143–150.

Papachristos, A., C. Wildeman, and E. Roberto. (2015). Tragic, but not random. *Social Science and Medicine* 125:139–150.

Parenti, C. (2000). *Lockdown America: Police and Prisons in the Age of Crisis*. London: Verso.

Parker, B. (2012). How the North Hollywood shootout changed patrol arsenals. *Police Magazine*. February. Accessed November 4, 2018. http://www.policemag.com/channel/weapons/articles/2012/02/how-the-north-hollywood-shootout-changed-patrol-rifles.aspx

Parker, K., J. M. Horowitz, R. Igielnick, J. Baxter Oliphant, and A. Brown. (2017). America's complex relationship with guns. Pew Research Center. June 22. Accessed February 11, 2020. https://www.pewsocialtrends.org/2017/06/22/americas-complex-relationship-with-guns/

Pascoe, C. J., and J. A. Hollander. (2016). Good guys don't rape: Gender, domination, and mobilizing rape. *Gender and Society* 30 (1): 67–79.

Payne, B. K. (2006). Weapon bias: Split-second decisions and unintended stereotyping. *Current Directions in Psychological Science* 15 (6): 287–291.

Petersilia, J. (2013). *Voices from the Field: Realignment in Review*. Stanford, CA: Stanford Criminal Justice Center.

Philadelphia Inquirer. (1986). Gun control: Round 2. *Philadelphia Inquirer*. May 12. Accessed November 4, 2018, from ProQuest.

Phillips, S. (2016). Myths, militarism and the police patrol rifle. *Policing and Society* 26:185–196.

Philly Voice Staff. (2017). Philly activist on 2nd Amendment: "I don't give a f*** who they meant it for. It's mine now." *Philly Voice*. December 26. Accessed January 29, 2018. https://www.phillyvoice.com/philly-activist-2nd-amendment-i-dont-give-f-who-they-meant-it-its-mine-now/

Pierce, J. E. (2018). *Making the White Man's West*. Boulder: University Press of Colorado.

Pilkington, E. (2018). Gun deaths in US rise to highest levels in 20 years, data shows. *The Guardian*. December 13. Accessed January 5, 2019. https://www.theguardian.com/us-news/2018/dec/13/us-gun-deaths-levels-cdc-2017

Plassmann, F., and J. Whitley. (2003). Confirming "more guns, less crime." *Stanford Law Review* 55 (4): 1313–1369.

Police buying own carbines. (1967). *The Sun*. September 16. Accessed November 4, 2018 from ProQuest.

Prassel, F. R. (1972). *The Western Peace Officer: A Legacy of Law and Order*. Norman: University of Oklahoma Press.

Primeau, A., T. G. Bowers, M. A. Harrison, and XuXu. (2013). Deinstitutionalization of the mentally ill: Evidence for transinstitutionalization from psychiatric hospitals to penal institutions. *Comprehensive Psychology* 2 (2): 1–10.

Prokos, A., and I. Padavic. (2002). "There oughtta be a law against bitches": Masculinity lessons in police academy training. *Gender, Work and Organization* 9 (4): 439–459.

Pugh, A. J. (2013). What good are interviews for thinking about culture? Demystifying interpretive analysis. *American Journal of Cultural Sociology* 1 (1): 42–68.

Pyle, L. (2001). The Second Amendment police department. *The Second Amendment Police Department.* Accessed July 17, 2019. https://web.archive.org/web/2017030 2225241/http://www.2ampd.net/Articles/Pyle/LeroyPyle-Biography.htm

Rahr, S., and S. Rice. (2015). *From Warriors to Guardians.* Laurel, MD: U.S. Department of Justice, Office of Justice Programs, National Institute of Justice.

Ralph, L. (2014). *Renegade Dreams: Living through Injury in Gangland Chicago.* Chicago: University of Chicago Press.

Ramey, D. M., and T. Steidley. (2018). Policing through subsidized firepower: An assessment of rational choice and minority threat explanations of police participation in the 1033 Program. *Criminology* 56 (4): 812–856.

Randles, J. M. (2013). Repackaging the "package deal" promoting marriage for low-income families by targeting paternal identity and reframing marital masculinity. *Gender and Society* 27 (6): 864–888.

Ray, L. (2011). *Violence and Society.* Los Angeles: Sage.

Rehm, D. (2016). *The Diane Rehm Show.* National Public Radio. July 19. Accessed January 23, 2019. https://dianerehm.org/shows/2016-07-19/update-on-the-gop -convention-in-cleveland

Reiner, R. (2010). *The Politics of the Police.* Oxford: Oxford University Press.

Reiter, K. (2016). *23/7: Pelican Bay Prison and the Rise of Long-Term Solitary Confinement.* New Haven, CT: Yale University Press.

Reiter, K., and T. Blair. (2015). Punishing mental illness: Trans-institutionalization and solitary confinement in the United States. Pp. 177–196 in *Extreme Punishment,* ed. K. Reiter and A. Koenig. London: Palgrave Macmillan.

Reiter, K., and N. Pifer. (2015). *Brown v. Plata.* Oxford Handbooks Online. Accessed November 7, 2018. http://www.oxfordhandbooks.com/view/10.1093/oxfordhb /9780199935383.001.0001/oxfordhb-9780199935383-e-113

Riddell, C. A., S. Harper, M. Cerdá, and J. S. Kaufman. (2018). Comparison of rates of firearm and nonfirearm homicide and suicide in black and white non-Hispanic men, by US state. *Annals of Internal Medicine* 168 (10): 712–720.

Rios, V. M. (2011). *Punished: Policing the Lives of Black and Latino Boys.* New York: New York University Press.

Rios, V. M., N. Carney, and J. Kelekay. (2017). Ethnographies of race, crime, and justice: Toward a sociological double-consciousness. *Annual Review of Sociology* 43:493–513.

Riots and guns. (1968). *Washington Post*. February 14. Accessed November 4, 2018, from ProQuest.

Roberts, D. (2009). *Shattered Bonds: The Color of Child Welfare*. New York: Civitas Books.

Roberts, J. (2004). Assault weapons ban expires. *CBS*. September 13. Accessed November 4, 2018. https://www.cbsnews.com/news/assault-weapon-ban-expires/

Robles, F. (2018). Florida's "Stand Your Ground" law applies to police, too, court rules. *New York Times*. December 13. Accessed January 28, 2019. https://www.nytimes.com/2018/12/13/us/florida-stand-your-ground-police.html

Roman, J. K. (2013). Race, justifiable homicide, and stand your ground laws: Analysis of FBI supplementary homicide report data. Urban Institute. https://www.urban.org/sites/default/files/publication/23856/412873-Race-Justifiable-Homicide-and-Stand-Your-Ground-Laws.PDF

Romero, D. (2014). The militarization of police started in Los Angeles. *LA Weekly*. August 15. Accessed November 4, 2018. http://www.laweekly.com/news/the-militarization-of-police-started-in-los-angeles-5010287

Rose, V. (2013). Firearms boards in Connecticut and other states. Connecticut Office of Legislative Research. February 20. Accessed January 27, 2017. https://www.cga.ct.gov/2013/rpt/2013-R-0138.htm

Rosenblatt, K. (2018). Broward County officials change shooting-response policy after lessons learned in Parkland school massacre. *NBC News*. December 26. Accessed January 29, 2019. https://www.nbcnews.com/news/amp/ncna952036

Ross, C. T. (2015). A multi-level Bayesian analysis of racial bias in police shootings at the county-level in the United States, 2011–2014. *PLoS One* 10 (11): e0141854.

Roth, R. (2012). *American Homicide*. Cambridge, MA: Harvard University Press.

Rothstein, R. (2017). *The Color of Law*. New York: Liveright.

Ruelas, R. (2017). He's a good guy with a gun who saved a cop's life—and he's for gun control. *AZCentral*. May 24. Accessed December 17, 2018. https://www.azcentral.com/story/news/local/arizona-best-reads/2017/05/24/thomas-yoxall-saved-trooper-arizona-gun-control/331711001/

Ruelas, R. (2018). Good guy with gun: Gabby Giffords shooting touts training. *AZCentral*. February 22. Accessed October 30, 2019. https://www.azcentral.com/story/news/local/arizona/2018/02/22/good-guy-gun-gabby-giffords-shooting-touts-training-if-teachers-armed/364647002/

Russell-Brown, K. (1999). Driving while black: Corollary phenomena and collateral consequences. *Boston College Law Review* 40:717–731.

Russell-Brown, K. (2009). *The Color of Crime*. New York: New York University Press.

Sampson, R. J. (2008). Moving to inequality: Neighborhood effects and experiments meet social structure. *American Journal of Sociology* 114 (1): 189–231.

Seamster, L., and V. Ray. (2018). Against teleology in the study of race: Toward the abolition of the progress paradigm. *Sociological Theory* 36 (4): 315–342.

Schenwar, M. (2014). Reduce gun penalties. *New York Times*. March 15. Accessed November 8, 2018. https://www.nytimes.com/2014/03/15/opinion/reduce-gun-penalties.html

Schmitz, J. (1967). State roundup. *Tustin News*. August 31.

Schuppe, J. (2016). Officer mistook Philando Castile for a robbery suspect, tapes show. July 12. *NBC News*. Accessed February 12, 2020. https://www.nbcnews.com/news/us-news/officer-thought-philando-castile-was-robbery-suspect-tapes-show-n607856

Sergel, R. P. (1962). Before the sale. *St. Louis Post-Dispatch*. September 25. Accessed November 4, 2018 from ProQuest.

Shannon, S. K., C. Uggen, J. Schnittker, M. Thompson, S. Wakefield, and M. Massoglia. (2017). The growth, scope, and spatial distribution of people with felony records in the United States, 1948–2010. *Demography* 54 (5): 1795–1818.

Shapira, H., K. Jensen, and K. H. Lin. (2018). Trends and patterns of concealed handgun license applications. *Social Currents* 5 (1): 3–14.

Siegel, R. (2018). Two black men arrested at Starbucks settle with Philadelphia for $1 each. *Washington Post*. May 2. Accessed December 12, 2018. https://www.washingtonpost.com/news/business/wp/2018/05/02/african-american-men-arrested-at-starbucks-reach-1-settlement-with-the-city-secure-promise-for-200000-grant-program-for-young-entrepreneurs/?utm_term=.c10a503ae673

Sierra-Arévalo, M. (2016). American policing and the danger imperative. SSRN. https://ssrn.com/abstract=2864104

Simon, J. (2003). Gun rights and the constitutional significance of violent crime. *William and Mary Bill of Rights Journal* 12:335.

Simon, J. (2007). *Governing through Crime: How the War on Crime Transformed American Democracy and Created a Culture of Fear*. Oxford: Oxford University Press.

Simon, J. (2014). *Mass Incarceration on Trial: A Remarkable Court Decision and the Future of Prisons in America*. New York: New Press.

Singletary, O. A. (1971). *Negro Militia and Reconstruction*. Austin: University of Texas Press.

Skolnick, J. H. (2011). *Justice without Trial: Law Enforcement in Democratic Society*. New Orleans: Quid Pro Books.

Skolnick, J. II., and J. J. Fyfe. (1993). *Above the Law*. New York: Free Press.

Slotkin, R. (1973 [2000]). *Regeneration through Violence: The Mythology of the American Frontier, 1600–1860*. Norman: University of Oklahoma Press.

Slutkin, G., C. Ransford, and R. B. Decker. (2015). Cure violence. Pp. 43–56 in *Envisioning Criminology*, ed. M. Maltz and S. K. Rice. New York: Springer International.

Smith, D. A., and C. D. Uchida. (1988). The social organization of self-help: A study of defensive weapon ownership. *American Sociological Review* 53 (1): 94–102.

Smith, J. (2018). Landmark California law curtails California prosecutors. *The Intercept*. November 23. Accessed January 28, 2019. https://theintercept.com/2018/11/23/california-felony-murder-rule/

Smith, J., and T. Linnemann. (2015). Whiteness and critical white studies in crime and justice. *Contemporary Justice Review* 18:101–104.

Smith, M., and G. Alpert. (2007). Explaining police bias. *Criminal Justice and Behavior* 34:1262–1283.

Smith, M., and T. Williams. (2016). Minnesota police officer's 'Bulletproof Warrior' training is questioned. *New York Times*. July 14. Accessed February 12, 2020. https://www.nytimes.com/2016/07/15/us/minnesota-police-officers-bulletproof-warrior-training-is-questioned.html

Snow, R. L. (1997). The birth and evolution of the SWAT unit. *PoliceOne*. April 1. Accessed January 28, 2019. https://www.policemag.com/338658/the-birth-and-evolution-of-the-swat-unit

Sontag, S. (2003). *Regarding the Pain of Others*. New York: Farrar, Straus, and Giroux.

Soss, J., R. C. Fording, and S. F. Schram. (2011). *Disciplining the Poor: Neoliberal Paternalism and the Persistent Power of Race*. Chicago: University of Chicago Press.

Soss, J., and V. Weaver. (2017). Police are our government: Politics, political science, and the policing of race-class subjugated communities. *Annual Review of Political Science* 20:565–591.

Spierenburg, P. 2006. Democracy came too early: A tentative explanation for the problem of American homicide. *American Historical Review* 111 (1): 104–114.

Spitzer, R. (2015). *Guns across America: Reconciling Gun Rules and Rights*. Oxford: Oxford University Press.

Steidley, T. (2019). Sharing the monopoly on violence? Shall-issue concealed handgun license laws and responsibilization. *Sociological Perspectives* 62 (6): 929–947.

Stein, A. (2005). Make room for Daddy: Anxious masculinity and emergent homophobias in neopatriarchal politics. *Gender and Society* 19 (5): 601–620.

Stern, R. (2017). Armed civilian praised for shooting undocumented suspect who attacked trooper. *Phoenix New Times*. January 17. Accessed December 17, 2018. https://www.phoenixnewtimes.com/news/armed-civilian-praised-for-shooting-undocumented-suspect-who-attacked-trooper-8997702

Stivers, C. (2007). "So poor and so black": Hurricane Katrina, public administration, and the issue of race. *Public Administration Review* 67:48–56.

Stoughton, S. (2014). Law enforcement's warrior problem. *Harvard Law Review Forum* 128: 225–234.

Stoughton, S. (2016). Principled policing: Warrior cops and guardian officers. *Wake Forest Law Review* 51 (30): 611–676.

Strain, C. B. (1997). "We walked like men": The Deacons for Defense and Justice. *Louisiana History* 38 (1): 43–62.

Stroud, A. (2012). Good guys with guns: Hegemonic masculinity and concealed handguns. *Gender and Society* 26 (2): 216–238.

Stuart, F. (2016). *Down, Out, and under Arrest: Policing and Everyday Life in Skid Row*. Chicago: University of Chicago Press.

Sugrue, T. J. (2014). *The Origins of the Urban Crisis: Race and Inequality in Postwar Detroit.* Updated edition. Princeton, NJ: Princeton University Press.

Swidler, A. (1986). Culture in action: Symbols and strategies. *American Sociological Review* 51 (2): 273–286.

Sykes, G. (1958). The pains of imprisonment. Pp. 63–78 in *The Society of Captives: A Study of a Maximum-Security Prison.* Princeton, NJ: Princeton University Press.

Thacher, D. (2019). The aspiration of scientific policing. *Law and Social Inquiry* 44 (1): 273–297.

Thompson, A., J. H. Price, J. A. Dake, and T. Tatchell. (2006). Police chiefs' perceptions of the regulation of firearms. *American Journal of Preventive Medicine* 30 (4): 305–312.

Terrill, W., E. A. Paoline, and P. K. Manning. (2003). Police culture and coercion. *Criminology* 41 (4): 1003–1034.

Tonry, M. (1995). *Malign Neglect: Race, Crime, and Punishment in America.* Oxford: Oxford University Press.

Tonry, M. (2011). *Punishing Race.* New York: Oxford University Press.

Tonso, K. L. (2009). Violent masculinities as tropes for school shooters: The Montréal massacre, the Columbine attack, and rethinking schools. *American Behavioral Scientist* 52 (9): 1266–1285.

Tuccille, J. D. (2018). Culture war is all that's left when gun policy battles become pointless. *Reason Magazine.* February 27. Accessed January 6, 2019. https://reason.com/archives/2018/02/27/culture-war-is-all-thats-left-when-gun-p

Turk, A. (2004). Sociology of terrorism. *Review of Sociology* 30:271–286.

Turner, F. W., and B. H. Fox. (2017). Public servants or police soldiers? An analysis of opinions on the militarization of policing from police executives, law enforcement, and members of the 114th Congress US House of Representatives. *Police Practice and Research* 20 (2): 122–138.

Uggen, C., and S. McElrath. (2013). Six sources of the U.S. crime drop. The Society Pages White Paper. Accessed November 8, 2018. https://thesocietypages.org/papers/crime-drop/

United Press International. (1983). Rifle Association against ban on "cop-killer" ammunition. *St. Louis Post-Dispatch.* May 9. Accessed November 4, 2018 from ProQuest.

United States Department of Justice. (2018). 112. Firearms charges. In *Criminal Justice Manual.* Accessed November 11, 2018. https://www.justice.gov/usam/criminal-resource-manual-112-firearms-charges

United States Fish and Wildlife Service. (2017). National hunting license report. Accessed January 22, 2019. https://wsfrprograms.fws.gov/subpages/licenseinfo/Natl%20Hunting%20License%20Report%202017.pdf

United States Sentencing Commission. (2016). Fiscal year 2016. United States Sentencing Commission. Accessed November 8, 2018. https://www.ussc.gov/sites/default/files/pdf/research-and-publications/federal-sentencing-statistics/quarterly-sentencing-updates/USSC-2016_Quarterly_Report_Final.pdf

Van Maanen, J. (1973). Observations on the making of policemen. *Human Organization* 32 (4): 407–418.

Van Maanen, J. (1978). The asshole. Pp. 221–238 in *Policing: A View from the Street*, ed. P. K. Manning and J. Van Maanen. Santa Monica, CA: Goodyear.

Van Maanen, J. (2011). *Tales of the Field: On Writing Ethnography*. Chicago: University of Chicago Press.

Van Sant, S. (2019). Philando Castile's mom wipes out school lunch debt, continuing son's legacy. *National Public Radio*. May 7. Accessed February 12, 2020. https://www.npr.org/sections/thesalt/2019/05/07/721142955/philando -castiles-mother-wipes-out-school-lunch-debt-continuing-son-s-legacy

Vargas, R. (2016). *Wounded City: Violent Turf Wars in a Chicago Barrio*. Oxford: Oxford University Press.

Verma, A. (2015). The law-before: Legacies and gaps in penal reform. *Law and Society Review* 49 (4): 847–882.

Vigdor, E. R., and J. A. Mercy. (2006). Do laws restricting access to firearms by domestic violence offenders prevent intimate partner homicide? *Evaluation Review* 30 (3): 313–346.

Vitale, A. S. (2017). *The End of Policing*. Brooklyn: Verso.

Voigt, R., N. P. Camp, V. Prabhakaran, W. L. Hamilton, R. C. Hetey, C. M. Griffiths, . . . and J. L. Eberhardt. (2017). Language from police body camera footage shows racial disparities in officer respect. *Proceedings of the National Academy of Sciences* 114 (25): 6521–6526.

Wacquant, L. (2001). Deadly symbiosis: When ghetto and prison meet and mesh. *Punishment and Society* 3 (1): 95–133.

Waddington, P.A.J. (1999). Thought, talk, and action. Pp. 97–120 in *Policing Citizens*. New York: Routledge.

Walby, S. (2013). Violence and society: Introduction to an emerging field of sociology. *Current Sociology* 61 (2): 95–111.

Washington Post Staff. (1975). A police chief in context. *Washington Post*. July 19. Accessed July 17, 2019 from ProQuest.

Weber, M. (1946). Politics as a vocation. Pp. 77–128 in *From Max Weber: Essays in Sociology*, ed. H. H. Gerth and C. W. Mills. Oxford: Oxford University Press.

Welch, K. (2007). Black criminal stereotypes and racial profiling. *Journal of Contemporary Criminal Justice* 23 (3): 276–288.

Western, B. (2018). *Homeward: Life in the Year after Prison*. New York: Russell Sage Foundation.

Westley, W. A. (1953). Violence and the police. *American Journal of Sociology* 59 (1): 34–41.

White, K. (2017). "I probably wouldn't be here": Arizona DPS trooper saved by Good Samaritan breaks silence. *AZCentral*. March 17. Accessed December 12, 2018. https://www.azcentral.com/story/news/local/southwest-valley/2017/03/17 /arizona-department-public-safety-trooper-ed-andersson-good-samaritan -thomas-yoxall-cnn-interview/99320010/

Whitten, L. H. (1963). Rifle group opposes D.C. ban on guns. *Washington Post.* March 25. Accessed November 4, 2018 from ProQuest.

Wilcox, P. (2002). Self-help? Examining the anti-crime effectiveness of citizen weapon possession. *Sociological Focus* 35 (2): 145–167.

Williams, R. F. (1998). *Negroes with Guns.* Detroit: Wayne State University Press.

Williams, W. E. (2015). The true black tragedy. *CNSNews.com.* May 19. Accessed July 21, 2019. https://www.cnsnews.com/commentary/walter-e-williams/true -black-tragedy-illegitimacy-rate-nearly-75

Willis-Chun, C. (2011). Strategic rhetoric in news coverage of the Columbine and Virginia Tech massacres. Pp. 47–64 in *Critical Rhetorics of Race,* ed. M. Lacy and K. Ono. New York: New York University Press.

Wilson, C. P. (2000). *Cop Knowledge: Police Power and Cultural Narrative in Twentieth-Century America.* Chicago: University of Chicago Press.

Winkler, A. (2011). *Gunfight: The Battle over the Right to Bear Arms in America.* New York: W. W. Norton.

Winsor, M. (2016). What we know about man Minnesota police killed in traffic stop. *ABCNews.* July 7. Accessed July 9, 2016. http://abcnews.go.com/US/man -minnesota-police-killed-traffic-stop/story?id=40402805

Wintemute, G. (2015). The epidemiology of firearm violence in the 21st century United States. *Annual Review of Public Health* 36:5–19.

Wood, K. (2017). Best states for gun owners. *Guns & Ammo.* November 3. Accessed January 22, 2019. http://www.gunsandammo.com/editorial/best-states-for-gun -owners-2017/247983

Woodward, C. V. (1955). *The Strange Career of Jim Crow.* Oxford: Oxford University Press.

Young, I. M. (2003). The logic of masculinist protection: Reflections on the current security state. *Signs: Journal of Women in Culture and Society* 29 (1): 1–25.

Young, K. M. (2017). Masculine compensation and masculine balance: Notes on the Hawaiian cockfight. *Social Forces* 95 (4): 1341–1370.

Zedner, L. (2005). Policing before and after the police: The historical antecedents of contemporary crime control. *British Journal of Criminology* 46 (1): 78–96.

Zedner, L. (2016). Penal subversions: When is a punishment not punishment, who decides and on what grounds? *Theoretical Criminology* 20 (1): 3–20.

Zimring, F. E. (1972). The medium is the message: Firearm caliber as a determinant of death from assault. *Journal of Legal Studies* 1 (1): 97–123.

Zimring, F. E. (2017). *When Police Kill.* Cambridge, MA: Harvard University Press.

Zimring, F. E., G. Hawkins, and S. Kamin. (2001). *Punishment and Democracy.* Oxford: Oxford University Press.

Index

active shootings, 52, 73, 85, 86–105, 128, 179; defined, 88; media coverage of, 88–89; and mental health, 92–95; numbers killed in, 88, 225n12; and off-duty guns, 99; and police chiefs, 22, 89–100; police feelings of shame/ failure over, 88, 97–98, 99, 100; police training and tactics for, 87–88; and race, 22; and social geography of violence, 91–92; and SWAT teams, 87; as terrorism, 89–90, 92, 93, 100; victims of, 88, 89, 90, 92, 93, 104. *See also* mass shootings; school shootings

African American family, 72, 161

African American ghettos, 30

African American men: arrest of, 232n10; and child custody and support, 165; and crime, 2, 8, 11; and degradation ceremonies, 169; and gun boards, 152, 154, 162, 169; and gun homicide, 193; and intimate partner violence, 165, 166–68; legally armed, 2; and police traffic stops, 164; sexuality of, 11, 145, 161; stereotypes of as criminal or lazy, 145, 151, 160–61; surveillance of, 232n10. *See also* race

African Americans, 34, 66, 77, 198, 233n32; and Charleston church shooting, 96; colonial whites as apprehending, 28, 109; and community policing, 30, 171–72; and crack epidemic, 42; criminal image of, 11, 133, 152; criminal records of, 59, 122, 143–44, 145, 146–49, 152–58; and federal gun crime convictions, 59; and Great Migration, 216n34; and gun boards, 143–44, 145, 146–49, 152–58, 160–68, 169, 186–87; and gun licenses, 1–3, 23, 118, 122, 143–44, 145, 147, 152–53, 186, 228n34; as gun offenders, 59, 72; gun rights for, 63; harassment of, 2; lynchings of, 39; and mass shootings, 89; and mental health problems, 93; in Michigan, 117, 118, 122; middle class reformers among, 171; as militants, 41; and militias, 193–94; and Mulford Act, 62; and nineteenth-century charities, 214n21; Northern policing of, 29–30; and Northern urban ghettos, 32; and NRA, 41, 217n71; numbers of guns owned by, 8; as police, 72; and police as militarized, 10–11; police assisted by, 127–28; police contact with, 162–63, 164–65; police killings of, 103, 175; police officers organizations of, 49; and police traffic stops, 1, 83, 149, 164, 211n41; and police training, 202–3; and post-bellum militias, 214n11; and poverty, 161; and Project Safe Neighborhoods, 58; and self-defense, 157–58; stereotypes of, 145, 158, 160–68, 169; and tropes of criminality, 133; and vice, 30, 32, 33; and warrants, 146–47, 149, 152–53, 154–55. *See also* blackness; race